WITHDRAWN

D1337190

THE LOGIC
OF POLITICAL BELIEF

THE LOGIC
OF POLITICAL BELIEF

A Philosophical Analysis of Ideology

Ian Adams

New College, Durham

HARVESTER WHEATSHEAF

New York   London   Toronto   Sydney   Tokyo

First published 1989 by
Harvester Wheatsheaf
66 Wood Lane End, Hemel Hempstead,
Hertfordshire, HP2 4RG
A division of
Simon & Schuster International Group

Printed and bound in Great Britain by
BPCC Wheatons Ltd, Exeter

British Library Cataloguing in Publication Data

Adams, Ian
    The logic of political belief: a philosophical analysis of ideology.
    1. Ideology
    I. Title
    145

ISBN 0–7450–0526–8

---

1 2 3 4 5   93 92 91 90 89

To Joyce

CONTENTS

I own I met these Protestants with a delight and a sense of coming home. I was accustomed to speak their language, in another and deeper sense of the word than that which distinguishes between French and English; for the true Babel is a divergence upon morals.

Robert Louis Stevenson
Travels with a Donkey in the Cevennes

ACKNOWLEDGEMENTS

I would like to express my thanks to those present staff and past students of the University of Durham Politics Department who have, wittingly or unwittingly, contributed to my thinking on political ideas. Special thanks are due to Mr Henry Tudor for all his help and kindness, to Professor Alan Milne for his encouragement, and to Dr David Manning whose important work on ideology stimulated my own. I should also like to thank Mrs Dorothy Anson and Mrs Jean Richardson for their excellent and speedy typing.

This book should have been completed a long time ago, and I can only offer a final apology to those whose patience I have tried.

Ian Adams

INTRODUCTION

This work is concerned with the nature and scope of ideology. The intense controversy surrounding the subject makes it a difficult one to deal with, but is equally a measure of its importance. While the origins of the concept may lie in political theory, its significance is much wider, embracing any form of activity where belief and theory might be involved, and therefore virtually our whole practical life within society. The problem of ideology goes to the root of the relationship between thought and action, theory and practice. In this sense, the nature of ideology touches all of us. We may ignore or be entirely ignorant of intellectual pursuits, but we cannot avoid the need to act, or to judge the consequences of our actions for others; and we cannot, unless our circumstances are peculiarly desperate, avoid making choices about how we ought to live. Such actions and judgements and decisions involve beliefs, and it is in this sphere of social belief that the nature of ideology lies. But for all its importance and all the attentions of theorists of various stripe, its nature has never been made clear. It remains, as Raymond Plant points out, a 'much invoked but little analysed concept'.[1] Blame falls particularly heavily upon philosophers whose professional concern is conceptual analysis. Bhikhu Parekh has correctly observed:

> we have not so far devoted enough thought to the analysis of the logical structure of political doctrines and inquired where precisely to locate their identity. Political doctrines are highly complex and fluid conceptual structures, with one foot in the world of abstract ideas and the other in the humdrum world of human practice. Unless we know where to look for their identity, we are bound to end up misunderstanding them.[2]

If the concept of ideology really is as important in human affairs as is here being suggested then the failure to analyse it implies that much of our thinking on a variety of important matters may be in a state of chronic confusion.

There may be any number of reasons for this failure, but one or two can be considered which might point to a more adequate analysis. First, and most important, is the relationship between political and moral philosophy. There is a great philosophical tradition, going back at least to Socrates, of substantive ethics, of seeking to determine the fundamental principles by which men ought to live. Indeed, it is widely believed that this is philosophy's central concern, an assumption summed up in the common phrase 'philosophy of life'. But there is a gulf between the popular conception of philosophy and its systematic pursuit as an academic discipline. This has arisen because the traditional pursuit of ethical certainty through philosophy has, in the twentieth century, faltered and almost come to a stop. Although the logic goes back to David Hume, modern philosophers have increasingly doubted that any moral system can be given a foundation in objective reality; and if this is taken away it is difficult to see upon what secure theoretical foundation of whatever sort morality can be based. And if there is no such basis, then it is questionable whether it is possible to have an objective decision–procedure of any kind that could determine whether one set of moral beliefs is any better than any other. Certainly none has been found that enjoys any degree of consensus among philosophers.

Not all philosophers accept that ethics cannot be given such a foundation, but it has been the dominant philosophical view for some time, and is embraced by a range of philosophers whose approach to ethics is in other respects radically different; they include Charles L. Stevenson, R. M. Hare, D. Z. Phillips,[3] and Bernard Williams, who has written:

> there cannot be any very interesting, tidy or self-contained theory of what morality is, nor despite the vigorous activities of some present practitioners, can there be an ethical theory, in the sense of a philosophical structure which, together with some degree of empirical fact, will yield a decision procedure for moral reasoning. This latter undertaking has never succeeded, and could not succeed, in answering the question, *by what right* does it legislate to the moral sentiments?[4]

This implies that it is not the business of philosophy to determine by which moral principles men ought to live, and that philosophers have nothing that qualifies them better than anyone else to pronounce upon substantive ethical questions. The point is elegantly made by Peter Winch: 'philosophy can no more show a man what he should attach importance to than geometry can show him where he should stand'.[5] But if this is correct then much that passes for philosophy, and much that has long been accepted as philosophy, is not strictly philosophy at all and must be something else.

This puts political philosophy in an odd light. For within the broad sphere of philosophy it might be said to be one of the last bastions of the traditional belief in the responsibility of philosophy for determining the correct ethical principles which men should follow. Any number of general books on political philosophy,[6] explicitly or implicitly, are recommending the author's own political values; that is, his views on democracy, freedom, justice and the like. But this is precisely the sphere of political doctrine or ideology. It is this failure of ethical detachment that is the root of the failure to analyse ideology. And only the rigorous observance of ethical neutrality is likely to make progress.

The traditional belief that it was the function of political philosophy to provide the rational and moral principles of political action was so ingrained that when Logical Positivism cast doubt upon the meaningfulness of moral statements political philosophy was promptly pronounced to be dead.[7] Theorizing about politics, it was thought, was now the proper province of empirical social science, and sociology in particular. But this was not a noticeably successful move. The quagmire condition of theory in this area tends to spread confusion to everything sociology touches. And nowhere is this more true than in the sociology of ideas. This is the second reason why the nature of ideology has remained opaque to us. The introduction of sociological conceptions has compounded the confusion.

It will be argued in the following chapters that the beginnings of wisdom in this matter lay in the recognition that determining the nature of ideology is a problem of political philosophy, understood here as an ethically neutral exercise in conceptual analysis that is sharply differentiated from normative political theory. Failure to make the distinction (and it is a common failure) involves a fatal confusion of the method of analysis with what it is supposed to be analysing. It will also be argued, on the other hand, that ideology is too closely identified with normative political theory. Ideology has commonly been thought to pervade all kinds of thinking, perhaps every kind, but its influence is always presumed, so to speak, to radiate from the political. But this assumption can be challenged, opening up the possibility of there being different kinds of ideology.

First, however, it is necessary to consider what others have said about the nature of ideology. Here the initial task of surveying the ground suggests that, despite many contenders, no adequate theory exists, and that philosophical analysis is the only likely means of reaching one. After sketching a background of identifiable forms of understanding, the analysis proceeds by way of attempting to establish an ideological type of thinking that might take its distinctive place within this array of forms. Various dimensions and possibilities are explored culminating in a conception of ideology as a form of moral understanding built upon conceptions of human nature. An attempt to deal with objections and possible counter-examples leads to a widening of the concept, increasing its applicability beyond the world of politics and illustrating the possibility of non-political ideologies. The concluding chapter attempts to draw the threads together and speculates on why it is that a demonstrably unsatisfactory form of thinking like ideology may nevertheless play such a large and seemingly necessary part in our thinking.

Notes

1. Raymond Plant, 'Scientific claims', *The Times Higher Education Supplement*, 28.6.85, p. 17.
2. Bhikhu Parekh (ed.), *The Concept of Socialism*, (Croom Helm, 1975), p. 2. See Robert Nisbet, *Conservatism*, (Open UP, 1986). For the contrary view that the concept of ideology is not problematic but is a 'quite clear and altogether useful' concept (p. vii); though he follows this up with only the very blandest of definitions. But see also Malcolm B. Hamilton, 'The elements of the concept of ideology', *Political Studies*, vol. XXXV, (March, 1987), where the view that in relation to ideology 'conceptual anarchy prevail' is rather better supported.
3. See, for example, C. L. Stevenson, *Ethics and Language*, (Yale, 1944); R. M. Hare, *The Language of Morals*, (OUP, 1952); H. O. Mounce and D. Z. Phillips, *Moral Practices*, (RKP, 1970).
4. Bernard Williams, *Moral Luck*, (CUP, 1981), preface.
5. Peter Winch, *Ethics and Action*, (RKP, 1972), p. 191.
6. See, for example all those quoted in note 47 on p. 25.
7. Perhaps most famously in Peter Laslett's introduction to the collection of essays, *Philosophy, Politics and Society*, (first series), (Blackwell, 1956).

CHAPTER ONE

IDEOLOGY AND CONFUSION

Among political concepts none is more muddled or more fraught than ideology. This is not for the want of theories to define and explain it. On the contrary, there is a perplexing array of definitions and usages which are all in strident competition. Escape from this confusion lies in determining what kind of theory can settle the matter, and the first step must be to assess the weaknesses and potentialities of existing types. There are broadly three of these, associated with the fields of normative political theory, social science and philosophy, each of which must be examined in turn.

Ideology and political theory

It was in the field of normative political theory that the modern debate about the nature of ideology originated and where it still centres. More precisely, it was Marx's theory of ideology that began the debate and which still tends to dominate it.

I

Marx's theory of ideology is a very large complex topic. This is partly because Marx conceived of ideology as an all-pervasive feature of human life and thought; but also, in part, because despite the concept's critical role in his overall system of ideas Marx never defined it, never gave a systematic account of it, never indicated which of the different ways he used the term were the significant ones. As Professor Allen Wood points out: 'Marx is conspicuously unclear as to what he means by "ideology"'.[1] Nevertheless, it is possible to outline broadly what Marx seems to have had in mind.

For Marx, ideology is thought that appears to be objectively true but which in fact is systematically biased in favour of a particular social class; it is the disguised expression of class interests. What at first sight may appear to be pure philosophy or theology or science, may in reality be ideological in that it obliquely but effectively promotes the particular interests and values of a class. This indirect promotion is achieved through the justification of the class's social dominance or aspiration to dominance. Thus, the medieval conception of the human world as a microcosm reflecting God's ordering of the universe effectively justified the dominance and power of the feudal aristocracy, while seemingly scientific classical economics effectively justified the power and position of the bourgeoisie. If the whole of society believes the ideology to be objectively true and the values of the class are upheld, then the position of the class is legitimated and secured or, in the case of an emerging class, its cause deemed just.

The Marxist concepts of ideology and class are intimately related. All ideology is class ideology. Only with the acquisition of an ideology is a class fully formed; only then is it a class for itself as well as in itself, is it fully self-conscious. The ideology expresses the class's view of the world, its *weltanschauung*; though it is a distorted view from a narrow, self-interested position. All classes may have ideologies, but in any given society it is the ideology of the ruling class that predominates:

> The ideas of the ruling class are in every epoch the ruling ideas, i.e. the class which is the ruling material force of society is at the same time its ruling intellectual force. The class which has the material means of production at its disposal, has control at the same time over the means of mental production, so that thereby, generally speaking, the ideas of those who lack the means of mental production are subject to it.
>
> (*The German Ideology*, p. 64)[2]

Within the ruling class there are those who are its 'conceptive ideologists, who make the perfecting of the illusion of the class about itself their chief source of livelihood' (ibid.). Their function, albeit unconscious, is to keep subordinate classes in thrall, so that they see their own exploitation and oppression as part of a just ordering of society. Ideology, therefore is as much an instrument of class domination as the state and its laws: indeed, it is a more insidious and effective one. Ideology is, for Marx, a vital piece of social mechanism, being a principal means by which the ruling class maintains its position, and social stability is preserved.

Class domination and the ideology that sustains it, along with the alienation and oppression of those subject to it, are features of every class society. But capitalist society is a special case. While the proletariat is destined to suffer more cruelly than any previous oppressed class, it is also destined to be the class that by the very harshness of its lot will, as a matter of brute survival, cease to be taken in by ideology and see its condition as it truly is. This will involve the recognition that capitalist society must be overthrown and replaced by a classless society where exploitation will no longer be possible and in consequence ideology will cease to exist. This truth about the world is of course Marxism, which, despite being the *weltanschauung* of a particular class, is nevertheless not ideology but true science.[3]

Marx's theory has much plausibility, but it cannot in the end be adequate. A great many objections can and have been levelled against it. But two kinds of objection are especially important in the present context since one or other tends to afflict most theories of ideology and generally bedevil and obscure the whole topic. These two sorts of objection relate respectively to the two dimensions of Marxism – as normative political theory and as sociology. Problems relating to

Marxism as social science will be dealt with a little later. The problem in relation to political theory is the problem of objectivity.

Marx's theory of ideology is of doubtful adequacy precisely because it is part of a normative political theory. An adequate theory of ideology must be an objectively true one. But no theory can be objectively true if it embodies political values, or if it depends for its sense and coherence upon a wider theory which is loaded with values and dependent on faith. Put another way, a political commitment to particular values and untestable beliefs cannot be a condition of the theory's acceptance. But this is just the case with the Marxist conception. The whole of Marxist theory presumes a vision of human nature which is necessarily distorted and degraded by the experience of class society, and will only flourish and fulfil its potential if a certain political programme is successfully pursued and society is organized in a particular way. None of this is open to scientific investigation or is demonstrable by any objective means. But it is just this kind of value-laden, non-testable network of ideas that the Marxist concept of ideology is firmly locked into. In consequence, ideology is necessarily an evil: it is a necessary part of the process by which class society dehumanizes people; part of the process by which human beings are prevented from enjoying their true relationship with nature. It is a function of inequality and oppression, in that it can only arise in unequal and unfree societies and can only be eliminated in a fully free and fully equal society. His concept of ideology is part of what Marx means by inequality and oppression, and these in turn are built into his concept of ideology. Consequently, to accept fully the Marxist concept of ideology involves accepting that capitalist society is an evil and that communist society embodies what is ultimately good for man.

David McLellan's recent book *Ideology*[4] illustrates some of these points. In it McLellan gives a brief but scholarly and fair-minded account of the development of different conceptions of ideology, both Marxist and non-Marxist. He acknowledges that the situation is confused and comes to no firm conclusion of his own. But he does make clear in the very last paragraph, and on the basis of no previous argumentation, that a satisfactory account must:

> preserve the concept's critical potential by linking it with analyses of control and domination.... [Because] ideology is ... an aspect of every system of signs and symbols in so far as they are implicated in an asymmetrical distribution of power and resources. [So that] although in principle there could be an end to ideology, it is certainly nowhere in sight – not even on the horizon.[5]

In other words, we live in a world characterized by class domination which generates ideological illusions. This must be analysed and criticized, but ideology's disappearance and replacement by a genuinely scientific understanding can only follow a social transformation in which class domination is eliminated. Thus, McLellan's essentially Marxist vision of social reality is contained in his concept of ideology, even though that concept is incomplete. In laying down limits to what is acceptable in an account of ideology he effectively affirms his Marxist faith.

Finally, it could be argued that the Marxist concept can be assessed independently of the rest of Marxism; that we can have a concept of ideology which simply says that it is a disguised expression of class interest. We can strip away the connections with untestable beliefs and excise the Marxist values. This is true. But the point is that while we might have a similar conception of ideology, it would not be a Marxist one.

II

If the Marxist conception of ideology is unacceptable on the grounds that it is bound up with a wider normative theory, then Liberal and Conservative conceptions must be similarly rejected if they are inseparable from Liberal or Conservative beliefs and values.

A clear example of the Liberal conception of ideology is provided by Louis J. Halle's *The Ideological Imagination*.[6] Of the meaning of 'ideology' Halle writes:

> I confine it to bodies of doctrine that present themselves as affording systems of beliefs so complete that the whole population may live by them alone, that are made known and interpreted by leaders ostensibly possessed of special genius or by organized elites not unlike priesthoods, that claim exclusive authority as representing something like revealed truth, and that consequently require the suppression of whatever does not conform. Perhaps I should put it that I am concerned here only with systems of belief that are implicitly totalitarian.
>
> It will be seen that 'ideology', so defined, not only excludes liberal democracy but is its opposite. For liberal democracy is based on the assumption that none of us mortals have a privileged knowledge of truth, that equally honest and intelligent men will disagree in their identification of it. Therefore, instead of undertaking to abolish diversity it seeks to accommodate it, providing an open marketplace in which men of varying beliefs may compete in offering their intellectual wares to the public. Such a marketplace, in order to accommodate diversity, requires freedom of speech and mutual tolerance. (pp. 5–6)

Thus, ideology is inseparable from totalitarianism, which is the antithesis of all the Liberal holds dear, embodying the very opposite of liberty, tolerance and rationality, of enlightenment and progress. An ideology is a 'closed' system of ideas which inevitably leads to a 'closed society' in which freedom has no place. Hence, Bernard Crick, in the course of a very similar account of ideology, insists that 'the idea of an ideology of freedom is a contradiction in terms'.[7] Like the Marxist, therefore, the Liberal defines ideology in terms of his own values, and in such a way as to embrace rival political beliefs but not his own. However, the Liberal does have to make an exception for Conservatism which does not fit his definition and which must be attacked on other grounds. F. A. Hayek, for example, dismisses Conservatism for its distrust of theory, obscurantism and imperviousness to fact and argument; the Conservative, he says, is 'essentially opportunistic and lacks principles'.[8]

Traditional Conservatives[9] do express their distrust in what they call 'abstract theory' in politics, and indeed this is precisely what the Conservative means by 'ideology'. Sir Ian Gilmour writes:

> No British Conservative has produced a system of abstract political ideas or an ideology.... The reason for the absence of British Conservative systems is the Tory dislike of abstract theorizing.... It is thus part of the essence of British Conservatism to be free from systems.[10]

This strand of Conservative thinking goes back to Edmund Burke's condemnation of the French revolutionaries, and of anyone else who based their politics on such abstractions as 'the rights of man'. Government is seen as a wholly pragmatic business, attending to the real needs and interests of real people. The metaphysical theories of 'speculists' and 'visionary politicians'[11] can only lead to 'wild and dangerous politics'.[12] Similar views can be found in the writings of modern Conservatives, as with Michael Oakeshott's warnings against the dangers of 'rationalism in politics'.[13] However, it is important to notice that what is involved here is more than just the notion that the application of abstract theories to politics is generally unwise, since this is a practical judgement that anyone might hold. What the Conservative thinks is that it *necessarily* produces evil consequences. This necessity in turn implies theory, so that despite what is claimed, Conservatism is far from theoryless. Gilmour, for example, claims that Conservatism is 'based on fact and human nature',[14] but the selection of appropriate facts[15] and the determination of what is essential human nature both require some kind of abstract theory to guide them; while Burke's view that politics derived from abstract theory is 'at war with nature'[16] must involve a sophisticated theory that explains what 'nature' in human affairs amounts to.[17] Thus, there is plenty of Conservative theory which expresses Conservative beliefs and values, and which defines rival beliefs and values as ideological.

Each of the three accounts of ideology so far discussed is partisan. They are each designed to defend a set of values and beliefs by characterizing rival values and beliefs as false and dangerous thinking. To hold any one of them as the true account of ideology involves holding the values and beliefs that go with it. Since it is an objective account of ideology that we are looking for, it is therefore necessary to look elsewhere.

Ideology and social science

The second major source of theories of ideology is social science, and particularly sociology. In considering such theories Marxism is again the obvious place to start, not only because of the theory's intrinsic importance but because other social scientific theories are frequently derivatives of it.

I

Putting questions of values to one side, the adequacy of Marx's theory of ideology, as a social theory, revolves around two related issues. The first is the problem of determinism and social mechanism, while the second question concerns the appropriateness of using sociological criteria to determine the nature of a form of thought.

Marx did not believe that human thought was autonomous but saw it as the automatic by-product of socio-economic processes:

> We set out from the real, active men, and on the basis of their real life-process we demonstrate the development of the ideological reflexes and echoes of this life-process.

The phantoms formed in the human brain are also, necessarily, sublimates of their material life-process, which is empirically verifiable and bound to material premises. Morality, religion, metaphysics, all the rest of ideology and their corresponding forms of consciousness, thus no longer retain the semblance of independence. They have no history, no development; but men, developing their material production and their material intercourse, alter, along with this their real existence, their thinking and the products of their thinking.[18]

Independent thought and intellectual progress are, therefore, illusory. Men's ideas and beliefs about the world are simply 'reflexes' of their class experience: 'It is not the consciousness of men that determines their existence, but, on the contrary, their social existence determines their consciousness.'[19]

Consequently: 'man's consciousness changes with every change in the condition of his material existence ... intellectual production changes its character in proportion as material production is changed'.[20] So that to every kind of socio-economic structure there 'correspond definite forms of social consciousnesses' (ibid.). Furthermore, if ideas and beliefs are strictly determined in this way then it must be possible to explain ideas and beliefs in terms of the material conditions that gave rise to them. Beginning with the 'real processes of production', it is possible to:

> explain all the different theoretical products and forms of consciousness, religion, philosophy, ethics, etc., etc., and trace their origins and growth from that basis ... not explain practice from the idea but explain the formation of ideas from material practice.[21]

Thus, Marx frequently insists that to understand the nature of most ideas one must ask whose interests are served by them. This will reveal their ideological nature. Ideologies, therefore, need to be 'unmasked', by showing that whatever their surface form may be, they are expressions of class interests. There can be no alternative explanations since men's ideas and beliefs are merely 'the direct efflux of their material behaviour'.[22]

On the basis of these passages, and many more that might be added, Marx would appear to be a thoroughgoing determinist. But if this is so then the Marxist account of consciousness is open to some very serious objections. If 'social existence' does determine consciousness – that is, if class position does determine the way we think – then it simply does not make sense to say that the 'ruling ideas of each age have ever been the ideas of its ruling class',[23] for that would mean that the vast majority of people throughout history did not have their thinking determined by their class position but in fact possessed the ideas and beliefs of a minority whose social existence they did not share. Still less does it make sense to claim (as Marx and Engels do of themselves) that people of one class can discover the ideas and beliefs appropriate to another class. Again, if social background determines consciousness then the same background must produce the same consciousness; but it is a matter of common observation that members of the same family do not always share the same beliefs, let alone whole social strata. Another point is that there is clearly something wrong with the notion that our social existence is the cause and our ideas and beliefs are the effects; this is because our social existence is largely constituted by our ideas and beliefs, leaving no room for the causal relation. It also makes little sense to recommend that people adopt

Marxism because it is scientific and therefore rationally superior to other ideas and beliefs about society. If what people believe is causally determined then they are not open to persuasion, and rationality does not come into it at all. We judge rational belief and action on the basis of whether they have been chosen for the best reasons; but since caused thought entails the absence of choice then it must entail the absence of rationality. If people are socially programmed to produce and respond to ideas by causal necessity then reason, meaning and understanding have no part to play, any more than they have to play within the computer. And if ideas have no meanings but only effects then no theory has any claim to be superior to any other. Indeed, any theory asserting the causal determinism of thought undermines itself in this way. It follows from this that if Marx is as deterministic as the above passages suggest then his account of consciousness, and therefore of ideology, is self-destructive and incoherent.

But although strict determinism is the official doctrine of Marxist–Leninists (for whom the keys were passed to Lenin via Engels), not all Marxists accept this. They point to passages where Marx insists that 'men make their own history'[24] and are 'both the authors and the actors of their own drama'[25]; that is, passages implying that men have free will. Such passages are a tiny minority of those that are relevant to the issue, yet are nevertheless sufficient to introduce a note of doubt. Wood points out that Marx never seriously addressed the question, and might be correct in suggesting that Marx was in fact a 'compatibilist', simply assuming that there was no conflict between free will and determinism.[26] Marx may have been a compatibilist first of all in the broad sense of being a determinist in respect of the workings of society and the movement of history, while believing in free will in the ordinary sense of our everyday thought and action which might conceivably advance or retard wider developments but not alter them. He may also have been a compatibilist in the narrower sense of believing that the communist revolution will release men from historical determinism. In the words of Engels:

> Man's own social organization, hitherto confronting him as a necessity imposed by nature and history, now becomes the result of his own free action. ... It is the ascent of man from the kingdom of necessity to the kingdom of freedom.[27]

Either version of compatibilism would make Marx a partial determinist. But it is determinism or non-determinism which is the main isue, and one which must be settled.

It is not numbers of passages leaning one way or the other that is the important criterion in this context, or even what Marx might have said had he been more forthcoming on the matter. Whether or not Marx was a determinist has to be judged according to what place free will or determinism has in Marx's system as a whole. The first and obvious point is that Marx was philosophically a materialist and ruled out the autonomy of mind or spirit, which consequently have no determining role in history. Furthermore, his stages of history are necessary stages; his sociology is founded on the principle that base determines superstructure; while the collapse of capitalism and the subsequent triumph of communism are guaranteed by the 'natural laws of capitalist production ...

working with iron necessity towards inevitable results'.[28] But none of this would be possible if the activities of free-thinking men could cut across the pre-ordained historical sequence, or even interfere with such secondary features as 'no social order ever disappears before all the productive forces ... have been developed'[29] and thereby set history off in a different direction. This argument works against full determinism and also against partial determinism. It is simply absurd to suggest that large-scale events are governed by 'iron necessity' if the individual human actions of which such events are composed could all have been different. Marx, therefore, has to be a determinist because otherwise his system of ideas will not hang together. To this extent Allen Wood is wrong in suggesting that because Marx never directly addressed himself to the question it is impossible to decide whether he was a determinist or not.[30] Wood is also wrong in maintaining that nothing turns on the issue,[31] since if the earlier arguments showing the incoherence of determinism are correct then it is not too dramatic to say that everything hangs on the issue. Even if compatibilism does express Marx's view this cannot alter the fact that there is no room for free will in his system and that without determinism the Marxist account of reality does not make sense.

Determinism is, therefore, essential to Marx's system of ideas as a whole. But more particularly, it is essential to the coherence of Marx's concept of ideology as the disguised expression of class interests. Without it the very notion of class interests is unintelligible, while determinism is further needed to link together the otherwise disparate elements that go to make up the concept: class interests; various kinds of ideas that are not logically connected with class interests; and false and distorted thinking.

Class interest is not the simple notion it may at first appear. One may speak in very broad terms about the interests of this or that class, but any attempt to be precise in these matters invariably runs into an array of difficulties. To take a very simple example, we may wish to say that it is in the present interests of the working class that it achieves a higher standard of living. But it is not self-evident whether a socialist, a social democratic or an unrestrained capitalistic society will best achieve this. Again, some would argue that the welfare state and the managed economy of the post-war world were manifestly in the interests of the working class; but some have argued that such policies have in the end only led to inflation and mass unemployment, while others still have insisted that prosperity and welfare services have only served to stifle working-class demands for a just society and have therefore worked against their true interests. Among the working class themselves, and among those seen as their representatives, there is profound disagreement on such matters; and this is always true of any class. There is disagreement about values and aims, about short-term and long-term interests, and about what policies will succeed and how events will turn out. And since the past is ambiguous, the present confusingly complex and the future a blank, who can say with certainty where anyone's real interests lay? The Marxist, however, makes just such a claim to certainty because he has a theory which purports to lay down the course of events past, present and future, and from which the 'objective' interests of any class can simply be read off. But the theory can only do this if it is a deterministic one. That is, in judging the interests of a class in the past the theory must rule out the possibility that history might have been substantially different if the class had behaved in a different way, and, more importantly, the theory must rule out the possibility of alternative futures, otherwise anything is possible and no one can be certain what the best course is. Thus, it is only because he has recourse to a deterministic historical framework that the Marxist can claim to know what the objective interests of any class are, irrespective of what the members of that class themselves think.

The same deterministic theory that is necessary for establishing what the objective interests of any class are, is also essential for picking out which ideas and persons, among the variety that may be available, best express those objective interests at a given time. But having identified these ideas the deterministic theory is essential yet again for demonstrating the necessary link between the ideas and the objective class interests they are supposed to represent. This is necessary because the kinds of ideas Marx and Engels deem to be ideological are not the explicit expressions of class interest but the disguised expressions of such interests. This has to be so, otherwise it would not make sense to talk of 'illusions' or 'unmasking' or even of 'false consciousness'. As Engels points out, not even the ideologist is aware of the true nature of the ideas he develops,[32] or their true origins:

> the jurist imagines he is operating with a priori propositions, whereas they are really only economic reflexes.[33]... Ideology is a process accomplished by the so-called thinker consciously, it is true, but with a false consciousness. The real motive forces impelling him remain unknown to him; otherwise it simply would not be an ideological process.[34]

The kinds of ideas that Marx and Engels characterize as ideological are those expressed in universal terms, such as metaphysics, jurisprudence, ethics and economic theory; and precisely because of this universality they display no necessary connection with any class and contain no element that can be logically identified as necessarily ideological. Consequently, no logical analysis can reveal what is and is not ideological. The only kind of analysis that can identify it is sociological analysis. What this kind of analysis consists in is the establishment of a congruence between the presumed social effects of a set of ideas (for example, to induce an acceptance of the status quo among the lower orders) and the supposed interests of a particular class. This would seem to be a very dubious methodology since the social effects of any ideas being widely accepted is quite contingent and wholly unpredictable. What makes it possible to establish any congruence by this means is that the sociological analysis is based upon a theory which sets out what the objective interests of classes are, what ideas are significant and what the social effects of these ideas must be; and the theory could do none of these things unless it were a deterministic one. The theory must show that there is a necessary relationship between a given set of ideas, irrespective of logical content, and the interests of a given class, irrespective of the views of its members; and it must also show that a certain class inevitably generates certain ideas in a given historical period. Without this deterministic framework the Marxian conception of ideology falls apart: what a class's interest are, what ideas are significant and what social effects these ideas will have, all become impossible to establish, and any relations between them simply dissolve.

However, the necessary relationship with a class's interests, which the deterministic theory establishes, is not in itself a sufficient condition for labelling a set of ideas 'ideological' on the Marx–Engels view, otherwise their own theory would fall into the category. Ideology must also be 'false consciousness'.[35] Marxists do tend to assume automatically that ideas presumed to favour, or are favoured by, any non-proletarian class must be ideological, and therefore false and distorted.[36] But there is no necessary relationship between false and distorted ideas and class interests; one cannot entail the other. What is in a class's interest must be a matter of circumstance and be subject to change, and it would clearly be absurd if ideas could be true and accurate at one time and false and distorted at another. It is therefore perfectly possible in principle that some true and accurate ideas be in the interests of the bourgeoisie or the aristrocracy. It is only within a rigid framework that allocates world-views to specific classes that the history of ideas can be so interpreted that only the proletarian world-view is scientific, objective, true and undistorted.

Thus, it is causal determinism that holds the Marx–Engels conception of ideology together. Marx may not have regarded himself as a determinist, and he may well have rejected any such description, but the nature of his system forces it upon him, and its logical consequences cannot be escaped. Since determinism in this context is incoherent, then Marx's system in general and his conception of ideology in particular must be incoherent. There is no way that either can be saved without causal necessity. If determinism is replaced by contingency then nothing will connect with anything else. Objective class interests cannot be demonstrated, and even if they could their relationship with universalistic ideas cannot be sustained, while the notion of false and distorted thinking cannot be firmly tied to either. If the human world is governed by contingent relationships then ideas cannot be explained by their social causes or identified by their social effects. We could still say that certain circumstances were conducive to the development of certain ideas; but we could not say that those circumstances necessarily produced those ideas, or determined what kind of ideas they were. Similarly, we can still say that the spread of certain ideas appears (we can say no more than 'appears') to suit the interests of a certain social group at a certain time; but we cannot say that *this* set of ideas is therefore *the* ideology of *this* social group; nor, again, that this relationship determines the nature of the ideas concerned.

Marxism has to have determinism if it is to make any sense at all, but the mechanical determination of human thought and action is demonstrably false and contradictory. It is only logical characteristics that can determine the nature of any ideas and distinguish one kind of thinking from another. Marxism provides no such logical criteria by which we can decide what is ideological and what is not, and this is true of all sociological theories. It is for this reason that no sociological theory that defines ideology in terms of social causality or social function (the promotion of group interests or group solidarity, for example) can succeed in identifying ideology as a distinctive form of thought. Sociology cannot produce a coherent theory of the ideological.

II

Non-Marxist social scientists with a view of ideology fall into two main types: those influenced by Marx and those not. Much the most influential among the former and much larger group is Karl Mannheim.

Karl Mannheim's *Ideology and Utophia*[37] is an attempt to rescue Marx's conception of ideology from its non-scientific trappings and to use what were taken to be its genuine insights as the foundation of a 'sociology of knowledge'. This new branch of social science would investigate 'the social or existential determination of actual thinking' (p. 239); that is, the 'causal determinants' (p. 54) of our knowledge, beliefs and categories. The most important, though not the only, causal factor is social class, which shapes 'our whole mode of conceiving things' (p. 239) and is responsible for the 'inherently ideological character of all thought' (p. 48). Marx is criticized for not recognizing the ideological character of his own thought, and for not realizing that ideology, in the broad sense of thought distorted by class interests,[38] is inescapable. This, of course, raises questions about the objectivity of Mannheim's own theory. He did not possess a theory of history and, unlike Marx and Hegel, could not present himself as the 'owl of Minerva' able to comprehend the whole process by virtue of being close to the end of it. Instead his views imply a relativism that makes objectivity impossible. His answer to this problem is his conceptions of the sociology and the sociologist of knowledge. Absolute objectivity may be impossible, but through the sociology of knowledge we can at least become more self-aware and self-critical and appreciative of the views of others. Furthermore, since every ideological viewpoint, every class's *weltanschauung*, has its insights, its fragment of truth, then the sociology of knowlege can be 'a constant renewed attempt at synthesis of all existent perspectives aiming at a dynamic reconciliation' (p. 152). But the achievement of these things is dependent upon the independence of mind of the sociologists engaged upon the enterprise. This independence is possible, Mannheim thinks, because his sociologists will be classless intellectuals who will not be unduly influenced by the narrow interests of class.

This very brief outline is sufficient to show that Mannheim's account of ideology possesses features earlier criticized in Marx, as well as features peculiar to itself that may be open to separate criticism. The obvious starting point is Mannheim's determinism about which he is more explicit than Marx, as well as more revealing about the method of uncovering ideology that determinism implies:

> proceeding to an understanding of what is said by the indirect method of analysing the social condition of the individual or his group. The ideas expressed by the subject are thus regarded as functions of his existence. This means that opinions, statements, propositions, and systems of ideas are not taken at their face value but are interpreted in the light of the life-situation of the one who expresses them. (p. 50)

This characteristically sociological approach to ideas, which ignores content and assumes social causality, is also capable of brushing aside mere observation. Behind the commonly observed variety of people's ideas the sociologist perceives an inner structure:

If we confine our observations to the mental processes that take place in the individual and regard him as the only possible bearer of ideologies, we shall never grasp in its totality the structure of the intellectual world belonging to a social group in a given historical situation ... its inner structure is not to be found in a mere integration of these individual experiences. As a totality the thought-system is integrated systematically, and is no mere causal jumble of fragmentary experiences of discrete members of the group. (p. 52)

Thus, whatever the variety or nature of ideas held among a social group may be, that group will have a definite ideology causally determined by its social circumstances. Sociology of knowledge would not make sense without deterministic assumptions of this kind. On the other hand sociology of knowledge cannot be coherent with such assumption since, as we say earlier, any causal theory of human action reduces all thinking to the same meaningless level and thereby denies its own rationality.

Mannheim is also vulnerable to criticism for his relativism. It is well known that assertions of the relativity of all thought are logically self-defeating, since in effect they assert the universal truth that universal truths are an impossibility. But if objective truth is not possible it is difficult to see how sociology of knowledge can achieve it, and if it is possible there seems no good reason why it should be confined to sociology of knowledge. As Bhikhu Parekh puts it: 'his sociology of knowledge is impossible if his theory of knowledge is correct. In other words, paradoxically, his cure is only effective if his diagnosis is wrong'.[39]

And much the same may be said of Mannheim's class of classless intellectuals who have no class interests but are dedicated to achieving the truth. Furthermore, it is far from clear that synthesizing elements from different ideologies will provide a better guide to political action than any of the ideologies discarded.

III

Most sociologists subscribe to a conception of ideology which comes more or less directly from Marx or Mannheim;[40] but this is not true of the majority of behavioural political scientists. They have, for the most part, adopted what was earlier described as the 'Liberal' conception which equates ideology with extremism, and have attempted to distinguish by various empirical means between 'ideological politics' and 'pragmatic' or 'civil politics'.[41] It was a distinction of this kind that underlay the 'end of ideology' debate of the 1950s, when it was widely argued by political scientists that extremist politics were in terminal decline and the pragmatic politics of interest-bargaining would triumph in most of the advanced world. But although those of the 'behavioural persuasion'[42] are positivists to a man and aspire to 'value-freedom', it is nevertheless clear that their usual conception of ideology is in fact based upon liberal values. One of the most distinguished behaviouralists, Seymour Martin Lipset, writes in his *Political Man*:

This change in Western political life reflects the fact that the fundamental political problems of the industrial revolution have been solved. ... This very triumph of the democratic social revolution in the West ends domestic politics for those intellectuals who must have ideologies or utopias to motivate them to political action.[43]

Ideological politics, the argument goes, is being replaced by the pragmatic politics of interest on the American model, a model Lipset calls 'the good society itself in operation' (ibid., p. 430). More recently, in his *Ideology and Politics*,[44] Martin Seliger admits that if values did distort judgement then 'even modern behavioural science would be hard put to it to claim any unbiased insight' (p. 156). But as we have seen, and will see again, it is value content that makes it impossible for any account of ideology to be objective and therefore satisfactory.

Seliger, however, is not one of those behavioural political scientists who equate ideology with extremism; and much of his book is devoted to revealing, with relentless thoroughness, the contradictions, conceptual imprecision and unacknowledged shifts of meaning characteristic of the standard behavioural view, which he calls the 'restrictive' conception of ideology, (though he does not criticize its value content and thereby misses the main point). Instead he offers his own 'inclusive' account of ideology. Seliger defines ideology in terms of both function and content. He explains that 'the function of ideology is to guide concerted action of a distinct social group or groups' (p. 146) in their political battles. There can be no such thing as a non-political ideology. Ideologies are political belief-systems, all of which have a common structure comprising six essential elements: moral prescription, technical prescription, 'implements' (i.e. ways and means of implementation), description, analysis and 'rejection' (i.e. of rival beliefs) (p. 106). Ideology also has two 'dimensions': what Seliger calls the 'fundamental dimension', which is basic doctrine where moral prescription is the central element; and the 'operative dimension', which is ideology in action and where technical prescription holds centre-stage (p. 100). However, it is moral values that are the essential element:

> the reference to 'higher' values is ineradicable from any system of political beliefs, however low our opinion of some such values and their tangible contents in general may be. Their presence in political belief systems, together with the other elements of the formal structure of content, requires us to classify all political belief systems as political ideologies in so far as the belief system can be said to guide identifiable group action. (p. 146)

But Seliger goes on to insist that not all political belief systems are ideologies. Political philosophies are not ideological, despite having the same structure and elements, and having both fundamental and operative dimensions (p. 112). The difference is that philosophy deals with 'ultimate' questions while ideology concentrates on what is 'immediately relevant for social and political action' (p. 113). Thus, while Plato, Aristotle, Locke, Mill and Marx are political philosophers, the ideas of the likes of Paine, Lenin and the authors of *The Federalist Papers* are merely ideological (p. 115).

Unlike that of most behavioural political scientists, Seliger's account of ideology cannot be rejected for being a manifestation of Liberal values. There are, however, other grounds for rejecting it. For Seliger's account to be plausible he must have clear and unambiguous criteria for distinguishing ideology from other kinds of theory. He says that 'any politically relevant belief system' will have the same essential elements and structure (p. 102). But 'politically relevant belief system' could mean practically anything, including Cromwell's Christianity or

Wallenstein's astrology or Machiavelli's 'historical method', none of which conforms to Seliger's structure. Then there is his baffling distinction between ideology and political philosophy, where the only difference is that one's concerns are more 'ultimate' than the other's. But how degrees of ultimacy are measured in this context is hard to imagine. Besides, it is far from obvious that the concerns of Tom Paine or the authors of *The Federalist Papers* were any less ultimate than those of Locke or Mill in their political writings. Furthermore, Seliger rather confusingly adds that as well as political philosophy the works of Plato, Aristotle and the rest also contain ideology (pp. 115–16), so that presumably a work such as Plato's *Republic* is composed of fundamental political philosophy, operative political philosophy, fundamental ideology and operative ideology. Some very subtle criteria would be needed to sort out these different elements; but Seliger does not provide them, and it is difficult to believe that he could.

What is really behind Seliger's distinction between his version of political philosophy (which is a travesty of what philosophy is, but that is a different matter) and his account of ideology is not degrees of ultimacy but the function of ideology in the political process. As a behaviouralist, Seliger's aim is 'above all' to establish: 'a definition which, in accord with the objectives of scientific endeavour, is suitable for the ordering of data and the formulation of confirmable hypotheses' (p. 87).

That is, to characterize ideology as a phenomenon that can be observed and measured[45] as a causal factor in the political process conceived in mechanical terms. To this end Seliger imposes a functional definition designed to screen out what does not fit into this pre-ordained scheme; and since some political philosophy (even as Seliger defines it) will not conform to the pattern, it is defined out. But as in this case there is no clear qualitative difference between what is included and what is excluded: the functional definition is an entirely arbitrary one. One of the reasons why defining the nature of ideas in terms of social function never works is that the same functions can be performed by different kinds of ideas. In the present case we have seen that non-political beliefs (Cromwell's Christianity, etc.) can guide political action, while political philosophy, since it apparently has an 'operative dimension', can also do the job of ideology. Seliger's definition of ideology, therefore, collapses. This in turn invalidates his determination of the content and structure of ideology by abstracting common features, for this only makes sense if there is an adequate definition that guarantees that the various examples are examples of the same thing. This is a bad procedure in any case since common features are not necessarily essential ones, and it does not show how the features relate to each other in a structure;[46] it is perhaps significant that 'ideological composite' is used as an alternative to 'ideology'. Despite what Seliger claims, his list of features is no more than a list, while the assertion that one feature is central does not constitute an analysis of structural relationships. His whole account of ideology must, consequently, be counted a failure. The nature of ideas is not governed by social function, nor is it laid bare by measurement, testing hypotheses or looking for 'causal concatenations' (p. 158). It can only be done by logical means. In other words, establishing the nature of ideology is essentially a philosophical exercise.

Ideology and philosophy

The nature of ideology is a philosophical problem. Yet little enlightenment on the matter can be gained from examining works of political philosophy. Most general works do not so much as mention it,[47] while those that do have tended to be dismissive[48] (at least until very recently, as we shall see). The few philosophers who have seriously attempted to analyse the concept have tended to fail for basically the same reasons as those discussed in the previous two sections. This is true of perhaps the most widely known philosophical accounts of ideology, those of John Plamenatz and Patrick Corbett, but it is also true of most later attempts.

In his *Ideology*[49] Plamenatz's way of dealing with the concept is a rather curious one for a philosopher. In his preface he writes: 'The first chapter is introductory; but the five that follow become progressively less philosophical and more sociological and political' (p. 12).

He begins with a minimal definition of ideology as: 'a set of closely related beliefs or ideas, or even attitudes, characteristic of a group or community' (p. 15). So from the outset the sociological aspect is built in. Later this definition is refined. 'Ideology' it is argued, covers a 'family of concepts', of which two are particularly important. There is 'total ideology'; this is: 'Ideology in the broadest sense, since it includes all the ideas and beliefs of a people ... [it] cannot be distinguished from thought that is not ideological' (p. 28).

However, there is the more usual sense: 'Ideology in the narrower sense can, of course, be distinguished from thought that is not ideological' (p. 29). The notion of total ideology has its own problems which need not concern us here, except we might note that Plamenatz is clearly willing to regard absolutely anything as ideological. But it is the narrower view we will concentrate on because since the weakness of Plamenatz's case is bound up with whether he can show that it is possible to distinguish between ideology and non-ideology. One of the things he says is not ideological is science. Indeed, he seems to think that, at least in principle, in social science and in any other discipline where there are 'definite, consistent and usable criteria for testing the truth or falsity of beliefs' (p. 30) this is sufficient to make them non-ideological. Yet he appears to contradict this when he comes to characterize ideology more fully:

> for beliefs to be ideological, in this narrower sense, they must be shared by a group of people, they must concern matters important to the group, and must be in some way functional in relation to it: they must serve to hold it together or to justify activities and attitudes characteristic of its members. Nor does it entail that no true beliefs are ideological, for true beliefs can also be functional in these ways. What makes beliefs ideological, in the sense we are now discussing, is their constituting a system of beliefs which is functional in these ways, and is accepted regardless of whether or not its constituent beliefs satisfy the criteria of truth. Ideologies, in this sense, often contain many beliefs that are false or unverifiable, but they nearly always contain some true beliefs as well. (p. 31)

Thus, not only untrue but true beliefs, presumably including scientific ones, can be ideological. More importantly, their truth or falsity is quite irrelevant since it is not logical features that define ideology but its social function. He goes on:

An ideology is not 'ideological' in respect only of the false or unverifiable beliefs contained in it, for it is 'ideological' as a whole set of beliefs that serves to hold a group together or to justify its activities and attitudes or to promote its interest. (p. 31)

Now since anything can serve one or other of these functions then literally any thought can be ideological, and there is clearly a conflict between this and Plamenatz's claim that science, among other things, can be distinguished from ideology. But perhaps Plamenatz can be saved from contradiction here by taking his meaning to be that while true beliefs may be embedded in an ideological system (as Spencer, Kropotkin and others made use of the theory of evolution) without changing their nature as true beliefs, just as a block of wood may be built into a wall and serve the office of a brick without thereby becoming a brick. But then Plamenatz would be wrong to say, as he does say, that such true beliefs are ideological; he can only say at best that they are being used ideologically.

On the other hand, there is not really much point in saving Plamenatz's position here since the question of what is and is not ideological has nothing to do with the logic of ideas, but with their social and, apparently, psychological function. He writes:

> to be ideological has nothing to do with the intentions of the theorists . . . it has only to do with the motives and feelings of the persons who accept the beliefs and with how they behave as a result of accepting them. (p. 73)

But if this is so he cannot then make general statements about the nature of ideological thought, such as that it is not science, or that it is always largely descriptive (p. 79) or that it is not fantasy or fiction (p. 80). He cannot talk as though ideological thinking is something that can be identified and analysed, when he has defined ideology in such a way as to allow any thinking to be ideological. In fact Plamenatz nowhere analyses any ideological position or even identifies a piece of ideological writing; (he discusses Marx at some length, but only as a sociologist). But he is hardly in a position to do so for he has not given himself a concept capable of picking one out.

The consequence of Plamenatz's position is that the philosopher has not the competence to judge what is or is not ideology, or to say anything about it; that must be left to the social scientists. Thus Plamenatz fails to come to terms with ideology and fails to identify the concept, simply because he fails to be sufficiently philosophical.

I

Turning to Patrick Corbett, his *Ideologies*,[50] though in some ways an intelligent and elegant book, is also philosophically weak. It has a kind of dialectical structure. The first part consists of a statement of three ideological positions: Marxist, American Democrat and Roman Catholic. The second part sets out the response of a thoroughgoing sceptic to these positions. Finally, the philosopher speaks: laying down a middle path between irrational faith and corrosive doubt, a path along which the sensible and rational are invited to follow. Corbett does not provide us with a systematic analysis of ideology, but rather an impressionistic portrait which we have to piece together from scattered remarks throughout the book. He does, however, have a working definition:

> By 'ideology' is meant here any intellectual structure consisting of: a set of beliefs about the conduct of life and the organization of society; a set of beliefs about man's nature and the world in which he lives; a claim that the two sets are interdependent; and a demand that those beliefs should be professed, and that claim conceded, by anyone who is to be considered a full member of a certain social group.
>
> On this usage Gandhism, Catholicism, Leninism, Nazism, American Democracy, and the Divine Right of Kings are, or were, ideologies, and so, on a smaller scale, are the myths of English Public Schools or Amazonian tribes. (p. 12)

Corbett thinks there are hundreds if not thousands of such ideologies active today: moral, political, religious and many other kinds. Then Corbett tells us that:

> It will escape none but the simplest devotee that ideologies serve the interests of certain institutions, and therefore of those who hold office in those institutions . . . the social function of ideologies is to condition man intellectually to obedience. (p. 57)

But this is not as obvious as Corbett seems to think. And still less is his next point, which is that all ideologies are fundamentally about freedom: 'each ideology purports to tell us how – by prayer, production, self-control, self-assertion or whatever else – we can be free' (p. 195). But it would take some fairly sophisticated reasoning to show that, for example, the theory of divine right of kings is fundamentally to do with liberation, still less the myths of public schools or Amazonian tribes. But though these two points do not seem to fit together too well (though they do not actually exclude each other) both are essential to Corbett's wider vision of human reality and the role of ideology in it.

Corbett sees human history as an endless striving for freedom, of which ideology is a by-product. There is overall progress towards human liberation, but it has been a zig-zagging, back-tracking, snakes-and-ladders sort of progress, and along the way men have expressed the miseries and frustrations of particular unfreedoms in terms of ideological absolutes. Thus Marx and Engels translated the particular need for freedom from economic oppression into the claim that such freedom constituted the ultimate freedom of mankind, a claim which, for all its erroneous metaphysics, bad logic and evil consequences, was nevertheless understandable and humane. Humane freedoms are multifarious and often contradictory; the theory which purports to point men towards a total freedom can only lead to dogma and, Corbett hints (p. 206), totalitarianism. But although reason can show the irrationality of these grandiose dogmas of freedom, Corbett feels that, shorn of their metaphysics: 'we may yet perhaps be able to accept them as explorations, perhaps essential explorations, of the power of man' (p. 170).

By interpreting ideologies as 'temporary distortions of a rational core' (p. 154), each making its contribution to a greater whole, we can see them, not as irreconcilably hostile, but as 'complementary probings of the potentialities of man' (p. 195). There is a distinctly Hegelian quality about this view since Hegel saw all past philosophical systems as having a core of truth, contributing its part to an ultimate comprehensive truth. Somewhat Hegelian also is Corbett's notion of a dialectic of faith and doubt which characterizes all spheres of intellectual achievement. In the sphere we are concerned with these are represented by ideology and scepticism.

Corbett's sceptic has a primarily destructive role. He is a positivist sceptic who 'shows' the irrationality of belief in God and historical inevitability; the lack of foundation for ethical systems and the impossibility of choosing between them; and concludes by insisting that all moral assertions are disguised expressions of personal interest and ideologies the instruments of the powerful.

In true Hegelian fashion, Corbett's own position is a synthesis of what he takes to be the best of both positions. He accepts the sceptic's scepticism but not his cynicism about values. He accepts that ideologies have been the 'consequences, vehicles and instruments of power' (p. 154) but he feels that this may not necessarily be the case in the future. Indeed Corbett sees mankind as entering upon a new epoch in which growing prosperity, technological change and the growing interrelatedness of all human societies will compel men, willy-nilly, to cooperate more and more and move increasingly towards ever greater economic, political and ideological unity. Differences of belief wil remain, but men will hold them less dogmatically and increasingly see them as contributions to a wider vision, which men will need to 'create and re-create the grand strategy of man's development' (p. 191).

Thus, Corbett has a grand vision of human progress remarkably similar to that developed in the eighteenth century by men of the Enlightenment, best represented in Condorcet's *Sketch for an Historical Picture of the Progress of the Human Mind*[51] (1795) which characterizes history as mankind's struggle for rationality and freedom against the traditional enemies of priest and tyrant who keep men enslaved in ignorance and false belief. But for Corbett there is one great disaster that could prevent this otherwise inevitable progress, namely a nuclear war. And this is only made possible by the hostility of seemingly irreconcilable dogmas. Hence the occasion for the book. Corbett believes philosophers cannot remain detached but must enter the debate and do what they can. His answer is that men need to cultivate wisdom, which he cannot define but which appears to consist in understanding history and ideology as he does and in opening a dialogue with the holders of clashing dogmas, so that with patience, humour, tolerance and showing respect for others, we can bring them to see the intellectual weakness of their position. He writes:

> In each of these doctrines there are thus soft points through which liberal society, persistently working with its solvents of toleration and analysis, can insinuate itself into their structure and complete in theory the liquefaction of ideology that scientific and industrial dynamism has begun in practice. (p. 193)

Ideologies is very much a book of the 1960s when the unending growth of prosperity seemed inevitable and the 'end of ideology thesis' was fashionable. But even allowing for this it is a very naive book. He does not really bother to analyse ideology, seemingly because he takes a very simple view of the relationship between men's social conditions and their beliefs, beliefs that will all melt in the warmth of growing prosperity and cooperation. And his notion of what good-natured (and perhaps rather patronizing) tolerance can achieve with the ideology entrenched seems positively simple-minded.

But a more fundamental criticism is that his own views do not seem any more rational, free of metaphysics, or independent of values and faith than any of those he criticizes. He too has a theory of history as man's quest for liberation, he too has a theory of man, he too is promoting a vision of the future and persuading men to strive for it, he too has values that have no more foundation than anyone else's. *Ideologies* is an expression of Corbett's political faith. He does not analyse ideology philosophically but interprets all others in terms of his own. This is why Corbett emphasizes ideology's social functions of solidarity and social control. Others are the victims of the powerful and the dogmatic, represented by church, party or state, in contrast to his own views which are characterized as the political beliefs of a free-thinking individual. To put it at its crudest, Corbett fails to come to terms with ideology because he is less concerned to philosophize than to preach. And what he preaches is Liberalism: that is, human progress through the pursuit of Liberal values. His account of ideology fails because, whatever its other faults may be, it is partisan.

Both these leading philosophical accounts of ideology fail because they are not sufficiently philosophical: one is too sociological, while the other is too much an expression of political belief. It is just these faults that a genuine philosophical account should overcome. However, the same faults recur again and again, though philosophers are usually less liable to wander into sociology than fail to be rigorously objective. The expression of personal political values is, therefore, the more common weakness. It can be seen, for example, in the work of Kenneth Minogue.

II

Kenneth Minogue's *Alien Powers: The Pure Theory of Ideology*[52] is a more recent attempt to 'explore the logical and rhetorical character' (p.1) of ideology. This 'pure theory' asserts that the:

> formal centre of ideological understanding ... consists in the view that the evils of life are not ... part of an immemorial human condition which is beyond human power to change, or a set of problems to each of which a specific solution may be hazarded, as politicians often suggest, but that they are part of a single system of dehumanization which determines everything that happens, and which cannot be changed except by a complete transformation. (p. 32)

The nature of the domination, the 'alien power' of the title, varies from ideology to ideology: for the Marxist it is the capitalist system; for the feminist it is 'patriarchy'; while for the nationalist it is imperialism. But whatever the alien power is conceived to be, its effect is to dehumanize man and prevent him realizing his full potential. It must therefore be overthrown by means of a revolution which will transform humanity. To merely reform the system is to compromise with evil, and will in any case fail given the system's great powers of self-defence through mystification and deceit. The outcome of the revolution, what Minogue calls the 'ideological terminus', will be a world free of all oppression and conflict and where all will be of one mind. This insistence on revolution and rejection of compromise amounts, in Minogue's view, to a wholesale rejection of politics as such, which, like Crick, he defines in terms of Liberal democratic politics. Ideologists, therefore, are hostile to the political process and to democracy, and are even 'categorically hostile to the state' (p. 215). There is a clear contrast with what Minogue calls 'ordinary political doctrines', such as Liberalism, Conservatism and Social Democracy, which are dedicated to pursuing their political aims through persuasion, election and reform, and which consequently are not ideological.

Minogue believes that ideology, as 'an independent mode of thought and practice' (p. 31) began with Marx, and indeed all subsequent ideology is but a 'footnote to Marx' (p. 31). He therefore confines his detailed discussion of ideology to Marxist arguments, and only illustrates certain points with examples from feminism and nationalism: and even here he has in mind only Marxist-inspired versions of these doctrines. As a result he talks of features that are characteristic of Marxism as though they characterized ideology as such. Dialectical reasoning, we are told, is a feature of all ideology (p. 45), while all ideologists believe that the outcome of history will be the 'practical unity of mankind' (p. 147) in an 'egalitarian society' (p. 151) 'which will have transcended the alienations from which we now suffer' (p. 147). Despite this it is insisted that 'ideologies are many and various' (p. 101), with such as Anarchism and National Socialism referred to as ideologies and Comte, Mazzini and others as ideologists. But, to take just one example, Hitler did not think dialectically, was not preoccupied with alienation, still less with equality or the unity of mankind, and was not noted for his categorical hostility to the state.

Minogue's failure to embrace all that he himself deems to be ideological must entail the failure of his whole analysis. It is also indicative of a general lack of logical rigour. For example, ideology is portrayed as striving for a perfect world of freedom and justice and of interpreting the world in moral terms (e.g., p. 110), yet elsewhere Minogue insists that the ideologist's perfect world 'should not be confused with a realized ideal' (p. 162) and that ideology 'is in fact quite beyond good and evil', being merely parasitic on notions of moral and political reform (pp. 151–2). Thus Minogue's account of ideology is arbitrary, it does not even cover all he takes to be ideological and is logically vague.

However, to insist upon too much academic precision is perhaps to mistake the real nature of Minogue's work. Despite much talk of logic and rationality, *Alien Powers* is not a serious attempt to establish a 'philosophy of ideology' analogous to the philosophy of science, as it claims to be (p. 68); its purpose is essentially polemical and partisan. It is a defence of Liberalism against what Minogue considers to be its greatest enemy, namely Marxism and its derivatives. He therefore wishes to portray the enemy as a manifestation of evil, and the first step is to equate Liberalism with modernity, progress and civilization: 'ideologists can be specified in terms of a shared hostility to modernity: to liberalism in politics, individualism in moral practice, and the market in economics'. (p. 4, c.f. p. 173).

The 'modern state' is represented as the true line of human progress, while the 'ideological state' (which appears to be a contradiction of Minogue's own terms) is, by implication, a degenerate version of the same thing (p. 218). Ideology looks to a mythic past, and by rejecting 'the very system of modernity itself' (p. 173) rejects all that is civilized and humane. It is against democracy, freedom, morality, individualism and ultimately it is against humanity itself:

> ideology is a dagger pointing to the heart of a modern Western civilization [p. 226] ... bent on ... the utter destruction of everything that constitutes the modern world. Ideology is the purest possible expression of European civilization's capacity for self-loathing [p. 221]. ... In pronouncing the rottenness of a civilization, it is actually declaring a hatred of any possible human life. What it proposes is the cosmic equivalent of a suicide pact. (p. 222)

Thus, the reader is not so much invited to accept a logical analysis as to affirm a moral commitment to one side in a conflict where there can be no neutrals. And the reader is not given much of a choice: it is either morality, civilization and all that is decent on the one hand, or chaos, evil and self-destruction on the other. Consequently, even if Minogue's account of ideology were more coherent than in fact it is, its unashamedly partisan character renders it unacceptable on grounds of objectivity.

III

Thus, these philosophical accounts of ideology are marred by being either too sociological or too partisan. They fail because they are not philosophical enough. Yet greater philosophical rigour has, until very recently, bred no more than a dismissive scepticism.

It is not difficult to see why this has been so. Discussion of ideology, though confused and contentious, has at least been shaped by a consensus that ideology is to be found within the area of prescriptive political theory, and in particular where theories, facts, values, prescriptions, ideals and visions of the future are all combined into discrete systems of belief. It is this combination that makes the sceptical philosopher suspicious; facts and values do not mix, while disputes between values cannot be settled. T. D. Weldon, for example, insists that ideologies (or 'political foundations' as he prefers to call them) are 'a delusion' that 'confuse and distort political thinking',[53] and which we can well do without. Ideology is not taken seriously and consequently is not properly analysed.

However, there has recently appeared two full-scale philosophical studies of ideology of appropriate rigour, which take ideology seriously but without falling into the traps of sociological explanation or partisanship. They are D. J. Manning and T. J. Robinson's *The Place of Ideology in Political Life*[54] and Gordon Graham's *Politics in its Place*.[55] Neither book can be dismissed easily and some of their arguments will need to be dealt with later in this work. Nevertheless, in keeping with the theme of this chapter both may be said to contribute to the confusion surrounding the concept of ideology. This is particularly true of Gordon Graham's contribution. Graham defines ideology as:

> those sets of beliefs which have or are meant to have wide implications for the conduct of political life and even, in some cases, for its complete refashioning. The principal instances are very familiar – socialism, liberalism, conservatism, nationalism, Marxism and Fascism. (p. 48)

This is not very helpful, particularly since Graham proceeds to backtrack on some of his examples. One case is Marxism, which he later insists is to be distinguished from Socialism because socialism is an ideology while Marxism is a 'theory of society' (p. 103). Another case is Conservatism, which is described as an ideology, a non-ideology and an anti-ideology all on the same page (p. 172). Then again, the Liberal tradition appears to be mainly composed of political philosophy (p. 79), but it is not made clear whether Graham distinguishes between political philosophy and ideology, and if he does whether he would count his own work as ideological.[56] Furthermore, Graham insists that ideologies 'cannot be reasonably understood to be sets of fundamental principles or values' (p. 48), but his discussion of various ideologies in the second part of his book seems to be precisely about fundamental principles and values. On the other hand, Graham appears to exclude nothing from ideologies (not fundamental values or social theory or philosophy) when he writes:

> in reality ideological beliefs are of many different kinds – factual, philosophical, theoretical, speculative, expressions of value, and political principle, subscription to ends, and belief in efficient means. (p. 58)

It is not in fact clear whether Graham has a theory of ideology at all; but if he has it must be a confused one. Part symptom and possibly part cause of his confusion is his inability to come to terms with the 'is – ought' problem. He refers to it several times (e.g., p. 10) but fails to say whether he believes there to be an unbridgeable gulf between them or not. Clarity on this matter may be a route to a less confused account of ideology.

Manning and Robinson have a much clearer and consistent view of ideology. They do see the value-content of ideology as central. For them ideology is a form of ethical understanding (p. 20); it is that aspect of ethical life that is concerned with political relationships. As such, they argue, it is essential to, even constitutive of, politics (pp. 16 and 18). Unfortunately, they assert this rather than demonstrate it, and do so to the neglect of the descriptive and theoretical sides of ideology (in terms of the later discussion they lack a theory of ideological language and a theory of ideological structure). Nevertheless, theirs is an important conception that warrants further consideration below. For the moment it is sufficient to observe that in the absence of an adequate account of how their central premise is arrived at makes Manning and Robinson's account just one more addition to the confusion.

What is needed is a suitable place to start and a clear conception of what an adequate philosophical account can achieve. One starting point that at least has the virtue of being neutral is the fact that 'ideology' is now widely used by practitioners and observers of politics in a largely non-partisan way. A politician says that his party needs to define its own ideology more clearly,[57] or another politician is described as pursuing a policy for ideological rather than pragmatic reasons, and we understand well enough what expressions of this kind mean. They refer to systems of political belief, such as the varieties of Marxism, Conservatism, Liberalism and the like, with their analyses of social life, visions of the good society and prescriptions to guide political activity. But the analysis of 'ordinary usage' in a Wittgensteinian manner will not get us very far, for such usage in this case is only recent and has only seeped into common political discourse out of a confused theoretical discussion. What is important is whether the rather vague notion in ordinary usage points to something that can be shown to be coherent. The proper role of philosophy here is to demonstrate and explore the logical possibility of a distinct form of understanding which is more than just a mixture of different kinds of thinking, and which embraces the ordinary conception of some kind of unity of theoretical knowledge, values and prescriptions. If this cannot be done then 'ideology' is an insignificant concept with no analytical utility. But if the logical possibility can be demonstrated then light may be shed on a number of problems, including which political theories are ideological and which are not; whether all ideology is political ideology; and how ideology relates to other kinds of theory.

However, before proceeding with the attempt to establish ideology as a distinctive form of understanding it is necessary to be clear about what exactly constitutes a form of understanding and what basic forms of understanding there already are. This will enable us to see what it is that ideology must be distinguished from, and it also might indicate where, within the broad realm of human understanding, ideology might find its proper place. This is the subject of the next chapter.

Notes

1. Allen Wood, *Karl Marx*, (RKP, 1981), 'The arguments of the philosophers', p. 117. Wood goes on here to suggest that there are three basic meanings of 'ideology' in Marx. Bhikhu Parekh, on the other hand, in *Marx's Theory of Ideology*, (Croom Helm, 1982), suggests that there are two basic meanings and a variety of 'sporadic usages' (p. 1, footnote 1 on p. 230).
2. Karl Marx and Frederick Engles, *The German Ideology*, C. J. Arthur (ed.), (Lawrence & Wishart, 1970), pp. 64–5.
3. Later Marxists differ from Marx and Engels and classify Marxism as a 'scientific ideology'. See note 35 below.
4. David McLellan, *Ideology*, (OUP, 1986).
5. Ibid., p. 83.
6. Louis J. Halle, *The Ideological Imagination*, (Chatto & Windus, 1971).
7. Bernard Crick, *In Defence of Politics*, (Penguin, 1964), p. 55. The most distinguished exponent of this view is Hannah Arendt, especially in her *Origins of Totalitarianism*, 3rd edn, (Allen & Unwin, 1966).
8. F. A. Hayek, *The Constitution of Liberty*, (RKP, 1960), p. 401
9. 'Traditional Conservative' is used here to refer to the distinctively Conservative view of the world, which must not be confused with views that may prevail in the Conservative Party at any given time. The view that currently prevails in the Conservative Party is best classified as 'neo-Liberalism', which, ironically, takes some of its inspiration from the works of F. A. Hayek. (See Raymond Plant, 'The resurgence of ideology', Henry Drucker et al., (eds), *Developments in British Politics*, (Macmillan, 1983). Henceforth the use of 'Conservative' will imply traditional Conservatism.
10. Sir Ian Gilmour, *Inside Right*, (Quartet Books, 1978), pp. 111–12.
11. Edmund Burke, 'A letter to the sheriffs of Bristol', in B. W. Hill (ed.), *Edmund Burke on Government Politics and Society*, (Fontana, 1975), p. 198.

12. Edmund Burke, *Reflections on the Revolution in France*, (Penguin, 1969), p. 156.
13. See the title essay in Michael Oakeshott, *Rationalism in Politics and other essays*, (Methuen, 1962).
14. *Inside Right*, op. cit., p. 112.
15. F.A. Hayek explicitly accuses Conservatives as being immune to facts (see *Constitution of Liberty*, op. cit., pp. 404–5), so that at the very least Gilmour's 'facts' are not Hayek's.
16. Edmund Burke, *Reflections* ... op. cit., p. 138.
17. Consider, for example, ibid., p. 195: 'Each contract of each particular state is but a clause in the great primeval contract of eternal society, linking the lower with the higher natures, connecting the visible and invisible world, according to a fixed compact sanctioned by the inviolable oath which holds all physical and all moral natures, each in their appointed place'.
    From this passage alone it is clear that Burke's 'method of nature' (p. 120) involves some very complex metaphysics. However, for a sophisticated account of this matter which does take the conservative claims to theorylessness seriously see Gordon Graham, *Politics in its Place*, (OUP, 1986), p. 181ff.
18. Karl Marx and Frederick Engels, *The German Ideology*, op. cit., p. 47.
19. Karl Marx, Preface to 'A contribution to a critique of political economy' L. S. Feuer (ed.), *Marx and Engels: Basic Writings on Politics & Philosophy*, (Fontana, 1969), p. 84.
20. Karl Marx and Frederick Engels, *The Communist Manifesto*, (Penguin, 1967), p. 102.
21. Karl Marx and Frederick Engels, *The Germany Ideology*, op. cit., p. 58.
22. Ibid., p. 47.
23. Karl Marx and Frederick Engels, *The Communist Manifesto*, op. cit., p. 102.
24. Karl Marx, 'The eighteenth brumaire of Louis Bonaparte', in David McLennan (ed.), *Karl Marx: Selected Writings*, (OUP, 1977), p. 300.
25. Karl Marx, *The Poverty of Philosophy*, (Progress Publishers, Moscow, 1955), p. 100.
26. Allen Wood, *Karl Marx*, op. cit., p. 116.
27. Frederick Engels, *Anti-Duhring*, (Lawrence & Wishart, 1975), p. 336. However, this passage admits of a fully deterministic interpretation which Engels himself would no doubt have given it, while Marx may well have not. C.f. George Lichtheim, *The Concept of Ideology and other essays*, (Vintage Books, 1968), p. 21. Absolute compatibilism, in the sense of men's wills being both free and determined at the same time, is simply self-contradictory. But the less rigorous and more plausible version of compatibilism being suggested here, whereby so long as men lived in class societies they were locked into a sphere of necessity from which only a communist revolution could release them, also has its problems. It is difficult to see, for example, why communist society should not determine men's thinking any less than class societies; it must, after all, be a strange metaphysics that can switch causality on and off according to social arrangements. Besides, Marx's remarks about men making their own history and writing their own drama refer to men in the realm of necessity, which brings us back to absolute compatibilism.
28. Karl Marx, *Capital*, vol. I, (Lawrence & Wishart, 1970), p. 8. This is at least as unambiguously deterministic as, for example, Engels's remark in *Anti-Duhring*, that history proceeded 'in the manner of a natural process and is subject to the same laws of motion', which is quoted by McLellan in his *Ideology*, (op. cit., p. 22) as evidence of 'the simplification of Marx's ideas into a general doctrine of economic determinism' (p. 21) by Engels and others after Marx's death.
29. Karl Marx, Preface to *A Contribution to a Critique of Political Economy*, op. cit., p. 85.
30. Allen Wood, *Karl Marx*, op. cit., p. 116.
31. Ibid. C.f. G. A. Cohen, *Karl Marx's Theory of History: a defence*, (OUP, 1978), p. 147: 'the issue of determinism will not be discussed in this book', which seems to suggest a similar judgement.
32. Bhikhu Parekh has a different account in *Marx's Theory of Ideology* (op. cit., pp. 12–14). But this does not detract from the point that follows.

33. Frederick Engels, Letter to Conrad Schmidt, 27 October 1890, in L. S. Feuer (ed.), *Marx and Engels, Basic Writings...*, op. cit., p. 443.
34. Frederick Engels, Letter to Franz Mehring, 14 July 1893, ibid., pp. 446–7.
35. Marxist–Leninists take a different view of this matter, which throws up problems of its own. See, for example, Maurice Cornforth, *Communism and Philosophy*, (Lawrence & Wishart, 1980), pp. 20–5, where he insists that 'the definition of "ideology" in terms of social function does not imply that ideology is necessarily of wholly false consciousness' and goes on to designate Marxism as 'scientific ideology'.
36. C.f. H. B. Acton, *The Illusion of the Epoch*, (RKP, 1972), pp. 115–16: 'Marxists do not normally argue against the religious and metaphysical theories of their opponents, but claim to "unmask" them as the expressions of class interests or socially determined wishes. Marxists do not, for example, give detailed "refutations" of the arguments put forward by theologians and philosophers to prove that God exists, or that the world is fundamentally spiritual, or that there are two main types of essentially different beings, the physical and the mental. Instead of doing this sort of thing, they argue that this or that theological or metaphysical theory was developed in order to support this or that class interest'.
37. Karl Mannheim, *Ideology and Utopia*, (RKP, 1936). Subsequent page references are to this edition.
38. Within the broad category of ideology Mannheim distinguished between 'ideology' as the defensive beliefs of a ruling class, and 'utopia' as the aggressive beliefs of an aspiring class. But it is only the broad category that concerns us here.
39. Bhikhu Parekh, 'The problems of ideology' in Robert Benewick *et al.* (eds), *Knowledge and Belief in Politics*, (Allen & Unwin, 1973), p. 72. Parekh gives fuller account of, and criticism of, Mannheim than is appropriate here. However, he goes on to draw some doubtful conclusions.
40. See almost any general sociology textbook or dictionary of sociological terms. See also Donald MacRae, *Ideology and Society*, (Heinemann, 1961).
41. See, for example, Edward Shils, 'Ideology and civility: on the politics of the intellectual', *The Sewanee Review*, vol. LXVI, 3 (1958) and 'The concept and function of ideology', in *The International Encyclopedia of the Social Sciences*, vol. VII, (1968); Seymour Martin Lipset, *Political Man*, (Heinemann, 1960); G. Sartori, 'Politics, ideology and belief systems', *The American Political Science Review*, vol. LXIII, 2 (1969); R. D. Putnam, 'Studying elite political culture: the case of ideology', *The American Political Science Review*, vol. LXV, 3 (1971); and others.
42. The phrase comes from Heinz Eulau's *The Behavioural Persuasion in Politics*, (Random House, 1966).
43. Seymour Martin Lipset, *Political Man*, op. cit., p. 406.
44. Martin Seliger, *Ideology and Politics*, (Allen & Unwin, 1976). Subsequent page references are to this edition.
45. Seliger engages in such arcane exercises as measuring the 'distance' between his different elements of ideology (p. 197) and between ideologies of the 'Left Right scale' (p. 217ff.). His approach involves a causal explanation of ideology (a multicausal not a monocausal one – see p. 168), which is also a fatal weakness of his conception. But this topic was dealt with earlier.
46. C.f. Malcolm B. Hamilton, 'The elements of the concept of ideology', in *Political Studies*, XXXV, no. 1, (March 1987), pp. 18–38, which uses the similar but even more doubtful procedure of abstracting a definition of ideology from the common features of previous definitions. The result is predictably vague, simplistic and unreliable.
47. For example, none of the following general works on political theory mentions ideology: Ernest Barker, *Principles of Social and Political Theory*, (OUP, 1952); G.C. Field, *Political Theory*, (Methuen, 1956); Stanley Benn and R. S. Peters, *Social Principles and the Democratic State*, (Allen & Unwin, 1959); J. R. Lucas, *The Principles of Politics*, (OUP, 1966); Felix Oppenheim, *Political Concepts, (Basil Blackwell, 1981); Norman Barry, An Introduction to Modern Political Theory*, (Macmillan, 1981).

48. See, for example, D. D. Raphael, *The Problems of Political Philosophy*, 2nd edn, 1976). Ideology is curtly dismissed without analysis as 'prescriptive doctrine that is not supported by rational argument' (p. 17).

49. John Plamenatz, *Ideology*, (Macmillan, 1970). Subsequent page references are to this edition.

50. Patrick Corbett, *Ideologies*, (Hutchinson, 1965). Subsequent page references are to this edition.

51. A.-N. de Condorcet, *Sketch for a Historical Picture of the Progress of the Human Mind*, (The Noonday Press, New York, 1955).

52. Kenneth Minogue, *Alien Powers: The Pure Theory of Ideology*, (Weidenfeld & Nicholson, 1985). Subsequent page references are to this edition.

53. T. D. Weldon, *The Vocabulary of Politics*, (Penguin, 1953), p. 172.

54. D. J. Manning and T. J. Robinson, *The Place of Ideology in Political Life*, (Croom Helm, 1985). Subsequent page references are to this edition.

55. Gordon Graham, *Politics in its Place*, (OUP, 1986). Subsequent page references are to this edition.

56. In fact from his criticism of various ideologies it is not particularly difficult to see which particular political values Graham favours; although it would be unfair to say that his work is partisan in the way that, say, Minogue's clearly is.

57. This is the avowed purpose of Roy Hattersley's *Choose Freedom: The Future of Democratic Socialism*, (Michael Joseph, 1987). See, for example, Chapter 1, 'In praise of ideology'.

CHAPTER TWO

UNDERSTANDING, KNOWLEDGE AND IDEOLOGICAL CONCEPTS

If ideology is a distinctive form of thought then it must be distinguishable from other distinctive forms of thought. But demonstrating this would seem to be a very difficult matter, since it implies having to survey and classify all human thinking to see if it is possible to isolate one kind that overlaps and partakes of many other kinds. However, if, as a first step, we can determine what we mean by 'a form of thought' and go on to identify those forms that have the most direct bearing on the problem, then at least we may be in a better position to assess what needs to be shown about ideology in order to establish a claim to distinctiveness.

Forms of understanding and kinds of knowledge

The first need is to distinguish between knowledge and understanding. Much of what is characteristic about twentieth-century philosophy arises from its preoccupation with the nature of language, which replaced an earlier preoccupation with the nature of knowledge. This change was at least partly due to a realization that the question 'How is language possible?' is logically prior to the question 'How is knowledge possible?, if only because you have to have language before you can have even a concept of knowledge. To have language is to share a system of meanings; to be able to understand others and participate in communication with them using that system of meanings. Having an understanding is to have a mastery of a particular branch or aspect or area of language. Thus, to have a scientific understanding is to have a mastery of scientific concepts and principles; that is, to know the meaning of such terms as 'cause ', 'law of nature', 'measurement' and 'prediction'; to know how these concepts relate to each other in a system, and the particular importance of such features as experiment and accurate measurement. One may, therefore, have a scientific understanding without having much in the way of scientific knowledge; one would have, so to speak, the equipment necessary for acquiring scientific knowledge to the extent of having a framework to accommodate and make sense of it.

To possess a form of understanding is to comprehend the world, to see it in a certain way. Science is just one way of looking at the world in general, and there are various others. To illustrate this in the very simplest manner, one might take someone's room and consider its contents in a number of ways. One might consider them in a scientific way, or indeed several scientific ways: the materials and chemicals of which the physical objects are composed; the various forces holding everything in its place; and others. Their various mathematical relationships, their proportions, geometrical shapes, etc., might be looked at. Or we might consider the room historically, in terms of the histories of the various objects, how they came to be made and how they came to be there. Or we might view the objects aesthetically, either individually or in relation to each other, or the extent to which the ensemble may be judged to be an expression of the owner of the room's personality. Or again, it will be possible to judge everything in terms of its practical significance, in the sense that each object will or will not be of some use to their owner or someone else. Thus, there is a variety of possible approaches to, a range of frameworks that can be brought to bear upon a collection of physical objects; each one being a discrete understanding, with separate concepts and principles being applied. Physical objects may also have moral or religious or political significance; though not necessarily. These are more likely when dealing with institutions, ideas and human relationships, where further frameworks are possible.

Among these various forms of understanding there is, however, a vital distinction to be made. Some are capable of generating objective knowledge, and therefore of being academic disciplines, and some are not. For a form of understanding to be an academic discipline it must contain a body of rules which have to be observed by those who practise the discipline if knowledge is to be achieved. These rules lay down what constitutes a valid claim to knowledge, and what are the proper forms of reasoning, and of fact, theory and explanation. Above all, the rules lay down a decision procedure for settling claims to knowledge, so that disputes between claim and denial, or between rival claims, can, in principle at least, be resolved. The distinction between academic and non-academic forms of understanding must lie precisely in these procedures for dealing with conflicting claims, for we cannot have knowledge where one person claims that something is so while another claims that the contrary is so, and there are no means, even in principle, to decide who is right and who is wrong. In that situation anything goes and nothing could count as knowledge. Crudely, those forms of understanding that have no such decision procedure cannot be counted as academic disciplines. This is not to say that within academic disciplines there are not unresolved disputes. There may be a lack of evidence. It may no longer exist, or the practicalities of gaining it insuperable, but at least we know in principle what would settle the matter. In the meantime we have an impasse that may or may not be permanent, but we do not have knowledge.

The crucial element is the decision procedure, but what form it takes varies from discipline to discipline. In science, for example, it is observation and experiment, although there may be supplementary principles (such as simplicity) when the evidence appears to support two theories equally well. In logic, as in mathematics, we have a self-enclosed system with fixed rules, and an appeal to the rules is all that is necessary. With history there is documentary evidence; and so on. Where an adequate decision procedure is lacking then there cannot be an academic discipline or objective knowledge, irrespective of how intellectually prestigious or scholarly, or successful in a practical sense, some way of studying the world appears to be. For example psychoanalysis is notoriously divided into different schools, rather like religious sects, each offering different diagnoses which cannot in principle be reconciled. This being so, psychoanalysis clearly cannot be generating objective knowledge, no matter how effective it may be at restoring its patients to mental health. The point is that knowledge is not just true belief but justified true belief. 'Justification', and therefore 'truth' in this context, means satisfying the criteria appropriate to a given discipline. This kind of rigour can be very limiting and often does not give us the certainty we seek. But certainty or absolute truth belong to matters of faith rather than to academic disciplines where all knowledge is necessarily provisional.

We have, then, a clear distinction, between that which is academic knowledge and that which is not, even though it may not conform to more usual classifications of subjects, such as those taught in universities. But if we are to get to the bottom of ideology, we will have to be as precise as possible in the use of terms like 'form of understanding' and 'objective knowledge'. We have to be especially clear about objectivity because we have to assess both the claims of ideology and the claims about ideology, both of which are highly contentious. The two things which in particular militate against objectivity are moral content and the lack of a decision procedure. The two are in fact connected. Moral content is destructive of objectivity because people disagree profoundly over values in ways that in the nature of things cannot be settled, and since such values influence judgements of all kinds, disputes involving such judgements can never be resolved. If there was a decision procedure in morals (or an absolute morality that was demonstrably true, which amounts to the same thing) there would not be this problem; but this is not the case. Thus, the incompatibility of moral content with objective knowledge can be seen as a special case of the absence of a decision procedure generally being incompatible with objective knowledge, and therefore with academic disciplines. It follows from this that we can evaluate claims to academic status in terms of the presence or absence of such a decision procedure. This may be illustrated in relation to social science, particularly sociology.

I

It is clearly believed by some that sociology explains just about everything; but the long-held and high hopes of sociology's powers to explain the world have never in fact come near to being fulfilled. This is because the subject has never developed the essential elements of an academic discipline. As a result, there is no characteristically sociological form of explanation, but only a variety of rival forms deriving from rival theoretical frameworks. There are structuralists, structural functionalists, phenomenologists, symbolic interactionists, ethno-methodologists, Durkheimians, Weberians, neo-Weberians, Marxists, neo-Marxists, neo-Marxist phenomenologists, and more. This confusion of tongues undermines the possibility of anything being properly regarded as sociological knowledge.

Sociologists are inclined to disguise or minimize this confusion with frequent talk of 'perspectives'. But this is a misleading metaphor. It implies looking at the same object from different points of view, just as we fully appreciate sculpture only by viewing it from different angles. But the sociologist's case is not comparable. The same-thing-from-different angles conception cannot work because the social phenomena sociologists deal with are, partly at least, constructs of the theoretical frameworks they employ; so that, despite appearances, they cannot all be said to be studying the same thing. Similarly, 'from different angles' only makes sense if the different sociological 'perspectives' are all compatible, which they are demonstrably not. Structural functionalists, for example, explain social phenomena in terms of structures and processes whose existence phenomenologists, among others, entirely deny. Or again, followers of Durkheim, among others, insist that there can be no knowledge without value freedom, while Marxists deny that value freedom is either possible or desirable. Given these conflicts the relative merits of accounts derived from different 'perspectives' cannot be assessed in relation to each other because they are incommensurable, they do not share the same language, they are not standing on the same ground.

Sociology is riven with incompatibilities of this kind because no means exists to resolve them. There is no overarching framework that lays down what constitutes a properly formed claim to sociological knowledge, nor any procedures for dealing with disputed claims. Consequently, 'perspectives' proliferate and confusion grows. This may, of course, only be temporary. It is possible for example, that some 'Newton of the social sciences' will show that one 'perspective', or a particular combination of them, is alone coherent. But this seems unlikely. Marxism rules itself out because of its moral content, while positivist approaches cannot overcome the problem of the inapplicability of causal explanation to human action. This is because people act for reasons, and as reasons are not physical objects they cannot be part of a causal sequence, and therefore reasons cannot be causes nor can they be caused. Furthermore, there is a logical connection between a person's reasons for acting, and the identity of what that person is doing, which cannot be legitimately encompassed by causal explanation. The main alternatives to positivism, such as phenomenology and ethnomethodology, would seem to be more promising since they deny the validity of positivist social science and insist upon understanding human action in terms of the individual's own understanding of his world. But these 'perspectives' go on to insist on the uniqueness of every individual's view of the world, the sociologist's interpretation of things being no more objective or true than anyone else's opinions about anything. It is not clear, therefore, what the status of the sociologist's findings could be, or how they could be said to contribute to a disciplined pursuit of knowledge. Nor is it clear what the sociologist might be explaining, as there would seem to be no scope for any general explanation of anything. Nor does any synthesis offer much hope. Weber, for example, argued that causal explanation must be supplemented by the social actor's own view of what he was doing. Weber believed, wrongly, that he had two half-truths which, put together, would produce the whole truth. But in fact he was never able to to show how his two explanatory principles related to each other.

It is sometimes thought that, whatever the difficulties we must stick with social science because it is all we have; that nothing else can explain human action. But this is not so. All the phenomenological sociologist appears to be doing is describing how certain unique individuals, each with their unique understanding, respond to unique situations. They can only be doing what the historian does perfectly well without the metaphysics or the jargon, and within a more adequate framework. Historical explanation is perfectly adequate to cope with the complexity of human activity; and what it cannot do in this respect cannot be done by anything else. Historical explanation simply explains events in terms of human actions, which are in turn explained in terms of the reasons the individual had for performing those actions. This may seem a very simple form of explanation, but it is sound enough as far as it goes. It is obviously not far enough for those who believe that social science will eventually explain all human behaviour and will therefore enable us to predict and control our circumstances and solve all our problems. But these are illusions that we could well do without. However, although social science explains very little, its investigations may nevertheless have great practical usefulness (to politicians, governments, advertisers, among others), as was noted above with psychoanalysis. This touches on the relationship between theoretical knowledge and practice which will be discussed below. Sufficient for the moment to say that history appears to be a form of understanding and an academic discipline, while sociology manages to be neither in any full sense, only being at best a very disparate and fragmented form of understanding which may be capable of generating bodies of more or less useful information.

Much of this also applies to psychology and other areas of social science. The one significant exception is economics, and it is important to understand why it is exceptional. Economics cannot be lumped in with the other social sciences because it is not 'scientific' in the same sense as sociology and psychology are, or aspire to be. The difference is that economics is not an empirical science, in that its conclusions are not generalizations based upon observed behaviour. Curiously, economics conforms to an old and long-abandoned conception of physical science that was left behind by the success of Newtonian physics. This was the view, held by Descartes, Hobbes and others, that the correct model for science was geometry. Scientific knowledge could be built by establishing a small number of basic truths about matter, and then deducing the laws of physics from those truths. This would give our knowledge of empirical reality the same degree of certainty as our knowledge of spatial relationships in geometry. Unfortunately for this view, causal relationships are not logical relationships and so cannot be deduced a priori. Geometry, on the other hand, is a self-enclosed deductive system whose theorems are true whether the world conforms to them or not. Given the axioms, the theorems are necessarily true. However, different axioms give different kinds of geometry, as with Euclidian and non-Euclidian geometries.

Economics is more like geometry than it is like physics. It is a self-enclosed deductive system resting upon axioms. Its axioms concern rational economic action, so that in a given economic situation what an actor must do to maximize his economic advantage (buy this or sell that, invest here or save there) can be deduced. The problem with economics is always the relationship between its conclusions and people's actual economic behaviour. Economic rationality would only work if economic actors were confined to a narrowly circumscribed situation of the kind described in economic models, where they all had perfect knowledge, and where they acted only for economic motives. But real life is nothing like this. Economics, therefore, has only very limited means to predict or say how an economy is actually working. As Robert Brown observed: 'It is a perennial criticism levelled at economists that they produce deductive systems or calculi without being able to apply them usefully'.[1]

But it is the nature of the subject that it is deduced from axioms (though the axioms may vary) and not from generalizations from actual human behaviour. Consequently, its predictive capacity is necessarily very limited, and only if these limitations are properly understood can economics be understood as a genuine academic discipline. This being so it might be thought that in principle there could be other kinds of human thinking which are subject to similar rules of rationality that could be the basis of further disciplines. This is possible in principle, but the only serious candidate had been games theory; which proved disastrously misleading when used by American military planners in Vietnam.

II

The relationship between form of understanding and academic discipline is not always straightforward. It will be worthwhile to consider some further kinds of understanding which are or which sustain academic disciplines, for even this very simplified and schematic account suggests ambiguous and borderline cases. Among these are art and religion.

The artist views the world aesthetically, while the religious believer views the world in terms of some concept of the divine. Both are forms of understanding for which empirical fact and practical usefulness are not central. In both cases we speak of knowledge or truth, though in a special sense. The deepest experience of religious truth appear to be incommunicable to others of the same faith, let alone those of other faiths; 'knowledge' here is not the sort that can be supported by argument. Something similar is true of 'artistic truth'. Whatever this may amount to it is not something coldly stateable: a painting is not an argument that could be refuted by another painting. Knowledge in these cases is something altogether different from academic knowledge.

On the other hand, both art and religion are connected with discipline-like studies, with artistic criticism and theology respectively. Within artistic criticism there are undoubtedly arguments and controversies, and undoubtedly a piece of criticism can be shown to be false and inadequate. Yet at the same time, two pieces of criticism of the same work can be equally insightful and cogently argued while coming to contrary conclusions, with no clear way of settling which is right. Indeed, we may legitimately feel that both are right. And this is related to the fact that we do not regard the history of criticism in terms of an accumulating body of knowledge, in the manner of science or history. Partly this is a recognition that different critics, particularly of different periods, can have different sets of aesthetic values, and that there is no decision procedure for deciding between these. We may be able to show John Keats to be a better poet than William McGonagall (although perhaps we might be relying here on some kind of technical evaluation rather than purely aesthetic); and we may grant that given a shared set of aesthetic values one critic may prove their case against another; yet in the end we have to recognize that as between such sets of values there is no ultimate test of truth. Artistic criticism may perhaps be fairly called a 'quasi-discipline', since such knowledge as there is would seem to be relative to a set of values. Indeed, we pursue the enterprise less in hope of knowledge for its own sake as of cultivated sensibility and judgement for their own sakes.

Theology is a rather different case. Here we do have argument and refutation and a decision procedure based upon a holy book, the authority of which can be decisive in settling disputes. On the other hand, this procedure does not cross faiths, and may not even cross sects. Hence, theological knowledge is not universal in the way that scientific or historical knowledge is, but is relative to particular faiths. Both aesthetic and theological knowledge, therefore, share some of the features of full academic disciplines, but not all; and 'quasi-discipline' seems an appropriate characterization of both. But it should be noted that in neither case is the 'discipline' coextensive with the form of knowledge, still less with the form of understanding.

III

Ideologies do not generally claim to be academic disciplines themselves, although they are given to pronouncing on what principles ought to inform particular disciplines. What all ideologies do claim is that at least their basic doctrines have the status of academic knowledge, that is, of demonstrable objective truth. Liberals, for example, claim to base their principles upon pure philosophy; Marxists claim that their analysis of society is fully scientific; Nazis claim their theory of universal struggle between Aryan and Jew to be demonstrable historical truth; and so on. What we need to discover is whether ideology's moral content fatally compromises all such claims a priori, or whether such claims can be detached and independently assessed. There may also be the possibility of disciplines attaching to ideologies, as we have seen in relation to art and religion: that is, deriving from but not identical with the form of understanding.

The answers to these and other questions relating to the identity of ideology turn, to a considerable extent, on the fundamental question of whether ideology can be a distinctive form of thought, or whether it is a composite of many forms. In particular, to what degree the descriptive and explanatory side of ideology is separate from the moral, practical and prescriptive side. This second side is arguably the most important. Ideology is, if nothing else, a guide to action. It tells us what ideals to strive for and by what means. Its claims to objective knowledge are subordinate to its practical objectives, they are meant to underpin its prescriptions. Therefore, before addressing the question of ideology's coherence, we need to survey briefly the sphere of practical understanding, and the possible relationship of other forms of understanding to it.

Practice and theory

Practical understanding is concerned with how we live and what we do. It involves seeing the world in terms of its relationship to our actions, individual and collective; that is, in seeing the significance or insignificance of anything and everything for our enterprises, needs and pleasures. It embraces all that pertains to acting and doing; to what is effective and what is right. It is upon these two dimensions of practical activity that we deliberate. We can engage in technical and moral reasoning, and, correspondingly, we can have technical and moral knowledge. However, the ability to reason in either is no guarantee of good performance. Technical knowledge must be supplemented with skill, or 'knowing how', and moral knowledge by character. Indeed, skill and character are essential to good performance, while knowledge, in the sense of what can be stated, is very much secondary. But leaving skill and character aside, there are several important questions to be asked concerning the nature of technical and moral knowledge, their relationship to academic knowledge, and the relationship of all three of them to practice.

I

Having practical knowledge is knowing what to do next. Technical knowledge is about knowing what to do next in terms of the most efficient means of achieving a desired result. This result might be anything from mending a puncture to ending a war. In practical matters experience is always important, but at the same time there is usually a role for technical guidance, which may be more or less formal and more or less related to academic knowledge. We might illustrate this by considering three cases: the apprentice plumber, the nuclear engineer and the schoolteacher.

The apprentice plumber goes to his local technical college to learn 'theory'. This 'theory' is the principle of good plumbing: how different systems work, which are the best techniques, why they are the best, and so on. As part of this he may be told a few very elementary scientific laws, but he would do nothing that could properly be called 'learning science'; and he would learn nothing that he could not be a good plumber without. His kind of theory is not a deduction from pure science but is derived from experience; it is a summary of good practice, the outcome of practitioners reflecting on their best work. It is 'knowing how' verbalized and formalized; it is a description of the skilled man's technique, his 'mystery', and cannot be a substitute for it. The skilled man has no need of theories.

On the other hand, there is clearly a relationship between theories of this kind, which tell us what to do next, and the theories of the physical sciences. At its simplest, a physical theory asserts a causal regularity of such a kind that if you do A then B will happen and this confirms the existence of the regularity, thereby making it testable and predictive. Technical theories recommend A as an effective means of achieving B, and this can be confirmed by experience which can indicate future usefulness. Thus, there is a certain logical overlapping. But here the differences emerge, for theoretical soundness is no guarantee that something will work in practice, whereas something may work excellently well in a way that no theory can account for. This may be progressively less true as we move towards the more sophisticated levels of, for example, nuclear engineering. Here the engineer must be closely bound to theory to make any sense of what he is doing (safety considerations alone would prevent him from experimenting much beyond what established theory will justify). At this level the traffic between science and technology is necesarily heavy and constant. Yet they remain separate. They do not become the same thing, nor can one be deduced from the other. It it true?' and 'Does it work?' are different kinds of questions with different criteria for evaluating answers. The point of scientific theory is to state a truth whose usefulness is neither here nor there; and point of a technical theory is utility, over which questions of truth and falsity do not arise because their function is not to explain anything but to guide our action. For this reason science can be an academic discipline while technical theory cannot. Though related, technical theory and scientific theory are different in kind.

But when we move away from the material world, the world of engineers and doctors and jobbing builders, and into the human world, then the nature and role of technical theory becomes controversial and confused. In all forms of human activity the practitioner deals with other people. In politics or salesmanship or entertainment or teaching, some techniques work better than others, and this suggests some role for technical theory. What is in question is what kind of technical theory: where on the technical continuum, from nuclear engineering to plumbing, would this kind of theory fit; or does it vary according to the kind of practice or the needs of the practitioner? Some people believe that the relationship should be close and tight, in human affairs as much as in engineering. But this is a mistake. It is one that usually arises from an exaggerated notion of the explanatory power of social science, of its being to government or teaching or management what physics is to engineering. There is, for example, a vast amount of educational theory designed to assist schoolteachers to do their job, which is of notoriously little use to the new young teacher. Of far more use are the hints and tips and rules of thumb of the experienced practitioner. What will and will not work in human affairs is not something that can be determined a priori by theoretical means. People are infinitely variable and inherently unpredictable. Being successful in human affairs is not a function of theoretical ability, but, as Aristotle points out, of experience. The best teacher (or manager or salesman or politician) is not the one with the best theories; and teaching, together with other activities dealing with people, belong to the summary-of-best-practice or plumbing end of the technical theory spectrum, rather than the nuclear-engineering end.

But even where this kind of theory is kept close to solid experience and is thick with practical examples, the problem of making good use of the theory is by no means as straightforward as is usually supposed. The point is well illustrated with Machiaevelli's *The Prince*.[2] This is a handbook on how to be an effective ruler in the viciou. world of Italian Renaissance politics, and is full of advice about what to do in a variety of likely situations which are amply illustrated with examples from classical and contemporary history. However, for the inexperienced ruler, for whom the book is intended, following its advice must always be problematic. The situation he faces will never be exactly the same as the examples given in the book, so he can never be exactly sure that any particular piece of advice is the right one for his immediate problem. What every prince needs, Machiavelli tells us, is an experienced and knowledgeable adviser. But then if he has such an adviser he presumably does not need the book. Machiavelli goes on to say that the prince must not only be able to choose good counsellors, he must know when to take their advice and when to ignore it. But surely if the prince has this amount of political shrewdness he hardly needs the adviser, let alone the book. If he does have it then he does not need the book, but if he has not the book will not give it him. The point is that dealing with people, in politics or management or teaching or any similar activity, involves judgement, and good judgement cannot be reduced to a formula.

II

What then of moral knowledge? If technical knowledge is knowing the effective thing to do next, then moral knowledge is knowing the morally right thing to do next. Our knowledge is of a code and how to apply it; and in this context we talk, for instance, of 'knowing the difference between right and wrong'. The thing about moral codes is that, at least in the day-to-day sense of honesty, decency, etc., they tend to vary between community and community, so that our knowledge is relative to a social context and is not universal. However, when we claim our values to be universal ones we are making claims of a different order, and one where claims to knowledge are far more questionable. The claim to universal knowledge comes with systems of ethical belief, whether purely moral or religious or political. The difficulty here is that claims to universality cannot be tested or measured against anything, they are incommensurable and cannot be compared. Hence, if one set of beliefs tells us to pursue enlightened self-interest, while another says to do one's duty in spite of self-interest; or one says love thy neighbour, while another says pursue martyrdom; or one insists that all men are equal while another that they are necessarily unequal; there is simply no means of establishing who is ultimately right or wrong.

To understand why this must be so it is necessary to rehearse, briefly and roughly, the distinction between description and evaluation. To describe is to state what is there, what is in the world independent of our describing it; it is to state facts. To do this we use descriptive terms whose utility lies in their reference to features of the world, so that we can use them to pick out the features we observe and construct descriptions. Since there is some sort of correspondence between descriptive terms and reality, disputes over the accuracy of a description can be settled by checking it against the facts. But when we evaluate – when we use terms like 'good' or 'bad', 'beautiful' or 'ugly', 'superior' or 'inferior' – we do not say what is there; we do not make statements that correspond to reality since there is no independent feature of reality to which terms like 'good', 'beautiful' or 'superior' can refer, and so these terms cannot be used to pick them out. And since there is nothing in the world to which these terms can be said to correspond, criteria for their application are indefinitely variable, deriving from people's values and beliefs, not from the world itself. (This is not usually a problem with technical evaluation, where there is general agreement on what constitutes a good tennis player or a good watch.) This being so, we can apply such terms freely according to what we believe is desirable, important or otherwise significant to us. That is, according to our evaluatory frameworks, which are things we bring to experience and not things we derive from it. The nature of these of frameworks is such that there is no way of showing that one is superior to another in any absolute sense. In consequence of this, when there is a dispute over an evaluation and the disputants have fundamentally different values, there is no way of settling it conclusively. Men, of course, frequently do differ in their fundamental values. But it is equally true that over large areas of experience, and certainly within communities, values are widely shared; and perhaps social life would not be possible if this were not so. It is only against such a background of shared values that disagreements over evaluations can be settled. But where there is no such background there is deadlock. Thus, all moral evaluations are endlessly contestable; they are always open to dispute, unsettleable dispute, by those of different values. Thus, while in some circumstances it may make sense to talk of moral knowledge, it is necessarily a relative knowledge. It could not be, or be part of, an academic discipline.

III

Practice, then, is an autonomous sphere of its own. It is also a complicated sphere with understandings and knowledge of different kinds, with practices and values, techniques, rules and traditions. It is arguably the appropriate sphere of religion and, if anywhere, ideology.

It might be said, then, that practice generates two distinct kinds of knowledge, very different from each other and very different, in several ways, from academic knowledge. Academic knowledge is concerned with objective truth; technical knowledge is concerned with practical effectiveness irrespective of formal truth; and moral knowledge cannot, in any absolute sense, claim objectivity. Yet all three may be necessary for effective action. To act in the world we need to know three things: the facts of the situation; what will work; and what is right. Academic, technical, and moral knowledge may answer to each of these respectively. This raises an obvious question as to where ideology fits into all this? It seems to fit in everywhere, or perhaps nowhere. It would seem that ideology aspires to provide all three kinds of knowledge. Marxism, for example, gives a factual/descriptive/explanatory account of the world, practical guidance and moral direction. Where, then, is ideology's place among these different kinds of thinking? Does it belong in the academic sphere, since ideologies, as we have seen, invariably make claims to academic status as good science or philosophy or history or whatever. Or does it belong in the sphere of the practical, whether as technical theory or moral? Or does it straddle several kinds of thought? And if the latter, can it be said to have any proper place at all, or is it essentially a confused mixture?

There are good reasons for plumbing for the latter. Ideology is, if anything, a disparate assemblage of all kinds of things; facts and values, explanations and prescriptions, myths, ideal societies and much else besides. All of this rather suggests that ideology is not so much a distinctive form of thought as a logical mess. However, this may be misleading. All the disparate elements can be reduced to, or related to, just two basic ones that appear to clash, namely fact and value. The question of the nature of ideological thinking, its logical identity and status, turns upon how these two basic elements are related.

The vocabulary of political belief

To be possessed of a set of political beliefs, an ideology, is to understand the world in a certain way. And to have an understanding is to be master of a vocabulary, to be able to apply it appropriately. Each of the various sets of political beliefs – Liberalism, Nazism, Marxism and the rest – has a distinctive vocabulary of its own. The terms to be found in these various vocabularies would seem to vary a great deal, and go together with various sorts of reasoning: the scientific, philosophical, historical, moral, technical and so on. But this appearance is illusory. Despite an apparent diversity, ideological concepts are of a single sort. The purpose here is to show what sort they are.

At first sight this seems an unlikely prospect. When we speak of someone's political beliefs we usually have in mind some system of ideas in which an apparently factual account of how things are in the world is combined with an account of how they could be and ought to be. But if this is so then it suggests that such beliefs must contain at least two sorts of concept, descriptive and evaluative. It also suggests that these beliefs must be based on a logical fallacy, and that with the aid of 'Hume's law' they can be easily analysed into two parts, with facts and theories on one side and values and prescriptions on the other. However, a close examination of ideological writings shows that illicit moves from fact to value are not common and that ideology does not in fact work in this way. How the fallacy is avoided, how the trick is worked, is central to the nature of ideology and to its distinctiveness as a form of understanding. The basis of that distinctiveness is the ethical element found in all political beliefs.

Whatever other characteristics political beliefs may have, they do have moral force: they tell us how we should live and what we should strive for. Insofar as we are Marxist or Nazis or Liberals, we are committed to beliefs about how the world ought to be, what relationships should prevail, what is just and what is conducive to human flourishing. Thus, despite the horrors that may be committed in its name, any system of political beliefs constitutes a moral vision, a set of ideals which provide a standard of what is right and what is important in social life, and consequently a yardstick against which the present world, the imperfect world we occupy, may be judged. These theories go on to suggest the means by which this imperfect world can be transformed into one in which its ideals are embodied – though revolution, democratization, the elimination of enemies or some other means – and as such act as a guide to right action in political life.

The moral force of an ideology is most clearly carried in certain of its concepts. Some of these are pecular to particular ideologies, as are 'progress', 'alienation' and 'master race'; while others, such as 'democracy', 'freedom', 'inequality' and 'justice', are common to several. 'Progress', 'alienation' and 'master race' seem to be quite definitely descriptive concepts, and yet at the same time are evaluative in the sense that progress involves improvement and so must be a good thing, alienation is necessarily an evil and master races cannot be other than superior. The other concepts – 'freedom', 'justice' and the rest – are more obviously moral, but nevertheless are thought to describe some state of affairs, whether actual or possible. But it is notorious that the realities to which these common concepts are thought to refer vary from ideology to ideology; Marxist and Liberals, for example, have very different notions of what realities correspond to such as justice and democracy. These concepts are, to use W. B. Gallie's phrase, 'essentially contested'.[3] We have, then, a group of concepts playing a central role in ideology which appear to combine both descriptive and evaluative elements, and this rather odd duality has logical consequences.

To see what these consequences are we might begin by looking at an ordinary moral concept, the relatively homely notion of murder. The term 'murder', in its moral sense (not its legal sense which is logically quite different), might be thought to refer to a specific kind of action, let us say unprovoked and premeditated killing, where correct application of the concept is merely a matter of establishing the facts, as in law. But this is not the case. What makes killing a case of murder is not any feature that can be empirically determined, but that the killing was wrongful or unjustified. This being so the application of the concept can vary from person to person and from society to society according to varying moral beliefs. Certain sorts of killing may be condemned by most societies, but there will be some society or sect in which it is permissible and hence not murder. But even if some sort of killing were universally regarded as murder this would not alter the logic of the case, which is that what we count as murder depends upon our moral beliefs and not upon the facts. The concept therefore has considerable elasticity and can be stretched to cover any kind of killing we disapprove of, far beyond the usual application. Some regard abortion as murder, others capital punishment, others still, the killing of animals for sport, while some animal rights activists proclaim the slogan 'meat is murder', and so on. The term 'murder', therefore, does not refer to any specific class of events in the world. It is 'quasi-descriptive', the appearance of descriptiveness coming from its assocation with the purely descriptive concept of 'killing', which determines its field of application. In consequence, when there is disagreement over whether some particular kind of killing, such as euthanasia, shall count as murder, there is little use in appealing to the facts since it is not the facts that are in dispute. Yet when the disagreement stems from fundamentally different moral beliefs it is difficult to see what else could be appealed to. For there is no logic that can demonstrate that one set of moral beliefs is true and another false, or prove one superior to another. However much we may wish it otherwise, there is no such decision procedure in this area. This is the basis of essential contestedness, and of the endless disputes over the 'true' meaning of justice, freedom and the rest. That such terms may have a descriptive content does not alter the matter. In all concepts which combine the descriptive and the evaluative, it is their evaluative content that determines their logic. These points are perhaps best illustrated with an example from outside the contentious sphere of moral evaluation.

Consider the concept of a weed. Let us imagine two people living side by side who are both gardeners. One is a lady who grows mint. She loves the taste of it, the look of it, the smell of it, and she rejoices to see it flourish. Her neighbour loathes the stuff and is forever tearing it out as it spreads persistently and anarchically across their common border, threatening to ruin his neatly ordered husbandry. He insists furiously that mint is a weed; she, equally furiously, insists that it is not. This is clearly not the kind of argument that can be settled. Within gardening weeds are bad things: they are what gardeners pull up. What counts as a weed is relative to what any gardener wants to grow. The point is that 'weed' is a term of evaluation, and as such there is nothing actually in the world to which it can refer. There is no essence of weedness of which mint may or may not, as a matter of demonstrable fact, partake; there are no fixed public criteria for its application other than the limits set by the concept of a plant. That 'weed' is, strictly speaking, non-referential is clear from the case of someone who refuses to count anything as a weed and is happy to see anything grow. On the other hand, because the term appears to be a descriptive one the unsettleability of the dispute between our two gardeners is not perhaps as self-evident as, let us say, two small children squabbling over whether baked beans taste nice or horrid. So it is possible to imagine our gardeners each setting out to prove their case and searching through books on botany for support. But they are inevitably disappointed since because 'weed' is an evaluatory term it could not be a scientific one, and could have no place in any system of scientific classification and description. However, though our two gardeners are theoretically naive they are nevertheless theoretically disposed, and proceed to rectify what they take to be a serious fault of current botanical desciption by constructing rival plant theories and classifications in which the concept of weed plays a central role, one proving the weedness of mint, the other the opposite. But however elaborate or comprehensive or systematic these constructions might be, they could not constitute rival botanies; they could only be rival horticultural ideologies, with no means of deciding which was right and which wrong.

There is a whole class of everyday concepts like murder and weed which are quasi-descriptive, where a descriptive appearance disguises an evaluative nature. But insufficient attention has been paid to them. However, Thomas Hobbes was aware of the phenomenon. In a section of *Leviathan* entitled 'Inconstant names' he wrote:

> The names of such things as affect us, that is, which please, and displease us, because all men be not alike affected with the same thing, nor the same man at all times, are

in the common discourses of man, of *inconstant* signification. For seeing all names are imposed to signifie our conceptions; and all our affections are but conceptions; when we conceive the same thing differently, we can hardly avoid different naming of them. For though the nature of what we conceive, be the same; yet the diversity of our reception of it, in respect of different constitutions of body, and prejudices of opinion, gives everything a tincture of our different passions. And therefore in reasoning, a man must take heed of words; which besides the signification of what we imagine of their nature, have a signification also of the nature, disposition, and interest of the speaker; such as are the names of Vertues, and vices; For one man calleth *Wisdome*, what another calleth *feare*; and one *cruelty*, what another *justice*; one *prodigality*, what another *magnanimity* and one *gravity*, what another *stupidity* &c. And therefore such names can never be true grounds of any ratiocination. No more can Metaphors and Tropes of speech: but these are less dangerous, because they profess their inconstancy; which the other do not.[4]

There are several features of Hobbes's account that are significant in respect of the sorts of concepts we have been considering. He is clear about the disguised nature of these terms; that where they appear to refer to some reality their application is in fact variable, being a function of the user's attitudes. He is also clear that, this being so, such terms 'can never be true grounds of any ratiocination'; or, as we might put it, are out of place in academic reasoning. However, there are weaknesses in Hobbes's account, at least in respect of the present purpose. That account bears the marks of two of Hobbes's characteristic doctrines which are in themselves highly questionable and which limit 'inconstant names' as a means of analysing political beliefs. First is Hobbes's mechanical psychology which interprets moral thinking in terms of personal self-interest; and secondly, his naming theory of language makes him see concepts in isolation rather than as part of a network of meanings. (This is why 'quasi-descriptive' and, as we shall see, 'pseudo-descriptive' are preferred to the more elegant 'inconstant names' and even 'essentially contested concepts'). To be fair to Hobbes, his 'inconstant names' can be used individually and as expressions of personal self-interest. But the dropping of his psychology and theory of language allows a wider understanding of how 'inconstant names' operate within moral and political thinking.

These points can be illustrated through a consideraton of one of Hobbes's own examples. In Chapter XIX of *Leviathan* he writes:

> There be other names of Government, in the Histories, and books of Policy; as *Tyranny*, and *Oligarchy*: But they are not the names of other Formes of Government, but of the same Formes misliked. For they that are discontented under *Monarchy*, call it *Tyranny*; and they that are displeased with *Aristocracy*, called it *Oligarchy*.[5]

Hobbes may be quite right in that 'tyranny' can just mean 'monarchy misliked' and used in a way that merely expresses an individual's personal discontent. But 'tyranny' can also be used, as it has been by thinkers before and after Hobbes, as part of a wider theory. It is this wider use in 'ratiocination' that Hobbes did not develop, and given his assumptions probably could not have developed, that is interesting in the present context. Locke's notion of tyranny, for example, is logically bound up with his theory of limited government and natural rights, and has to be defined in terms of these. Rousseau, Mill and others have their own quite different conceptions of tyranny which are connected with their respective notions of freedom, democracy and similar concepts. 'Tyranny' is the wrongful use of power; as with 'murder', its badness is built into it. Why these theorists differ in their conceptions of tyranny is because they have different values, different conceptions of political right and wrong. The important point about this is that just as 'weed', because of its evaluative nature, could not be part of an objective theory about plants, so for the same reason 'tyranny' could not be part of an objective theory about politics. 'Tyranny', like 'alienation', 'democracy' and similar concepts, has a moral content and so behaves evaluatively rather than descriptively, and because of the tight interconnectedness of language within theory must influence all the concepts that are connected to it. It makes some difference, therefore, whether or not particular usages of terms like 'tyranny' are part of a theory or not.

The meaning of 'weed' does not come from any theory, but from the practice of gardening (the person who would not count anything as a weed could hardly be called a gardener), and other practices have concepts of this type. There are also concepts of a similar logical kind whose evaluative content is moral and which relate to human conduct as a whole, to social life and to politics. Some of these also take their meaning from a practice or way of living – like 'murder' or Hobbes's virtues and vices – but others are the product of theory. That is, either they are pure theoretical products, such as 'alienation', or, like Locke's notion of 'Tyranny', have been brought into a theory from outside and given a fresh coat of meaning. Concepts that have grown out of practice and form part of our common language, like 'murder' and 'weed', may be called 'quasi-descriptive', for they seem to make no claims for themselves beyond what they are. But for concepts that owe their meaning to a theoretical system that purports to describe and explain the world, such as 'democracy', 'alienation' and 'master race', the term 'pseudo-descriptive' would seem more appropriate. It is pseudo-description that characterizes the nature of ideological concepts.

In employing such concepts the ideological believer is understanding the world in terms of morally charged categories. He has what appears to be a descriptive account of the world, but one which points in a certain moral direction and from which prescriptions can be drawn. It is in this way that the Humean objection is overcome, but at a price. The seemingly smooth transition between fact and value is only possible by building the values into the supposed facts, so that in ideology we do not have genuine descriptions or explanations of the world but only disguised evaluations of it. Only for the believer do the descriptions describe and the explanations explain; they have no purchase on the rest of us. In ideology, therefore, there is no illicit inference of values from facts. Description and evaluation are fused in the same concepts, with the effect of turning concepts which retain their descriptive appearance into evaluative ones with no genuine descriptive force. Yet this suggests a new dichotomy. For not all the terms in the vocabulary of a given ideology would seem to be morally charged, in which case it seems that we must have a mixture of the ideological and the non-ideological and not a set of concepts of a single sort. To examine this question we need to look at one ideology as a whole.

A Marxist commitment necessarily involves an understanding of society and its development in terms of class conflict and class oppression. Western society is characterized as 'capitalist society', which, despite its surface complexity, is fundamentally divided between a dominant bourgeois capitalist class and an exploited and oppressed proletariat. The state, with its apparatus of oppression, and the prevailing set of ideological beliefs, with its rationalizations and justifications, both serve in their different ways to maintain the system. The educational process also plays its part by reproducing the labour force which has been indoctrinated into passively accepting its position as inevitable and right. The victims of the system are exploited, oppressed and deprived of their humanity, a condition summed up in the concept of alienation. However, the system cannot be reformed but only destroyed by a revolution of the oppressed, who, having achieved revolutionary consciousness, thereby have the means to rebuild society on the basis of humanity and justice.

In Marxist eyes capitalist society thus stands condemned and its overthrow a moral necessity. It is precisely the function of the whole elaborate structure of Marxist theory to give substance to this vision of a morally incoherent world that can be transformed into a coherent one. The Marxist view of the world can be seen as essentially ethical. It is a moral vision that informs all Marxist thought and determines the nature of its distinctive concepts. Centrally important terms such as 'exploitation', 'oppression', 'dehumanization', and 'alienation', whatever their descriptive content, are clearly terms of moral evaluation, since anything to which they are applied (and their application can vary somewhat as between the different strands of Marxism) counts as an evil which socialist society will eliminate. It may seem possible to contrast such terms with others such as 'state' or 'class' or 'ideology' which, on the face of it, have no moral content. But this is a mistake. These apparently neutral terms do have moral import which comes from being defined by means of the overtly moral ones. Marxists define the state in terms of class oppression, while exploitation is built into the definition of class, as it is of capitalism. To be possessed of ideological beliefs may appear to be a neutral fact, but within Marxist discourse to have such beliefs is to be a victim of class distortions, which is an aspect of alienation. All the concepts of a Marxist understanding have a moral content; all take their meaning from, and are expressive of, the Marxist moral vision. It is this vision that makes Marxism an ideology and its concepts ideological. Ideologies are a form of ethical understanding and their vocabularies are made up of concepts of a certain sort, namely pseudo-descriptive ones. The theoretical framework links together concepts in such a way that its moral force is carried by the whole vocabulary; that vocabulary consists of a network of pseudo-descriptive concepts in terms of which the Marxist understands the world.

Given the kind of concepts involved, the Marxist account of capitalist society could not be an objective one. It is not a neutral description from which a condemnation is inferred or tagged on, so that a non-Marxist could accept the description while rejecting the condemnation. The condemnation is built into the description, or, more accurately, it is not really a description at all: it is an evaluation masquerading as a description. And that is true of all the individual descriptions and explanations which the theory makes possible; that is, of individual institutions, practices and situations. An account of a classroom situation, for example, might be given in terms of the operation of the 'ideological state apparatus', or the class distribution of 'cultural capital' (there are variations here according to whether the observer is a phenomenological Marxist, an Althusserian, or one of several other varieties). But whichever it is the pupils are seen as being yoked to a system that will oppress them and deny their humanity. Such accounts purport to tell us in some objective way what is really happening behind the immediate appearance that might be given in a humble description, of a maths lesson or whatever it might be. But an account of this kind can neither describe nor explain the situation in any objective sense. What it does, under the guise of description, is to endow the thing observed with a particular moral signnificance, so that those of the same beliefs will know how to regard such situations in the correct light, and, if appropriate, act accordingly. In this way the believer's evaluation of the world is extended to a new situation and his understanding thereby refined and developed. However, the important point is that the same situation 'described' by a Marxist observer would be 'described' differently by an observer with a different moral or political commitment. Instead of giving his account in terms of alienation and oppression, this other observer may do so in the entirely opposite terms of some kind of liberation, from the slavery of the passions, original sin, unenlightened short-term interests or whatever; education being, for this observer, the means to human happiness and fulfilment. These rival accounts of the same situation may present themselves as rival claims to knowledge, but are in fact rival evaluations which no amount of empirical research or neutral reasoning could decide between. They are incompatible and incommensurable; the dispute is, in principle, unsettleable.

That disputes between rival ideologies cannot in principle be settled is an extension of the fact that as between fundamentally different sets of moral values there is no decision procedure, no way of demonstrating that one is true and the other false, or that one is superior to the other. But because in ideology believers might be said to conceive the world in terms of their values, they not only evaluate it differently but experience it differently. Consequently, in disputes between rival beliefs the disputants are not standing on the same ground, are not talking about the same things, even though they may be using the same words. There is no possibility of objectivity and so ideological concepts, theories and explanations are necessarily incompatible with academic disciplines. That is, they can 'never be true grounds of ratiocination', and so, strictly speaking, notions such as 'Marxist history' and 'Liberal philosophy' are contradictions in terms. This is not to say, however, that words cannot be taken from their ideological context and neutralized. A sociologist may wish to use a notion of ideology as disguised expression of class interest, yet shorn of its connections with alienation, class oppression and the rest. But though derived from Marxism this would not be a Marxist concept, but a neutralized version. Conversely and more commonly, just as concepts may be divested of their ideological meaning, words can also be taken from ordinary usage and invested with ideological meaning. We noted this above with the case of 'tyranny', though in the present century examples such as 'proletarian', 'Jew' and 'rational' have been more common. In making this transition these words change their meaning and their logical nature.

If a Nazi and a non-Nazi both make the statement 'Freud was a Jew' it would seem that they are saying the same thing, being just as accurate. But this is not so. For the Nazi 'Freud was a Jew' means the same as 'Freud was an enemy of civilization', while it does not have this meaning for the non-Nazi. Further, the Nazi, unlike the non-Nazi, can go on to make the inference: 'Freud's works are Jewish, therefore Freud's works are degenerate'. Conversely, since Christianity was deemed a contribution to civilization it followed that Christ must have been an Aryan, and those aspects of Christianity which Nazis disliked or found inconvenient could be attributed to Jews like St Paul. In the Nazi vocabulary 'Aryan' and 'Jew' are not descriptive terms but evaluative They are used by the Nazi to indicate what is approved and disapproved of, in the same way as 'bourgeois' and 'proletarian' are used by the Marxist.

That ideological concepts are evaluative while appearing to be descriptive explains how ideologists make the transition from their accounts of the world to their prescriptions without apparent logical violence. Given their beliefs, the Nazi can make the inference 'Freud is a Jew, therefore his work should be destroyed'; the Marxist can say 'the police are the instrument of state oppression, therefore we should try to discredit them'. Arguably the crucial concept in any ideology is that of man, and the crucial inference is '*this* is the nature of man, therefore *this* is the kind of society that is appropriate to his nature'. Such inferences are possible because in these contexts the concepts of Jew, state and man are pseudo-descriptive. It is the nature of concepts such as these that integrates the seemingly disparate elements of ideology. And ideology is a distinctive form of understanding because it employs a distinctive vocabulary composed of concepts which, despite their apparent heterogeneity, are of a single sort.

Notes

1. R. Brown, *Explanation in Social Science*, (RKP, 1963,) p. 183.
2. Niccolo Machiavelli, *The Prince*, (Penguin, 1961).
3. W. B. Gallie, 'Essentially contested concepts', in *Proceedings of the Aristotelian Society*, vol. LVI, 1955–6, pp. 167–98. However, the analysis that follows differs somewhat from Gallie's.
4. Thomas Hobbes, *Leviathan*, (Penguin edn, 1968), p. 109.
5. Ibid., p. 239.

CHAPTER THREE

IDEOLOGY, SCIENCE AND THEORY

In looking at ideologies as theoretical structures it will be useful to relate them to, and compare them with, scientific theories. This is not as simple as it might seem, for both the nature of science and its relation to ideology are contentious matters which will need some untangling before we can get a clear view. We will begin by considering the views that ideologies may be partially scientific and that they are bad science.

Ideology as bad science: Karl Popper

Against the account of ideology given in the previous chapter it may be argued that to characterize such as Marxism as an ethical understanding is to ignore the obvious fact that, whatever its prescriptive implications, it does provide us with a description of capitalist society, and a very powerful one; and that as such it does have a place in academic enquiry. Of course, a whole sociological theory can be abstracted from Marx's thought, but as a set of hypotheses about the workings of society, shorn of any moral or political implications and made subject to empirical disconfirmation the result would be a long way from Marxism as a system of belief, and strictly speaking would have no logical connection with it. Certain terms such as 'class' or 'ideology' (though not 'alienation' or 'exploitation'), retaining something of their Marxist sense, could be used purely descriptively as part of an objective account of contemporary society, one that could figure in academic study. But then they would have to be neutralized, stripped of their moral content. In which case they would cease to have Marxist meanings, and the resulting account would not be a Marxist account, no matter how much it resembled one.

Such an argument, however, may not satisfy those who contend that ideologies are essentially bad science, belief in which is therefore irrational, just as, given present evidence, belief in phlogiston or a geocentric universe is irrational. Nazism is frequently dealt with in this way, implying that if its racial theories had better supporting evidence it would be rational to be a Nazi. But because there is no supporting evidence, Nazi belief is irrational and it is the irrationality that produced the horrors of Hitler's Germany. Indeed, it was all so irrational that we can only make sense of it by saying that Hitler was mad. However such vulgar simplicities do not characterize all attempts to view ideologies as bad science.

Perhaps the best known and most successful approach to ideology in terms of its scientific status is Karl Popper's account of Marxism. But Popper's attack is upon an attenuated Marxism, one where the ethical dimension is deliberately ignored.

> The position is, simply, that whoever wishes to judge Marxism has to probe it and to critize it as a method, that is to say, he must measure it by methodological standards. He must ask whether it is a fruitful method or a poor one, i.e. whether or not it is capable of furthering the task of science.[1]

Marxists do of course make claims to scientific status (as do other ideologies, though not all of them) and Popper's case against such scientific pretensions is both powerful and important. Yet if, as we have argued, the ethical dimension is the essence of the matter, then it must be said that Popper's case does to a considerable extent miss the point. Marxism is not just bad science like astrology and alchemy, any more than religion is bad science. Besides, Popper's case is not perhaps as sound as it is usually assumed to be.

Popper has two main arguments. First, that Marxism is non-science because it is unfalsifiable,[2] and secondly, that its historicist method is mistaken and dangerous. On the first count Popper argues that for Marxists, as for Freudian and Adlerian psychologists in their field, all facts verify the theory because the theory has an explanation for every circumstance. But the consequence of this is that the theory can never be tested because there are no possible facts that could show it to be wrong. Thus:

> The most characteristic element in this situation seemed to me the incessant stream of confirmations, of observations which 'verified' the theories in question; and this point was constantly emphasized by their adherents. A Marxist could not open a newspaper without finding on every page confirming evidence for his interpretation of history; not only in the news, but also in its presentation – which revealed the class bias of the paper – and especially of course in what the paper did *not* say.[3]

Thus every fact 'verifies' the theory. But the point about scientific theories, Popper insists, is that they can be tested; that is, they are so constructed that they exclude certain circumstances which, if they are then found to obtain, will falsify the theory. Thus, whereas true scientific theories are falsifiable, pseudo-scientific theories like Marxism are not.

However, Popper is ambiguous in his dealings with Marxism on this point. A couple of pages later Popper writes:

> The Marxist theory of history, in spite of the serious efforts of some of its founders and followers, ultimately adopted this soothsaying practice. In some of its earlier formulations (for example in Marx's analysis of the character of the 'coming social revolution') their predictions were testable, and in fact falsified. Yet instead of accepting the refutations the followers of Marx re-interpreted both the theory and the evidence in order to make them agree. In this way they rescued the theory from refutation; but they did so at the price of adopting a device which made it irrefutable. They thus gave a 'conventionalist twist' to the theory; and by this stratagem they destroyed its much advertised claim to scientific status. The two psycho-analytic theories were in a different class. They were simply non-testable, irrefutable. (*Conjectures and refutations*) p. 37)

By 'soothsaying practice' Popper means 're-interpreting the theory *ad hoc* in such a way that it escapes refutation'. But the implication of this is that the fault lies with Marx's later followers and not with Marx himself, and that Marxism, as it left the hands of Marx, was perfectly good social science, and that it in some sense still could be. So on this argument Marxism, as such, would seem to be scientific; it is Marx's followers adapting the theory to explain away inconvenient facts which renders Marxism unscientific. But this seems hardly fair, since, as Kuhn has pointed out (as we will see below), no scientific theory fully fits the facts and much scientific activity consists in developing theories in order to produce a better fit. As Popper himself says:

> In point of fact, no conclusive disproof of a theory can ever be produced; for it is always possible to say that the experimental results are not reliable; or that the discrepancies which are asserted to exist between the experimental results and the theory are only apparent and that they will disappear with the advance of our understanding.
>
> (*The Logic of Scientific Discovery*), p. 50)[4]

No scientist abandons lightly a theory he thinks is basically sound in the face of counter evidence, and the attempts by Lenin and others to show that capitalism had yet to go through a higher stage of development than Marx could have foreseen can be seen in this light. And this would not be unreasonable because it could be argued that the falsification of Marx's predictions do not essentially affect the core of Marxist theory: the class basis of society, necessary historical stages and the rest. Popper does have a point about the way Marxists automatically adjust their theory, but by approaching Marxism as social science the point is weakened by the fact that it is difficult to draw the line between legitimate persistence and illegitimate dogmatism.

Popper is stronger on the second count. His account of the methodological inadequacies of what he calls 'historicism' (i.e. discovering the 'laws' of 'patterns' of historical development in order to predict the future course of history – see *Poverty of Historicism*, p. 3)[5] is convincing. Yet the force of his argument is undoubtedly weakened by the fact that he thinks small-scale prediction is quite acceptable, and indeed gives us a slightly embarrassing example of the sort of thing he means (embarrassing because this is clearly in line with his own political beliefs). He writes:

> There can be sociological laws, and even sociological laws pertaining to the problem of progress; for example, the hypothesis that, wherever the freedom of thought, and of the communication of thought, is effectively protected by legal institutions and institutions ensuring the publicity of discussion, there will be scientific progress.
>
> (*The Open Society and its Enemies*, vol. II, p. 322)

Now it could be argued that there is a rather better case against historicism as a part of the broader case against positivist social science and the possibility of predicting human action, as discussed in Chapter 2. But this line of reasoning is not open to Popper because he is himself a convinced positivist in these matters (though not of course a logical positivist). Purely on the methodological issue Popper seems to be arguing over a matter of degree, and contributing to just one more methodological dispute by which the social sciences are notoriously plagued (and which are, if the analysis of Chapter 2 is correct, somewhat redundant anyway). But then, Popper's case against Marxist historicism is not purely methodological. He writes:

> Why, then, attack Marx? In spite of his merits, Marx was, I believe, a false prophet. He was a prophet of the course of history, and his prophesies did not come true; but this is not my main accusation. It is much more important that he misled scores of intelligent people into believing that historical prophecy is the scientific way of approaching social problems. Marx is responsible for the devastating influence of the historicist method of thought within the ranks of those who wish to advance the cause of the open society.
>
> (*The Open Society and its Enemies*, vol. II, p. 82.

This makes clear that Popper's main objection is a moral or ideological one: belief in historicism leads to the 'closed society' with its attendant evils, while belief in Popper's own scientific methodology leads to the 'open society' which is the good society. But there are few things in human affairs more uncertain than the effects of ideas, and Popper's beliefs concerning their good or evil influence can only be based upon faith. This is quite apart from the problem of what constitutes good and evil in social affairs, a problem about which Popper is remarkably naive and unsubtle, seemingly unaware that his own moral beliefs could be very different from those of any other reasonable person.

Thus, in seeking to exclude Marxism from science it could be argued that Popper is only partially successful, and that he does not really get to the heart of the matter. The heart of the matter being that Marxism, like any other ideology, constitutes an ethical understanding which by its very nature is incompatible with all academic disciplines, including science.

Science as ideology: Thomas Kuhn

The conception of physical science as objective knowledge, which is common to Popper and others, is not one that is universally accepted. A very different account has been developed by a number of radical theorists, the best known being Thomas Kuhn. In his book *The Structure of Scientific Revolutions*[6] Kuhn argues that a study of the history and sociology of natural science reveals that it is not the rational, consistent and progressive activity it has been traditionally assumed to be. It is rather a rigidly conservative activity, narrowly applying a received wisdom, though subject to periodic convulsions when, for what seems no very good reason, a new wisdom replaces the old; after which, following a fit of group amnesia, the scientific community returns to blinkered normalcy. One implication that some have drawn from this account is that: 'from a sociological perspective there is no value in a fundamental distinction between "science" and "ideology"'.[7] Clearly, Kuhn's ideas pose a threat to the view of ideology being developed here, and consequently require close attention.

I

In *The Structure of Scientific Revolutions*, Kuhn argues that the traditional conception of science, as a cumulative and consistent progress towards ever-greater truth, is simply false. This conception is propagated through scientific textbooks and the popularizations derived from them. But what these works picture is only what Kuhn calls 'normal science', which is a situation where a branch of science is governed by a dominant theory or paradigm. Such 'normalcy' is the condition to which all sciences aspire, for it is the mark of maturity and a guarantee of fruitful work for the scientist, provided he is able enough. Such necessary security is reinforced by the traditional conception of scientific progress where the present is seen as the culmination of the common enterprise of scientists through the ages. But this is a false picture. It is not deliberately so, but such is the power of the scientific community's self-image, and so functional is this image for the coherence and sense of common purpose of the community that the distortion of history that the traditional conception involves is more an unconscious reflex than any deliberate attempt to deceive.

Nevertheless it is false, because 'normal science' is not science, as such, but is the product of 'revolutionary science', which is a period of dispute and some confusion when a new paradigm is established at the expense of an old one. Such changes are revolutionary because acceptance of a new paradigm necessarily involves the wholesale transformation of the scientific world which the old theory dominated. The crucial point here is that dominant theories are never just theories, as scientific textbooks and philosophers of science would have us believe, but are a complex of concepts, relationships, model achievements of analysis and experiment (hence 'paradigm'), methods and instrumentation. They provide a theoretical framework and a set of procedures which define the problems and lay down standards of success for their solution. Normal science is not the investigation of the paradigm but its articulation, solving the puzzles involved in fitting it more closely to nature. They are puzzles rather than problems because the paradigm stands as a guarantee that there is a solution if only the scientist is clever enough to find it. The paradigm itself is beyond investigation: it is a 'given', a dogma,[8] a matter of faith. The paradigm is constitutive of the world which the scientist, as scientist, occupies, defining both science and its object: 'paradigms are constitutive of science...[and]...constitutive of nature as well' (p. 110). This being so, a change of paradigm is necessarily a great trauma, a total disruption of the scientific community with much conflict and passion. But once it has been accomplished the community reunites around its new conception of science and the world, and a new era of normal science begins.

This picture raises an obvious question: if normal science is the narrow, paradigm-bound activity Kuhn claims it is, then how are revolutions possible? Kuhn argues that no paradigm solves all its problems, there is never a perfect fit with nature – a situation which provides the puzzles of normal science. Most puzzles are solved in time, but a puzzle may, despite the best efforts of the best minds, defy solution and become an anomaly. This may come to be conceived as crucial, as calling into question the authority of the paradigm. In this state of crisis scientists are prepared to look at any potential solution within or beyond the paradigm. In such a situation a rival paradigm may emerge which appears to solve the anomaly but at the price of calling into question much that has been achieved under the old paradigm. In the ensuing conflict the new paradigm may triumph and issue in a new period of normal science under its aegis. When the dust has settled the whole field will be redefined and the textbook writers and popularists will set about explaining science in terms of the new paradigm and rewriting history in its image, showing it to be the natural outcome of steady, linear, cumulative scientific progress, and ignoring its revolutionary origins.

Thus far Kuhn is reasonably convincing, at least when speaking of Newton or Einstein or Darwin (less so when paradigmatic status is conferred on almost any theory or discovery). The more controversial and less acceptable aspects of his view – and which turn an interesting theory of scientific development into a radical theory of science itself – comes with his account of the relationship between rival paradigms and the process of paradigm change. The key point is his insistence that competing paradigms are necessarily incommensurable. In a crisis when the scientific community must decide between old and new paradigms, Kuhn argues that the conflict is not of a kind that can, as one might suppose, be settled by scientific means, such as a critical experiment. There is instead a breakdown in communication; the rival camps are talking past each other. This is a consequence of incommensurability. They are in a sense talking different languages: their conceptual schemes differ; their standards of what is problematic and what can count as a solution differ; to use Kuhn's striking metaphor, they live in different worlds. And because each paradigm carries not only its own theoretical structure but its own ontology and standards and conception of science, there is no higher framework in terms of which rival theories can be assessed. Kuhn writes:

> Like the choice between competing political institutions, that between competing paradigms proves to be a choice between incompatible modes of community life. Because it has that character, the choice is not and cannot be determined merely by the evaluative procedures characteristic of normal science, for these depend in part upon a particular paradigm, and that paradigm is at issue. When paradigms enter, as they must, into a debate about paradigm choice, their role is necessarily circular. Each group uses its own paradigm to argue in that paradigm's defence. . . . Yet, whatever its force, the status of the circular argument is only that of persuasion. It cannot be made logically or even probabilistically compelling for those who refuse to step into the circle. The premises and values shared by the two parties to a debate over paradigms are not sufficiently extensive for that. As in political revolutions, so in paradigm choice – there is no standard higher than the assent of the relevant community. (p. 94)

Thus, the superiority of one paradigm over another cannot be demonstrated, cannot be proven: 'The competition between paradigms is not the sort of battle that can be resolved by proof' (p. 148). Since there is no logical basis for choice, then other, non-scientific factors must play a part in determining which paradigm the community opts for: social factors, the persuasiveness of those promoting the new paradigm, and so on. (Kuhn makes the point that to any problem there is, in principle, an infinite number of possible answers, and there is the question as to why the scientific community chooses one rather than the others. But this is really a separate question.) It is impossible, Kuhn argues, for a scientist to achieve understanding of a new paradigm gradually by following logical steps: 'Just because it is a transition between incommensurables, the transition between competing paradigms cannot be made a step at a time, forced by logic and neutral experience' (p. 150).

It requires a 'gestalt switch', something akin to a religious conversion. But how, Kuhn asks, does a whole scientific community come to change its mind? There are a variety of answers. Sometimes the new paradigm is a 'better fit' than the old; Lavoisier's theory of oxygen was superior to Priestly's in this respect and so was accepted (p. 147). Some are converted because the new paradigm solves the problems of the old. Sometimes the new theory is more quantitatively accurate. Another criterion that may operate is the aesthetic; the new view may be 'neater' or 'simpler'. But none of these, Kuhn insists, is logically compelling. They will not shake everyone from their commitment to the old paradigm. The scientific community moves on leaving them isolated until they eventually die off. Such holding out is possible because a decision to adopt a new paradigm is not a matter of acknowledging a proof; in the last analysis: 'A decision of this kind can only be made on faith' (p. 158).

II

Thus Kuhn presents a vivid and dramatic picture which, if true, has profound implications. The first is that the traditional picture of science as a body of knowledge which is steadily accumulating, brick upon brick, is false. Secondly, if the superiority of one paradigm over another cannot be shown according to any scientific or logical criteria then it is questionable whether science can be said to be rationally progressive at all. Paradigms cannot be checked against nature independently of any paradigms, for it is only through a paradigm that nature can be approached, and each paradigm confirms itself. There is no superior and inferior, only differing conceptions of nature and science. Why one paradigm prevails at any one time is more to do with historical and sociological factors than scientific ones; and the notion of science progressively getting nearer to the truth is an illusion. Finally, and most importantly in the present context, the dividing line between science and ideology is brought into doubt. Kuhn's whole case must be shown to be substantially false if the main arguments of the present work are not to be fatally undermined.

The Structure of Scientific Revolutions is in many ways a brilliant book, intelligent, original and lucid. And yet its most dramatic assertions are by no means as unambiguous as Kuhn's admirers (especially sociologists) usually suppose. He tends to make a bold assertion, then qualify it drastically, only to reaffirm the original assertion as though the qualifications made no difference. There are several examples of this but the most important is in respect of the crucial issue of incommensurability and paradigm choice. As we have seen, Kuhn insists that rival paradigms are incommensurable and that there are no rational grounds for choosing one rather than the other; and yet superior problem-solving ability, better fit with nature, more quantifiability and greater simplicity are all cited (pp. 147 and 153–6) as reasons scientists may have for changing their allegiance to a new paradigm. But these are perfectly rational reasons, and so Kuhn appears to be claiming both that there are no rational means and that there are rational means of choosing between paradigms. But it must be one or the other. If we are to take the notion of incommensurability seriously then these non-paradigm-dependent decision-criteria would be an impossibility. Nor would it be possible for the achievements of one paradigm to be taken up by another; but Kuhn admits: 'though new paradigms seldom or never possess all the capabilities of their predecessors, they usually preserve a great deal of the most concrete parts of past achievement' (p. 169).

It would not be possible for a scientist to say, as they sometimes do, that: 'so-and-so is doing some interesting work which could transform the whole field'; and the scientific past would be incomprehensible.[9] There may perhaps be some plausibility in some of Kuhn's examples of incommensurable concepts, but he cannot have it both ways; he cannot have partial incommensurability and then pick and choose examples to suit his argument. If he accepts, as he does and cannot avoid doing, the existence of rational decision-criteria then his case for incommensurability must fall, and with it his case against the rational progressiveness of science.

However, Kuhn feels that he has one argument which outweighs all the rest, which is that in a revolutionary situation there are those who resist the change and never accept the new paradigm. This may be a frequent phenomenon, but it would not follow from this that only incommensurability could explain it. It is probably best explained in terms of stubbornness and failure of understanding. But the contingent facts of human obduracy and obtuseness do not determine any logical relationships, and the logical status of science cannot be dependent upon how a number of scientists behaved in particular historical circumstances when faced with the difficult business of coming to terms with new ideas. Both Kuhn and (as we saw in the previous section) Popper agree that a theory cannot be absolutely disproved, which suggests that the scientist who stubbornly holds out despite the evidence is being unreasonable rather than irrational. It is not irrational to believe that new evidence will eventually swing the balance of probability back to the old theory; though no doubt faith in paradigm regained can be taken to strange lengths. But it does not follow from this, as Kuhn seems to think, that paradigms must be incommensurable or that there cannot be adequate grounds for choosing between them. Perhaps it does require a 'gestalt switch' to comprehend a new theory (and no doubt this was true of quantum mechanics, relativity and others), but again this does not preclude rational choice. Kuhn seems to confuse the business of understanding a theory with the business of assessing its merits. It may be quite impossible to say whether the picture is really a duck or a rabbit, but given the decision-criteria that Kuhn himself cites, this does not apply to scientific theories. (Where they are not decisive, rival theories may both be accepted until such times as there is conclusive evidence for one or the other, or some reconciling theory is found, as is most famously the case with wave and particle theories of light.) Yet Kuhn insists that the decision-criteria are not compelling, and in an absolute sense this may be true. But this is not necessary; it is only necessary that they be sufficient to make a rational choice. And since they clearly are, Kuhn's stubborn scientist is neither here nor there.

Thus, there are rational decision procedures in science; indeed, without them science would be a shambles. It would certainly be so on Kuhn's account, where paradigmatic status is conferred on a bewildering variety of phenomena from the cosmic theories of Newton and Einstein to the discovery of Uranus and the development of the Leyden jar;[10] and where every new paradigm – that is, every significant new theory, discovery and technical innovation – carries its own conception of nature and science which is incommensurable with every other. If science really did go on in this way it would be a chaos which not even the most congenitally obtuse writer of science textbooks could fail to notice. But science is not like this. Paradigms may be incompatible (no one would wish to argue with that) but they are not incommensurable, while the decision-criteria bring order and coherence to the process of development. However, these decision-criteria are only part of the wider framework of scientific understanding which Kuhn denies by insisting that every paradigm has its own peculiar conception of science. What Kuhn does is to conflate understanding and theory. But a wider framework of understanding above and independent of the paradigms is something Kuhn does occasionally appear to make reference to without explaining what he means. He writes:

> at a still higher level, there is another set of commitments without which no man is a scientist. The scientist must, for example, be concerned to understand the world and to extend the precision and scope with which it has been ordered. (p. 42)

and again:

> Observation and experience can and must drastically restrict the range of admissible scientific belief, else there would be no science. (p. 4)

Now clearly these suggestions of a notion of 'science as such' would appear to conflict with Kuhn's insistence on incommensurable conceptions of science attaching to every paradigm, yet he discusses them no further. They imply a body of concepts and rules which constitutes the scientific understanding and gives science its logical identity over and above any paradigm. Part of that identity – the part that makes science an academic discipline – is a procedure for choosing between conflicting theories or paradigms; and the decision-criteria, which Kuhn accepts without recognizing their importance, are the basis of just this procedure. Thus, Kuhn's conception of science is false. It cannot challenge the traditional notion of science as productive of objective knowledge, a notion from which ideology can be sharply distinguished.

In truth, Kuhn overstates his case. He has a plausible thesis about the history of science (though not an incontestable one), but then makes an illegitimate jump to the logic of science which results in confusion and contradiction. On the other hand, Kuhn has created an interesting set of ideas that might prove useful if applied to a different and more suitable object. But discussion of this possibility will need to be postponed until we have a more adequate account of the nature of science.

The nature of ideological theory

Neither Popper nor Kuhn can provide us with a satisfactory account of the relationship between science and ideology. Yet we must clarify this matter before a full account of ideological theory can be given. We may accept Popper's view that, given appropriate criteria of testability, science is capable of generating objective knowledge[11] in contrast to ideology, which, because of its pseudo-descriptive nature, cannot. But there is more to the problem than this. To understand ideology as a theoretical structure it is first of all necessary to see that theory plays a quite different role in it than it does in science.

I

Within science there is an essential distinction between scientific understanding on the one hand, and scientific knowledge, usually in the form of true (that is, provisionally true) theories, on the other. An understanding is a body of concepts and principles in terms of which we comprehend the world or some aspect of it. Certain forms of understanding constitute academic disciplines, of which science is one. The scientific form of understanding is composed of a set of principles and concepts – including the uniformity of nature, the principle of causality, experiment, prediction and covering law explanations – all of which are intimately related and defined in terms of each other, and together constitute a framework by means of which the scientist can conceptualize any problem. This framework is not itself true or false, just as the rules of a game are not true or false: rather it sets up the possibility of making true or false statements. It is not itself the object of scientific investigation, but is the 'given' which allows scientific investigation to take place. Theories are only true or false within the framework. The framework determines their identity as scientific, and provides procedures for determining whether they are true or false scientific statements. This is what guarantees that a particular theory can count as knowledge.

The situation is analogous to law. The distinction between the form of understanding and the theories generated within it is not unlike the distinction between the constitution of a state and the laws passed under that constitution. The legality of any particular law passed in the proper way is guaranteed by the constitution, while the constitution itself is not legal in the same way, its foundations being extra-legal. Similarly, scientific theories have to be 'constitutional' and successfully 'passed' as true, while the 'constitution' itself is of a different logical order. The exception to this in the legal sphere is constitutional amendments which must be passed in the proper legal way. Though even here there is arguably an analogy in physical science, since certain theories could be said to have changed or developed the conceptual framework, as quantum mechanics has, although these are rare.

The distinction between theory and understanding is crucial to the nature of science, and the absence of just this distinction is equally crucial to the nature of ideology. In ideology there is no division between theory and understanding: the two are conflated so that the theory *is* the understanding. That is, the theory is the unquestioned 'given' in terms of which the world is conceptualized. There is no overarching framework of understanding that gives to theory its identity and truth status (or, incidentally, for settling revisionist disputes), none for any particular ideology and none for ideology as such; these theories are self-validating. The statement 'All history is the history of class struggle' is not, within Marxism, a theoretical statement in the same way that '$E=mc^2$' is a theoretical statement in science. It is, in Wittgenstein's terminology, a statement of logical grammar; it states a rule of Marxist discourse not a putative fact, and thus has more in common with 'nature is uniform' than with '$E=mc^2$' Marxists no more investigate whether society is class-based, or Liberals whether freedom does increase rationality, or Nazis whether Jews were responsible for the ills of Germany, than scientists investigate whether nature really is uniform. This is the significance of Popper's remark (quoted earlier) about the Marxist with the newspaper seeing Marxism confirmed on every page. Everything is automatically 'seen' in terms of the all-explaining theory, such that the world so 'seen' appears to be further evidence of the theory's truth. The ideological adherent is not, as Popper's view seems to suggest, a would-be scientist with a defective methodology, or someone who happens to think a particular theory happens to be true, but someone with a moral commitment to a view of the world that embodies his moral beliefs. That view of the world may resemble some form of objective theory, but is of a different order; even though it may be an essential part of the adherent's commitment that he accepts the theory as objective knowledge. Thus, it is part of the Marxist's moral belief that Marxism is a scientific theory; but that cannot be taken at face value. Nor can the 'research' that Marxists do as historians or sociologists, for it cannot be research in the academic sense (i.e. the disinterested pursuit of knowledge) but could be no more than a further articulation or extension of the moral understanding in its range and detail – puzzle-solving in the Kuhnian sense – such that the believer can more effectively apply his understanding and comprehend the significance of situations and events in terms of his prior beliefs.

This not only applies to internally developed theories such as Marxism, but also to those taken from elsewhere, such as evolutionary theory borrowed from biology. Taken out of context and embedded in an ideological framework such theories change their nature. They have to be, so to speak, 'wired up' to the rest of the ideology, becoming pseudo-descriptive in the process. But beyond this, they no longer have the context which guarantees their status as scientific or some other kind of knowledge; nor, in consequence, is it any longer provisional knowledge. It is religions and ideologies that deal in certainties, not science. In Kropotkinian Anarchism and Spencerian Liberalism evolutionary theory is made part of the unquestioned given, in terms of which the world is interpreted.

II

Returning to Kuhn, we can now see the significance of the contradiction he falls into whereby he argues that each paradigm carries its own peculiar and incommensurable conception of science, implying that adherents of different paradigms are not engaged in the same activity, while at the same time allowing that there is a higher view of science to which all scientists must be committed. It results from a failure to recognize the distinction between understanding and theory which exists within science but which is noticeably absent in the sphere of ethical belief. But while for this and the other reasons discussed, Kuhn's account of science must be counted a failure, this is not to say that his ideas are without utility. Several writers have attempted to apply his ideas to matters of political understanding.

In his paper 'Paradigms and political theories',[12] Sheldon Wolin uses Kuhn to attack the pretensions of contemporary political scientists who dismiss traditional political theory for being normative, incapable of generating reliable knowledge and therefore 'pre-scientific'. Wolin's strategy is to suggest that the history of political thought is very similar to the history of science as revealed by Kuhn, and that the behaviouralist revolution in political studies is just one paradigm among many (p. 139). Their attack upon traditional theory merely reveals an ignorance and lack of sophistication about the history and logic of science. Unfortunately, Wolin's faith in Kuhn's account of science is unwarranted, and the behaviouralist case is therefore left unscathed (though it does fall for quite other reasons). This leaves Wolin with a Kuhnian account of the history of political thought which, upon examination, is far from convincing. All Wolin in fact does is to draw a few suggestive parallels, such as the observation that political theorizing tends to flourish in times of crisis, in a way similar to Kuhn's 'revolutionary science'. But this is merely redescribing what we already know. Indeed, Wolin is not even consistent in this, for he has two versions of the equivalent of 'normal science'. One of these is that it is lesser thinkers developing the thought of a great thinker – as the Scholastics did of Aristotle – a view that Wolin thinks opens up the possibility of 'cumulative knowledge in the history of political theory' (p. 141), whatever that might mean. But Wolin also offers the view that actual political systems may be viewed as paradigms, so that their workings would be equivalent to 'normal science'. But these views are not consistent, and each alone raises more problems than it solves. Furthermore, Wolin fails to answer the behaviouralist charge that traditional theory is value-laden and incapable of producing objective knowledge. He appears to assume that the adoption of a Kuhnian model overcomes that objection and so does not discriminate between political theories with an ethical content and those without. Wolin in fact uses Kuhn as a set of metaphors to play with and not as any kind of genuinely explanatory theory. Had Wolin not seen Kuhn as a useful stick with which to beat the behaviouralists it is difficult to believe he would have had any genuine use for Kuhnian ideas[13].

In his paper '"Normal" science or political ideology?',[14] Alan Ryan claims to be taking up Wolin's suggestion of applying Kuhnian paradigms to political theories. However, unlike Wolin, Ryan quite properly rejects Kuhn's account of science. But Ryan is not concerned with traditional political theory; instead he wishes to deploy a notion of paradigms as sets of social definitions, norms and expectations which we all need to understand our own and others' behaviour in the practical world, and how these relate to the theories social scientists bring to the understanding of social life. But not only are these 'social paradigms' a long way from anything in Kuhn, Ryan also makes clear that it would be a mistake to attribute to them such characteristically Kuhnian features as universal and enforced acceptance. Again, as with Wolin, Ryan could perfectly well say what he has to say without reference to Kuhn, which he makes no genuine use of.

But these rather abortive attempts to make use of Kuhn do not exhaust all the possibilities. It has been said that Kuhn destroys the distinction between science and ideology, and if Kuhn does not tell us anything about science then perhaps he can tell us something about ideology. In his contribution to *Criticism and the Growth of Knowledge* (p. 33), J. W. N. Watkins makes the interesting point that Kuhn treats science as though it was religion. Indeed it can be argued that Kuhn fails to understand science precisely because he attributes to it features that only properly belong to ethical belief, that is to religion and ideology, and that this is why those (like Barnes quoted earlier) who accept Kuhn's account of science have confused the scientific with the ideological. If this is so, then it is reasonable to suppose that Kuhn's ideas might provide the basis of an adequate account of ideological theory. This is indeed the case, but only given certain important modifications.

We have already noted two features of Kuhn's ideas applying to ideology: the fusion of theory and understanding, and the notion of puzzle-solving within the context of a theory that guarantees a solution but which itself is beyond investigation. These are, one might say, by-products of the two central notions of paradigm and incommensurability. The paradigm is the unquestioned framework, providing explanations, concepts, vocabulary and model analyses. Each ideology has its unique complex of theory, concepts and intellectual techniques and instruments, and each is different from and incommensurable with that of other ideologies (though the relationship between ideologies can sometimes be more complex than this). Each ideological theory is constitutive of both the world and the way the world is to be understood. However, this picture of ideological theory is incomplete. Two further dimensions must be added, which will not only complete the picture but will explain why ideological theory has such distinctively Kuhnian features. These extra dimensions are first of all ethical content and secondly metaphysical status.

It was stressed in the previous chapter that the fusion of the factual and the ethical was the nub of ideology, and in fact virtually everything that is distinctive about ideology can be traced back, more or less directly, to this central feature. Incommensurability as between different ethical beliefs can be explained in this way. Rival theories and the concepts they contain are incommensurable because of differences of values that cannot be reconciled. It was noted in the earlier discussion of Kuhn that he admits that in the last analysis 'observation and experience' are decisive in science. But because ideological statements are pseudo-descriptive (that is, morally charged and without reference) they are not corrigible by facts; the flexibility of pseudo-descriptiveness mean that facts never need be embarrassing. This is a sphere of faith where evidence is of little significance. What the believer 'sees' in the world is a function of his values, which are embodied in the concepts he uses. The Liberal and the Marxist can 'see' the same situation quite differently, but there is no rational choosing between them, no proving one is right and the other wrong. There is no kind of logic that could settle their dispute; no decision-procedure as there is in science. It is thus the ethical content which explains this Kuhnian feature of ideology which Kuhn himself does not explain in respect of science but merely asserts. Kuhn only seeks to explain why scientists do not really attempt to settle their paradigm problems through discussion by insisting, implausibly, upon the blindness and obduracy of all scientific communities. But the kind of passionate commitment Kuhn attributes to every scientific community is far more characteristic of rival groups of ideological adherents, and for good reasons (that is, good logical reasons, not the dubious psychological reasons that Kuhn relies on). As between rival ideological beliefs there really is no common ground, there really are no public criteria that could settle the question of who is right. Ideological disputants are talking past each other and seeing past each other; they speak a different language. If one man sees freedom all round him while another sees oppression, or if one sees his fellow men as essentially good while another sees them as congenitally evil, then they are living in different worlds in a much more profound sense than any two scientists with rival theories.

This is why ideological and religious conversions have to be 'gestalt switches' that are dramatic and wholesale, while conversion to a new scientific theory need not be. The scientist may indeed be 'forced by logical and neutral experience' in the very way that Kuhn denies. It may happen that for reasons that are nothing to do with the logic of science, some particular scientific community is strongly attached to some theory, but this is not of the same order as the moral commitment which is a necessary feature of all ideological belief. Ideological beliefs are genuinely incommensurable and can genuinely bind a community together. Equally, they can divide a community. Curiously, Kuhn illustrates his contention that paradigm disputes cannot be rationally settled by using the analogy of a society divided by a conflict of political belief, where, he says the issue can only be settled by which side the community decides to support. This is indeed true in the case of ideology where there are no decision-procedures, but not so of science which does have such procedures which Kuhn cites but does not recognize. Ideological belief is a more powerful commitment that goes much deeper than any factual theory, since it goes to the roots of our identity: it is concerned with all aspects of our lives, with who we are and what our place is in the world, with what values we should hold and how we should live. The community sees itself and the world in a certain way, and so sees the past in a certain way; and consequently the ideology must rewrite history in its own image, which adherents to a scientific theory may or may not do.

A second feature of ideological theories or paradigms that must supplement a Kuhn-based view is their metaphysical status, and this too is bound up with their ethical content. There are different accounts of what constitutes metaphysical theories and concepts, but common to all accounts is the idea that metaphysical statements about the nature of reality are beyond the reach of empirical confirmation or disconfirmation, not only in practice but in principle. Now if the analysis of the previous chapter is correct and ideological statements and concepts necessarily have a value content and in consequence are pseudo-descriptive and non-referential, then this must put them beyond empirical test and make them necessarily metaphysical. As with incommensurability, Kuhn cannot explain why it is necessarily the case that scientific paradigms are not themselves subject to investigation (a view that is in any case demonstrably false), but in the case of ideological theories there is, again, good reasons why this is so. In the first place, ideological commitment is to the theory alone and not also to some higher framework of understanding, as is the case with science (which Kuhn both denies and acknowledges). Secondly, ideological adherents not only do not put their theories to the test, because of their ethical/metaphysical nature they could not if they wanted to. Thirdly, ideological commitment involves a moral commitment to see the world as the theory describes it. Because the theory is also the understanding, to investigate it is to acknowledge another and higher understanding; it is to step aside from the commitment, deny the faith and accept the authority of a higher truth which the theory does not comprehend.

Thus, we have a picture of ideological theory where theory and understanding are fused, and where ethical and factual are fused, and which are, in consequence, both metaphysical and incommensurable. But there is more to the matter than this. If this analysis is correct then we have to ask how this affects other aspects of theory (at least of scientific theory) to which ideological theory also lays claim: that is to be explanatory, to be predictive and to be true.

III

Not all ideological theories take physical science as their model. Yet all such theories claim to be dealing in factual truths about the world, to be describing it accurately; and like scientific theories they claim to explain and predict. However, the same ethical element that vitiates their descriptive power also denies the possibility of proper explanation and prediction. But more important than this is that, at least where the explanations and predictions are central to the theory, they are part of the framework of belief that is not open to question; that is, they have the status of necessary truths.

What ideologies seek to explain, potentially at least, is nothing less than the whole of human experience; though the immediate concern is the present situation of mankind. The theory an ideology contains is concerned with the identification, explanation and remedy of social ills. Thus is Marxism concerned with the inequality, exploitation and dehumanization inherent in capitalist society and with how this is an inevitable outcome of the historical class struggle which will only be cured by the socialist transformation of society through revolutionary action; thus is Liberalism concerned with the oppression and denial of individual rights in so much of the world where irrational ideas and institutions prevail and where progress must be made towards liberty and justice; thus was Nazism concerned with the pollution and debilitation of the Aryan race by the historical race-enemy, the Jews, against whom the struggle had to be intensified to restore that racial hierarchy which is the natural and just ordering of mankind and the foundation of true civilization. Each ideology centres on an explanatory and prescriptive theory of social ordering in terms of which all other social manifestations – law, art, economy, etc. – and any ideas, institutions or events can be interpreted. Each ideology gives an all-embracing picture of the human condition.

As we have seen, ideologies purport to describe the world but their descriptions can only be pseudo-descriptions. Similarly, ideological explanations are pseudo-explanations; although explanation is a more complex case than description. Take the Nazi belief that Germany's sufferings in the 1920s were the consequence of an international conspiracy of Jewish capitalists and communists. Now, however widly implausible this explanation may be, it is nevertheless logically possible that a group of capitalists and communists who happened to be Jewish were in fact responsible in some way for the horrors that Germany suffered. Though it is an extreme case it does suggest that it is possible for ideological explanations to be factually true. But it depends on what is meant by 'explanation'. In an academic discipline what is recognized as a true explanation is not one that merely corresponds to the facts, but one which is adequately supported by appropriate evidence; that is, knowledge is *justified* true belief and only certain kinds of justification can count. But in ideological explanation evidence has no such essential role. For the Nazi, Germany's plight *had* to be attributable to the machinations of the race-enemy. It was a necessary truth and a confirming instance of a universal truth about Jews being the source of all evil. Any confirming evidence was no doubt welcome, but not essential; any counter-evidence could be interpreted as an extension of the original Jewish plot. In Marxist theory class struggle is all pervading and all explanatory. If we point to conflict not based on class the Marxist will tell us that we are being superficial and that class struggle is the deeper reality; and if we point to periods of social tranquillity when there is no apparent struggle of any kind we will be told that the class struggle is there, only 'latent'. These explanations, which have nothing to do with falsifiability or demonstration or even evidence, are only explanatory for the believer. For the rest of us they are only pseudo-explanations.

If ideologies can only produce pseudo-descriptions and pseudo-explanations we can hardly deny them the title of pseudo-theory, (taking academic theory as the standard). Yet they always claim the status of academic theory, that is, to be good science, good philosophy or whatever. But these claims cannot be sustained. Descriptions which only describe, explanations that only explain and truths which are only true if and only if one believes that a certain set of values is embodied in the world, can hardly count as objective knowledge. No values are embodied in the world, and no set of values can be shown to be absolute, and so no evaluations are absolutely true either. The Liberal enters the factory of a commercial firm and sees factory owner and workers in an economic relationship freely entered into in a free market and so he is seeing the good society in action; while the Marxist observing the 'same' situation sees exploitation and dehumanization. Their disagreement is not of the sort that can be settled; there is simply no procedure for settling which is right; their views are irreconcilable and incommensurable. To hold a view like this is not a matter of proof of evidence. You either see the world that way or you do not.

Much the same is true of prediction. A prediction is related to the prescriptions of the ideology, with the consequences of following or not following them. Not all of these are of central importance, but those that are have a special status, and are in fact pseudo-predictions. As we noted earlier, ideologists weld together contingent relationships into necessary ones in order to preserve the coherence of their theory, and this is especially true of future events. Thus capitalism *must* collapse through the weaknesses of its own structure; the Germans *must* flourish in war and civilisation once the race enemy has been destroyed; democratic participation *must* make people more rational and tolerant. In each case a contingent possibility is turned into a necessary truth, an article of faith, such that no failure of expectations is allowed to challenge belief. Evidence can always be interpreted: if the extermination of the Jews does not promote Germany's greatness then there must have been more Jews in the world than originally thought and the secret Jews must then be eliminated; if capitalism does not collapse in the predicted manner then it must be because it has a yet higher stage to pass through first; if democratic participation has not made men rational and tolerant then more time is necessary before the educative process can fully work. Thus, ideologies claim to determine what in fact no theory can determine, namely inevitable outcomes. But the price of this is to render these determinations untestable, irrefutable and lacking any strong grip on empirical reality. Although this really only applies to structurally essential relations. Those failures that do not challenge the basic theory are obviously less vital and can be replaced, so if one tactic fails another can be employed.

The point of this whole apparatus of theory, explanation and prediction is not the disinterested pursuit of truth but to give substance and authority to the ideologist's vision of what is wrong with the world and what needs to be done about it, to his values and ideals and prescriptions. And, whatever the scientific pretensions of his theory, this comes first. As Ernest Barker says of Herbert Spencer:

> He did not really approach politics through science, without preconceptions drawn from other sources, and with the sole idea of eliciting the political lessons which science might teach. On the contrary he was already charged with political preconceptions when he approached science, and he sought to find in science examples or analogies to point a moral already drawn and adorn a tale whose plot was already sketched.[15]

Hitler was a similar case. As Jackel points out,[16] at 30 Hitler was a conventional nationalist and anti-semite, but around these practical attitudes he built a theory of some originality, in order that he might 'deduce' the policies he had already decided upon. Locke's *Second Treatise* is a theoretical defence of prior Whig principles; and Lenin was a revolutionary before he was a Marxist. Given his principles, his moral vision, the ideologist seeks to make the world of objective knowledge serve his practical purposes in a way that cannot logically be done; that is, deducing from the facts of the world the direction in which we ought to go. This is not to say that the ideological enterprise is an unintelligent or ignoble one; but it is logically flawed.

Tolstoy once remarked that science was meaningless because it gives no answer to the only important question: 'What shall we do and how shall we live?'[17] But whatever the profounder point Tolstoy was making, the remark does have its degree of mundance logical truth. From the point of view of practice, science itself can give no guidance. But ideologists are, so to speak, professionally committed to an opposite view. They characteristically perceive their task as revealing the practical implications of some body of established knowledge or putative knowledge – scientific, philosophic, historical, etc. – which they embody in their theory. But they are not extending academic knowledge, as they often claim to be doing, but using it, making it do work for which it was not designed, embracing or absorbing it within a practical vision which already has value commitments.

Their ideological understanding is a practical understanding, and the categories of such an understanding are quite different from those of the academic. From a practical standpoint objects and events in the world are viewed in terms of what is useful, efficient, possible, beneficial, morally right or wrong; and the ideologist views the sphere of the academic in the same light. The facts of the world are useful or irrelevant; ideas are judged in terms of the effects of believing them rather than their intrinsic truth or coherence; while the purpose of history is to illuminate our present concerns, not the past itself. Many examples could be cited. The efforts of Socialists, Anarchists, Liberals and others to demonstrate that the theory of evolution underpins their particular view of the world is a striking and obvious example. There is Bentham's use of classical economics as a model of society, and Popper's use of scientific method as a model of social reform, and many more. As to ideas, as we saw in Chapter One both Marxist and Liberal accounts of ideology are based on the classification of ideas in terms of their effects, good or ill. The Liberal uses philosophy as a source of universal values, while the Marxist even condemns neutral conceptual analysis as disguised support for the status quo. But in some ways the most important case is history, since all ideological positions must have some view of it and the view is of a particular kind. Herbert Butterfield called it 'reading the past backwards'. His concern, in *The Whig Interpretation of History* and elsewhere, is with bad history done by unwitting historians:

> The study of the past with one eye, so to speak, upon the present is the source of all sins and sophistries in history. .... It is the essence of what we mean by the word 'unhistorical'.[18]

But the distortions he is attacking arise from ideological influence. Following Butterfield, Oakeshott insists that to pursue history in order to discover how we arrived at our present plight, where we went wrong, or to reveal past glories that might yet inspire us, or from any similar motive, is to pursue 'practical history' not academic history.[19] This is precisely the ideological approach to history. It is history interpreted in terms of the ideology's values and theoretical categories. As Kuhn alleges of scientific paradigms, ideologies recreate the past in their own image.

The ideologist creates a world, embracing past, present and future. The world he constructs from a variety of intellectual materials, often structured on quite different principles, is a world which men can occupy and, from a practical point of view, find satisfying. That is, a world that is morally comprehensible; a world where fact and value form a continuum, where man has a place and a direction. None of this would be possible without a framework of theory. Values, ideals and prescriptions are not enough; they cannot constitute a world. A theory is needed to hold the structure up. But as we have seen, a special kind of theory is necessary. It is a theory that is imbued with values; one that has been taken out of the sphere of investigation and criticism (the sphere that guarantees its academic truth and coherence), and which shares no common ground, no common language, with rival theories. It is a theory which explains the world, but only to the believer to whom it guarantees the future. It is a theory which, whatever its origins – whether borrowed like Spencerian evolution or purpose-built like Marxism sociology – is wholly immersed in the practical.

Notes

1. Karl Popper, *The Open Society and its Enemies*, 5th edn, (RKP, 1966), vol. II, p. 84. Subsequent references are to this edition.
2. The obvious objection that Popper's charge against such as Marxism and Freudianism is not that they are 'bad science' but that they are 'non-science' is strictly true. On the other hand, Popper's attitude to Marxism in particular is more complex than this, as we shall see. Besides, 'bad science' can be taken to mean either 'poor science' (which seems to be Popper's view of historicism), but also, at a stretch, work that aspires to be scientific but fails (which Popper accepts as being true of Marx himself and perhaps some others). 'Bad science' best sums up Popper's view of Marx and Engels, while 'non-science' best characterizes his view of their latter-day followers who treat their works as holy writ.
3. Karl Popper, *Conjectures and Refutations*, 5th edn, (RKP, 1974), p. 35. Subsequent references are to this edition.
4. Karl Popper, *The Logic of Scientific Discovery*, 6th edn, (Hutchinson, 1972), p. 50.
5. Karl Popper, *The Poverty of Historicism*, 2nd edn, (RKP, 1960), p. 3.
6. Thomas Kuhn, *The Structure of Scientific Revolutions*, 2nd edn, (University of Chicago Press, 1970). Subsequent references are to this edition.
7. Barry Barnes, *T.S. Kuhn and Social Science*, (Macmillan, 1982), p. 107.
8. See Thomas Kuhn, 'The function of dogma in scientific research', in A.C. Crombie (ed.) *Scientific Change*, (Heinemann, 1963), pp. 347–69.
9. C.f. S.E. Toulmin, 'Does the distinction between normal and revolutionary science hold water?' in I. Lakatos and A. Musgrave (eds), *Criticism and the Growth of Knowledge*, (CUP, 1970), pp. 37–47. Subsequent references are to this edition.
10. *The Structure of Scientific Revolutions*, op. cit., pp. 115–16 for the discovery of Uranus, and pp. 61–2 for the development of the Leyden jar.
11. It is only the immediate point that is being accepted here. It does not imply acceptance of Popper's entire account of science, which has been subject to a certain amount of legitimate criticism, and which at best is only partially correct. The account of some aspects of the logic of science, that is being offered here does favour Popper's view that science is rationally progressive, but is neutral as between Popper and Kuhn on whether science is moving ever closer towards the 'truth' in the absolute sense of correspondence.
12. Sheldon Wolin, 'Paradigms and political theories' in Preston King and B.C. Parekh (eds), *Politics and Experience*, (CUP, 1968), pp. 125–52.
13. See also Sheldon Wolin, 'Political theory as a vocation', in Martin Fleisher (ed), *Machiavelli and the Nature of Political Thought*, (Croom Helm, 1973), pp. 23–75. In this

later paper Wolin takes a slightly different line on behaviouralism, but his view of Kuhn is the same.

14. Alan Ryan, "'Normal'' science or political ideology?', in P. Laslett, *et al.*, (eds), *Philosophy, Politics and Society*, 4th series, (Basil Blackwell, 1972), pp. 86–100.
15. Ernest Barker, *Political Thought in England from Herbert Spencer to the Present Day*, (Williams and Norgate, 1915), p. 85.
16. Eberhard Jackel, *Hitler's World View*, (Harvard University Press, 1981), p. 117.
17. Quoted in Max Weber, 'Science as a vocation' in H.H. Gerth and C. Wright Mills (eds), *From Max Weber*, (RKP, 1948), p. 143.
18. Herbert Butterfield, *The Whig Interpretation of History*, (Pelican Books, 1973), p. 11.
19. See in particular Michael Oakeshott, 'The activity of being an historian', in *Rationalism in Politics and Other Essays*, (Methuen, 1962), pp. 137–67.

CHAPTER FOUR

IDEOLOGY AND ETHICS

The discussion of the nature of ideology so far points to the dominating influence of its ethical content, and therefore to the conclusion that it can be best characterized as a form of ethical understanding. The purpose of this chapter is to examine where ideology fits in to, and in what ways it relates to, the wider ethical field. However, the nature of this wider field is much disputed so that it is necessary to begin by offering a general account of it, starting with the most basic question of what constitutes ordinary morality.

The nature of ordinary morality

I

Much of twentieth-century moral philosophy has centred on the question of the relationship between fact and value. Accounts of the nature of morality may be grouped into three broad types according to their response to this problem. Several, such as Emotivism and Prescriptivism, have taken as their starting-point Hume's strict separation of fact and value, which denies any possibility of deriving one from the other. The most notable exponent of this view over the last thirty years has been R.M. Hare.[1] His account of morality is roughly that moral statements are characterized by their universality and their prescriptivity, particular judgements being syllogistically derived from these general statements. If an individual decides that certain rules of conduct should apply to all, including himself, then these rules constitute his morality, irrespective of their content. All moral rules ultimately derive from such individual decisions. An individual may, of course, simply accept prevailing norms, but that is still his decision, and besides, the origin of these norms must have been the decisions of individuals in the past. But once an individual has decided on his principles then no one can prove that he has the wrong ones, or that some other set are morally superior. Consequently, there is no decision procedure for solving fundamental moral disputes.

This view of morality has been very influential, but it has come under increasing criticism in recent years. Hare's position has certain similarities with that of Kant, and many critics have argued that it shares the same weaknesses in its over-formality and lack of content, such that it can be manipulated in ways that can produce absurd and contradictory results. It does indeed seem absurd that, to use the example of Phillips and Mounce[2] 'everyone should clap hands every two hours' could, on its own, count as a moral rule. Furthermore, we could think of practical rules – 'everyone should be selfish' – which would cut across Kant's important distinction between the prudential and the truly moral. With sufficient ingenuity we can even, as with Kant, think up sets of rules which effectively allow us to do what we want while others may not, which destroys the whole point of universality. But though important, these criticisms do not actually refute Hare's position; rather they reveal its inadequacy as a comprehensive account of moral thinking.

Hare's main critics – including G.E.M. Anscombe, Peter Geach and perhaps most notably Phillipa Foot[3] – have taken a quite opposite view of the fact–value relationship. Their starting-point has been a rejection of Hare's notion that absolutely anything can count as a moral rule, provided it has the right logical characteristics. Instead, they argue that morality derives from certain basic facts about human existence: Anscombe speaks of the facts of 'human flourishing', while Foot of the facts of 'human good and harm'. Both have in mind an analogy with plants, which have certain basic needs such as water and sunlight, the provision or denial of which represents good or bad for plants.

Human beings have equivalent needs in terms of which moral good and bad can be assessed. An individual action can, therefore, be morally evaluated according to whether it promotes or denies the basic needs of a human being or beings; doing either of these things will be a factual matter which will entail a moral judgement. Thus, we have a universal morality applying to all men at all times irrespective of circumstances, since all men have the same basic needs. Such universalism has undeniable advantages. There are no problems (as there are for Humeans) with other people's beliefs and practices that we find abhorrent – like Nazism or primitive ways of dealing with unwanted babies – which can simply be dismissed as immoral. If alternative moralities cannot be reduced to the universal one, they can be rejected as wrong. Finally, there is a decision procedure that can, in principle, resolve all moral disputes. This approach has much in common with that of traditional Natural Law thinkers like Thomas Aquinas, from where perhaps the inspiration came, but for the purposes of this discussion it can be grouped along with other universal moralities which have much less in common with Natural Law. The obvious example here is Utilitarianism, where the absolute good is not human flourishing but human happiness. (It should be noted that the only concern here is with Utilitarianism as an account of what morality necessarily is; choosing to regard human happiness, or human flourishing, etc., as one's ultimate good is a separate matter.)

But although the universalists rightly emphasize the problem of content in Hare's position, they cannot provide an adequate solution. Their alternatives are either too narrow or too broad. If 'happiness' or 'flourishing' or 'good and harm' are taken in the narrow senses we often take them in everyday conversation, then they could not possibly cover all that people value or regard as morally significant. Philippa Foot sometimes talks as though the most important moral consideration was physical injury, but many would regard any physical injury and even death, as a trivial matter compared with the loss of their souls or their honour. We might even conceive of a society where it was believed that a person's reward in heaven was directly proportional to the physical suffering they had endured in this life, and where, in consequence, physical injury was not regarded as a bad thing. On the other hand, if we interpret 'happiness' or 'flourishing' or Foot's 'good and harm' sufficiently widely to embrace most people's highest values, then the terms would become meaningless. We cannot talk of the 'facts' of human flourishing or happiness or good and harm if different people have quite different conceptions of these things. Anscombe, in the article where she proposes 'human flourishing' as the absolute good, goes on to admit that she cannot define it;[4] and as we saw in the previous section, there are any number of different and incompatible accounts of what human flourishing is.[5] But if this is so, then how can the 'correct' account of human flourishing (or happiness or good and harm) be established? We cannot use the 'facts' of flourishing or happiness or good and harm as a standard, for it is just these 'facts' that are in dispute. And if a particular interpretation is simply laid down as the 'correct' one, then this can only be a narrow and partisan view, which has to answer the question of Bernard Williams (quoted in the Introduction) which asks by what right anyone legislates in these matters; to which no remotely adequate answer seems possible.

Thus, we have two broad positions, Humean and universalist, which are diametrically opposed. There is, however, a third position lying somewhere between the two. This has been developed by such philosophers as Peter Winch, D.Z. Phillips and Howard Mounce and R.W. Beardsmore,[6] and derives largely from the work of Wittgenstein. W.D. Hudson offers reasons for believing that Wittgenstein would not have agreed with them;[7] nevertheless it will be convenient to refer to this group as 'Wittgensteinians'. What they have done is to take Wittgenstein's analysis of the rules of language and applied it, as far as possible, to the rules of morality. Just as Wittgenstein argued that the essence of the rules of language is that they are shared and grow out of shared practices and a shared way of life, so they have argued that moral rules only have meaning within the context of shared moral practices, a shared way of life. Phillips and Mounce (who we may take as representative of this group) state, somewhat baldly, that there are no such things as 'theories of goodness' (*Moral Practices*, p. 60) and what they seem to mean by this is that an abstract set of rules, divorced from any practice, can have no sense, cannot constitute a morality. Hare's position implies that an individual can, so to speak, step outside of the jurisdiction of the prevailing moral norm and make a choice of commitments; but Phillips and Mounce deny this possibility. For them, one can no more step outside of morality than one can step outside language, and one can no more have a private morality than one can have a private language. They argue that a morality must be embedded in a way of life so that our moral understanding is part of our understanding of the world. Facts and values do not come in separate boxes but are bound together within moral practices. We do not learn the facts of lying, stealing, cruelty and murder, and then go on to learn that these things are wrong.

We learn fact and evaluation together, and employ concepts that are both factual and possess moral import: 'deceit', 'kindness', 'murder' and the rest. These concepts have a crucial role in moral reasoning.:

> Such concepts as sincerity, honesty, courage, loyalty, respect and, of course, a host of others, provide the kind of background necessary in order to make sense of rules as moral principles. It does not follow that all the possible features of such backgrounds need to be present in every case. The important point to stress is that unless the given rule has *some* relation to such backgrounds, we would not know what is meant by calling it a moral principle.
>
> (*Moral Practices*, p. 47)

To make moral judgements some such background needs to be taken for granted:

> In order for a man to hold a moral position at all, there must be certain things it does not make sense for him to question. In our society, for example, it does not make sense to ask whether honesty is in general good, or murder bad, or generosity admirable.
>
> (*Moral Practices*, pp. 17–18)

Phillips and Mounce argue that moral judgements are not syllogistically derived from moral principles, but are applications of these concepts. Thus, to call something 'lying' or 'murder' is both to describe and evaluate at the same time. There is, then, no gulf between fact and values; though this can only be true within the context of particular moral practices. What can count as a morally significant fact varies from practice to practice, and there can be no facts of this kind that have a necessary moral significance for all men independent of any moral practices. There is, therefore, no position outside moral practices from which different moralities can be compared and judged. This means that fundamental moral disputes involving different moral practices may end in a deadlock which no facts or form of reasoning can overcome. And this is not only true of disputes between different cultures, but also of disputes within a culture.

II

It should be clear from previous chapters that it is the last of these three positions that is closest to the view of morality that informs this work. But the Wittgensteinian position will not do as it stands. It has substantial weaknesses that need to be overcome before it can be accepted. The Wittgensteinians go to some lengths to refute the positions represented by Foot and Hare. But though they are effective against Foot, their attempts to refute Hare are rather less successful On two issues especially – the fact–value relationship and the possibility of individual moral autonomy – their arguments seem to create more problems than they solve. Phillips and Mounce in particular attack Hare vigorously for maintaining a strict divorce between fact and value. But this does not seem entirely fair, for their own position insists, in sharp contrast to that of Anscombe and Foot, there can be no necessary connections between facts and moral conclusions independent of moral practices. But it is just at this absolute level, the same level as Foot and Anscombe, and in direct response to views such as theirs, that Hare is dealing; whereas Phillips and Mounce are dealing in relative terms, at the level of societies and social groups. All they are doing is substituting social convention for individual decision, and to suggest that within moral practices people fuse the descriptive and the evaluative in various ways does not necessarily contradict Hare's view that ultimately there are no necessary connections.

In other words, the two positions are not strictly comparable because they are operating on different levels. They are also not comparable in a second sense. When Phillips and Mounce speak of deriving moral judgements from fact within moral practices, they are not using 'fact' in the way Hare uses it. The sort of 'facts' they have in mind would include such as 'he is lying' and 'she has committed murder'. But as we saw in Chapter 2, the use of morally charged terms such as 'lying' and 'murder' alters the logic of apprently descriptive statements, so that although they may have a descriptive element they cannot, strictly speaking, be descriptive or factual statements at all. It is, therefore, highly misleading of Phillips and Mounce to speak of 'facts' in this way. It would be better, perhaps to speak of them, as was suggested in that earlier chapter, in terms of 'quasi-description' and 'quasi-facts'; and from which moral conclusions can be derived because there is a moral content there already. Thus Phillips and Mounce are not refuting Hare on this point, as they seem to think they are.

The second point upon which the Wittgensteinians seek to refute Hare is the possibility of the individual stepping aside from whatever morality he has inherited and choosing the principles he shall henceforth live by. They want to deny this completely and to insist that personal decision has no part to play in a person's moral commitments. Thus Bearsmore writes:

> Morality does not depend on decisions. On the contrary, if it means anything at all to speak of someone making a moral judgement or reaching a moral decision, this is because what he says can be understood as part of an established morality ... no one decides what is to be regarded as having moral significance ... what does and does not count as a moral consideration is determined by the way of life to which an individual belongs. Outside some such way of life, there can be no connection between facts and values, no connection between the reasons we give and the judgements that we make. That is to say, there can be no such things as a moral judgement ... whatever a man's convictions, they can only be understood in so far as they are founded on socially accepted standards. Otherwise they would not be moral convictions at all.
>
> (*Moral Reasoning*, pp. 134 and 130–1[8])

Decision, therefore, is confined to choice of action within a morality, and the notion of deciding between moralities, or principles or practices, is unintelligible since such deciding cannot of necessity form part of an established morality, an established way of life.

The impossibility of detachment, or standing aside from one's values, is connected with the Wittgensteinian's insistence that only by taking certain things for granted is morality possible at all. Together, these rule out any deliberation upon, or questioning of our commitments; as Beardsmore makes clear:

> Would it, for instance, make sense to suppose that a man brought up to regard suicide, murder and adultery as evils, might somehow get outside these values and ask himself whether they were not perhaps virtues. It should be clear that on my account such a question would be incoherent. I am maintaining that the events in a man's life,

the decision he makes, his problems and judgements, have the significance for him that they do, only by reference to his moral viewpoint. So it is by no means clear what it could mean to suppose that he might simply set himself to question the worth of his viewpoint.

(Moral Reasoning, p. 79)

This is not to say, however, that no questioning of basic principles is possible, but it is only possible from within the embrace of another moral commitment; so that the mere questioning of our assumptions implies that we have already abandoned them in favour of others. Phillips and Mounce show this in their discussion of family commitments (*Moral Practices,* p. 116); and they go on to argue that because modern society is so complex it is possible to judge one moral practice from within another, which gives rise to the illusion that we can deliberate upon and choose our moral principles, an illusion which is the basis of Hare's mistaken account. Hare's case, they insist, 'involves the assumption that moral values come into our minds from nowhere' (p. 117), which cannot be the case.

The overwhelming emphasis of the Wittgensteinians on the morality we are brought up to accept suggests some difficulty in explaining moral change, both individual and social, and also moral communication. Beardsmore can only understand a change of moral view as something like a religious conversion, where: 'Though the change in the convert's views may be a radical one, it is clear that it does not depend on a "decision of principle" in Hare's sense' (*Moral Reasoning,* p. 90).

Individual moral change can, on this account, only be explained in terms of some kind of wholesale Kuhnian 'gestalt switch'. And Beardsmore reinforces this conclusion by insisting that our values 'determine our ideas of reality' (p. 79). But if this is so, and inhabiting a different morality involves inhabiting a different reality, then it becomes very difficult to see how, on this account, people with different moral views can make sense of each other. This is not in fact what the Wittgensteinians say. Phillips and Mounce speak of dialogue between different moral points of view, and of the diversity of moral influences people feel (p. 108). Yet such is their stress upon intelligibility, upon things only making sense in the context of the practices to which people belong, that the thrust of their argument seems to point in the opposite direction, such that intelligibility is at least a problem. Their argument rather moves towards the conclusion that the kind of detachment Hare requires can only put the individual in a position: 'like that of man who has no moral practice of his own, and who can only look upon the practices of others. ... To such a person, moral judgements would be unintelligible' (ibid., p. 18). They see moral change as evolutionary, dependent upon the evolution of practices in which individuals play no conscious part. Man does not decide his morality, but has it determined by his social circumstances:

Furthermore, any set of values which one can imagine will have a similar relation to some set of social conditions. This is why we have said that values are to be understood as they arise within ways of life, or, as we have described them, moral practices, which occur at definite times and at definite places.

(Ibid., p. 117)

This could be interpreted in the sense of Hegel's remark that a man can no more

jump out of his own time than he can jump out of his own skin, and as such might
pass as a general insight into the human condition. But as a necessary truth it is
quite unnacceptably deterministic. Taken in conjunction with the rest, it would
appear that we are all locked in cultural cages from which there is no escape,
while if a person could step outside he would be condemned to a moral wilderness
from which there is no return.

This is hardly credible. Phillips and Mounce, like all Wittgensteinians, put
great stress on how we learn things. But they seem to stop at a point somewhat
short of maturity. We do, after all, grow up; we do reflect upon our moral
inheritance, sometimes modify it or even reject it; we do deliberate and make
moral choices, and sometimes we are influenced by 'theories of goodness'.
Furthermore, if we are confined to practices outside of which we cannot step, and
if practices are inseparable from established ways of life, then it would seem that
a revolutionary new morality is a logical impossibility. But this also seems
implausible in the light of some fairly obvious historical examples: Stoics, Cynics
and Epicurians, Christianity and Utilitarianism, Marx and Neitzsche. Phillips and
Mounce do not, and perhaps cannot, take account of these, though R.T.
Beardsmore, in his *Moral Reasoning* does make some attempt, at least admitting to
the problem. Beardsmore says a little about both Christianity and Neitzsche. In
both cases he stress the continuity with what he has gone before, but essentially
missing the point, at least the point being made here. He cannot say in either case
that those aspects that are not continuous, that are radical departures, were based
upon established ways of life.

Part of the reason why the Wittgensteinians fail to cope with radical moral
change is that they dismiss any alternative source of morality beyond established
practices as an absurd conjuring of values out of nowhere, thereby denying the
possibilities of moral reflection and moral imagination. But even given their strict
interpretation of the relationship between meaning and social context there seems
nothing impossible, or even implausible about an individual reflecting upon his
duties and coming to conclusions at variance with his inherited code. An
individual may, for example, reflect upon and reject an obligation to pursue a
vendetta by killing another for the sake of family honour. He may convince
others of the stupidity and waste of the practice and help to bring about what
amounts to a moral revolution in his society, without any recourse to values
plucked from the air. The likeliest outcome is not the assertion of new values, but
a change in what that society counts as 'honour', etc. Radical differences between
moralities very rarely turn on absolute contradictions, such as Aristotle's view of
pride as a virtue compared with Augustine's view of pride as the fundamental sin.
Rather, they turn upon differences of priority and differences of application. The
Wittgensteinians ignore this fact and distort the nature of moral difference by the
way they develop their doctrine of the necessity of certain things having to be
taken for granted, having been drilled into us at childhood, for there to be any
morality at all. The sorts of things they believe need to be taken for granted is
apparent from a passage quoted earlier

> In order for a man to hold a moral position at all, there must be certain things it does
> not make sense for him to question. In our society, for example, it does not make

sense to ask whether honesty is in general good, or murder bad, or generosity admirable.

(Moral Practices, pp. 17–18)

But this is a most pecular way to characterize our morality, since it would be difficult to find any morality that does not regard honesty as good, or murder bad, or generosity admirable. Where the differences lie is in the fact that other societies and other moralities have different ideas as to what counts as murder or honesty or generosity, and this goes for a host of other such concepts; and they differ too in what values they take to be more important than others. Furthermore, as the Wittgensteinians themselves emphasize, we do not learn morality by learning principles such as 'cruelty is wrong' or 'honesty is good', we learn that *this* action is cruel and *that* action honest. In other words, what we learn is a set of applications identified in particulars, which in due course we learn to express in terms of principles.

Now if moral differences do not depend upon disagreements over such principles as 'murder is wrong' and 'honesty is good' but upon the interpretation of such principles, then it puts the problem of individual decision and creativity, and the possibility of radical moral change, in quite a different light. While it may be true that we cannot question that murder is wrong or honesty is good, we can perfectly well question the interpretation of those principles which we have inherited. There is no reason why the individual cannot decide to extend or modify or reject and replace any given set of applications, without having to wait for new practices to have established themselves to give his ideas meaning. Nor is there any reason why the individual cannot look ahead to possible futures, and possible practices, more ideal in his eyes than those which prevail, and adopt new values accordingly. The Wittgensteinians do not demonstrate the impossibility of any of this. Their attempt to deny any role for individual decision, or meaning to any moral view not embedded in established practices, must therefore be counted a failure.

The failure of the Wittgensteinians to bring out the crucial significance of differences of application and priority is a major flaw in their theory, and it is connected with a more serious weakness. This arises from a failure to distinguish properly between moral statements that are tautologies and those which are genuine judgements. We have just seen Phillips and Mounce make the point that the goodness of honesty or the wrongness of murder could not be sensibly questioned in our society, as though they could be in other societies. But this is to treat the goodness of honesty and the badness of murder as though they were moral judgements, when earlier in their work (see *Moral Practices*, Chapter 1) they treat such statements, quite correctly, as tautologies. Beardsmore is similarly in error in a passage quoted earlier where he denies the possibility of anyone brought up to believe in the evil of murder, suicide or adultery changing their mind on these matters. Again this is wrongly equating 'murder is wrong', which is tautologous, with 'suicide is wrong' which is a genuine moral judgement; one could not change one's mind about the first, but one could about the second (as people do), but this is nothing to do with upbringing. In a similar way, Beardsmore uses the impossibility of anyone 'deciding' that murder is wrong quite illegitimately to suggest the absurdity of anyone deciding on their own moral principles:

> While it makes perfectly good sense to talk of someone having decided to watch television or go to the pub, or of his having been forced to decide between doing his duty or taking the easy way out, I think that we should be less willing to talk of having decided that murder is evil, for example, or of his having adopted this as his standard. We should not know what to make of someone who talked as if the content of moral laws were dependent on the individual will in this sort of way.
>
> (*Moral Reasoning*, p. 31)

This is more than just a simple mistake, since these writers all go on to assume that because the goodness of honesty and the badness of murder cannot be questioned, then things which are moral judgements – such as the wrongness of abortion within Catholicism and the special treatment of fathers within family life – cannot be questioned either. In other words, they are using one piece of logic to justify assumptions about matters which are governed by quite different logics. In fact several very different things are being confused; on the one hand there are tautologies like 'murder is wrong', while on the other there are principles which we are brought up to accept, and could be otherwise; and then there are systems of belief. In consequence, they are confusing what cannot be questioned because it is illogical to do so, with what people do not question because it is part of their way of life and/or part of their faith; the former cannot be questioned, while the latter can be.

Part of the reason for this confusion is that the Wittgensteinians are systematically ambiguous about systems of belief, which they do not properly distinguish from practices and their associated concepts and principles. They insist that a moral concept or judgement can only have meaning against a certain background. But sometimes this background is a network of similar concepts, while at other times they talk, seemingly interchangeably, of ways of life, practices, moralities, traditions and beliefs; and sometimes these beliefs appear to be of the 'murder is wrong' sort (i.e. tautological), sometimes of the 'parents are entitled to respect' kind (i.e. genuine moral judgements), while at other times they seem to have in mind entire systems of belief such as Roman Catholicism or 'scientific materialism'. Yet, as we saw above, Phillips and Mounce are dismissive of 'theories of goodness', and what they seem to be saying is (a) no theory can demonstrate any absolute value or set of values, and (b) that abstract moral theories divorced from ways of life are effectively meaningless. The first is true and the second half-true (as we shall see below), but one or both would seem to catch Roman Catholicism and 'scientific materialism', both of which they appear to regard as legitimate moralities. (They might argue that these have grown out of religious and scientific practices, unlike more abstract theories, but this hardly bears examination.) Also caught would be Utilitarianism, Marxism, the theories of Anscombe and Foote and many more. It is difficult to see how the line is drawn between acceptable and unacceptable moral theories. Furthermore, it would be hard to maintain that these theories of goodness, however they are distinguished, necessarily cannot influence people's thought and action; and if this is possible it needs explaining. Both these problems could be, if not solved, at least illuminated by a clear distinction between ordinary moral thinking and systems of belief.

A related area of difficulty surrounds the problem of intelligibility. If moral rules are only intelligible within an established practice, then any kind of stepping aside is necessarily self-defeating, since the individual must render himself incomprehensible to his fellows. But for this to be true, one would presume that it would also have to be true that incomprehension reigns as between conflicting moral practices and points of view. But as we have suggested, the Wittgensteinians are ambiguous on this point, insofar as they speak of understanding, even dialogue, while the thrust of their arguments seem to point in the opposite direction. They cannot have it both ways: if other practices are incomprehensible, then it would simply be consistent to deny intelligibility to stepping aside; but if other practices do make sense, then so should stepping aside. On the other hand, there is problem about intelligibility, but it only becomes clear when we separate ordinary moral rules from related systems of belief. Another culture which equates kindness with weakness may not be attractive to us, but it presents no problems of understanding: nor would a Spartan who rated physical courage above honesty baffle an Athenian whose priorities were different. Where comprehension is much more difficult is at the level of belief. Mutual incomprehension between Pagan and the Christian or the Communist and the Nazi is much more understandable because they see the world so differently; in a very real sense – to use Kuhn's image which is more appropriate here than it is among scientists with different theories – they occupy different worlds. Thus, intelligibility is only a problem at the level of systems of belief, not at the level of ordinary morality (that is the level of ordinary human intercourse that involves such concepts as honesty, kindness, promise-keeping, murder, hypocrisy, etc.). The Wittgensteinians are ambiguous on this matter because they run the two levels together.

The heart of the matter is the denial of the possibility of stepping aside from or thinking beyond our moral commitments, which effectively rules out any moral autonomy or radical moral change. But the price of this denial is a denial of the obvious. People do on occasion choose their principles and moral revolutions do occur. Furthermore, Phillips and Mounce cannot talk of 'any morality we can imagine' or use Wittgenstein's technique of conceiving exotic societies with strange beliefs and practices, which they do, and then go on to deny that the individual can imagine and choose what has been imagined. They cannot maintain their own moral detachment (which they would consider, rightly, was essential for philosophy) and deny a similar detachment to others who do not happen to have philosophical purposes. In short, the Wittgensteinian attempt to confine morality to shared practices seems to deny the individual any possibility of freedom, choice, decision, deliberation, self-consciousness or creativity in moral matters, to an extent that is entirely implausible.

III

All of this rather brings us back to Hare. But not pure Hare. The Wittgensteinians are right to insist that not anything can count as a moral rule, and also right to insist that universalism will not do as an alternative. Stressing the social nature of morality, they can properly rule out 'clap hands every two hours' on its own as a moral rule which someone can, upon a whim, simply choose; and also rule out the equally absurd notion that we can have a society of morally autonomous individuals all of whom have different values and follow different rules, which Hare's position does allow. They give the most convincing account of ordinary morality and how we learn and sustain it. What they cannot do is deny the individual the capacity to step outside, deliberate and choose moral commitments that he has not been brought up to, or are beyond his experience, or are embodied in his own or another's 'theory of goodness', in the way that Hare allows. Phillips and Mounce may well be right to say (if it is indeed what they are saying) that in practice one cannot escape one's own times, or even that, as a matter of fact, individuals never think much beyond what is available in their society; but philosophy is about the logically possible not the practically possible. On the other hand, Phillips and Mounce are surely right in insisting that morality is a social matter, concerned with relationships between people, and adherence to a theory of good that applies only to oneself and is incomprehensible to others is in some way empty and without validity. If, then, there is some truth in the position of Hare on the one hand, and Phillips and Mounce on the other, a compromise or synthesis would seem to offer the best chance of a clear understanding of morality.

In attempting to work out such a compromise we can begin by accepting Phillips and Mounce's analysis of what can be called 'ordinary moral concepts' – honesty, murder, courage and the rest – and also Winch's argument, which they refer to approvingly, that certain of these concepts, lying and integrity for example, must exist in some form for there to be any society at all.[9] Though different societies may mean different things by 'honesty', 'murder' and the rest, and though not all societies will possess all the concepts, most will be common and some indispensable in any community. These basic concepts are essentially social. They are embodied in and take their meaning from practices and ways of life such as family, friendship, exchanging goods, playing sports, pursuing occupations, etc. They are quasi-descriptive concepts and we learn them through examples in a manner that does not distinguish between fact and value. We may live our lives and never question them, muddle through conflicts and dilemmas, and teach our children just what we were taught. But not necessarily. For a multitude of reasons or for no reason at all, we may reflect and reconsider and change our minds. We may speculate, entertain theories, use our moral imagination to conjure up ideal societies with ideal values which we may adopt as our own. Yet clearly there are limits. If we had a man before us who claimed to have a fully worked out personal morality, but when asked what he understood by 'honesty', 'courage' or 'kindness' replied 'clapping my hands every two hours' we would dismiss him as a fool and conclude that he did not know what morality was. The concepts of ordinary morality, embedded in and deriving their meaning from practices to which we belong, are the means by which we acquire a moral understanding in the first place; and it is these which are necessarily the foundation of our speculations. In other words, the speculations of Hare's choosing individual are parasitic upon and limited by the conceptual background which he has inherited, even though his final commitments may be very different from those he has been brought up to value. This suggests a two-level view of morality, with the Wittgensteinians accounting for the basic level and a modified and limited version of Hare at a second level to account for the speculating, choosing individual.

A two-level theory of morality is hardly new: examples can be found from Plato to the later writings of R.M. Hare. Hare's version, most fully set out in his book *Moral Thinking*,[10] bears an initial resemblance to the theory being suggested here. His first level is the level of 'intuition'; that is, knowing directly that something is right or wrong. This is not Intuitionism, which misinterprets this phenomenon, since, as Hare points out in an earlier work: 'We have moral "intuitions" because we have learnt how to behave, and have different ones according to how we have learnt to behave' (*The Language of Morals*, p. 64).

The intuitive level derives from the morality we are brought up to accept and reinforced by social convention; it is similar, therefore, to what we have termed 'ordinary morality'. The second level is what Hare calls the 'critical' level, and it is the level at which the individual submits his intuitions to rational scrutiny, to what Hare calls 'logic and the facts', and accepts such principles as survive such scrutiny. It is this second level that Hare regards as the superior; indeed, he goes further: 'Because intuitive moral thinking cannot be self-supporting, whereas critical thinking can be and is, the latter is epistemologically prior' (*Moral Thinking*, p. 46).

However, Hare has a rather narrow view of what constitutes 'logic and the facts' which is closely connected with the growing tendency towards moral universalism which characterizes his later work, as is evidenced by his remark that: 'if we assumed a perfect command of logic and the facts, they would constrain so severely the moral evaluation that we can make, that in practice we would be bound all to agree to the same ones' (*Moral Thinking*, p. 6).

It is also evident from his tendency to dismiss those who do not share his values as 'fanatics'.[11] But apart from the naivety of his beliefs in a single universal rationality and a realm of pure facts together pointing to unambiguous moral conclusions, it cuts straight across his formal position, since it appears to deny the individual the freedom to choose his own values and is a clear violation of Hume's law. If an individual does go beyond the morality he has inherited, and beyond whatever alternatives may be available in his society, he does not step into a world of pure rationality and pure fact, but into the world of theory. If the speculations of this individual are to be genuinely moral and universal (as Hare would demand), he must engage in some form of theorizing, usually involving general considerations about the nature of man and the world. This is because new values and principles require justification. The important point here is that ordinary morality has no need to be justified theoretically; as supportive of and partly constitutive of a way of life, further justification is unnecessary, (and thus has an arguably better claim to epistemological priority than Hare's 'critical' morality). To justify new values and new principles it is necessary that facts and values be fused artificially, a process that necessitates a theoretical framework to relate the concepts in a coherent whole.

Put another way, theory-based concepts must replace or be grafted onto the quasi-descriptive concepts that are naturally at home in practices. However, acceptance of these pseudo-descriptive concepts involves belief in the wider theory, which is not the case with ordinary morality. Hence the second level may be seen as predominantly one of ethical theory and belief, the domain of the moralist, theologian and political theorist, as well as of the individual in search of fresh principles. This second level is not conceived of as being in any way superior to the first. Indeed, being abstract it lacks the fullness of meaning characteristic of ordinary morality, it has its boundaries of intelligibility set by ordinary morality and to that extent it is parasitic upon ordinary morality.

Morality and ethical belief

We now have a two-level theory of morality, with a concept of ordinary morality based on practices, and a second level of ethical belief within which ideology may be located. However, neither Hare nor Foot nor the Wittgensteinians seem to see any point in distinguishing between ordinary moral rules and ethical belief. One of the few recent thinkers who do, and who can therefore give us a point of depature for looking at ethical belief, is Peter Strawson.

I

Peter Strawson examines this question interestingly in his paper 'Social morality and personal ideal',[12] though he does not come to any very definite conclusion. Several examples are offered of ideal images of forms of life that may capture our 'ethical imaginations' at different times:

> The ideas of self-obliterating devotion to duty or service to others; of personal honour and magnanimity; of asceticism, contemplation, retreat; of action, dominance and power; of the cultivation of 'an exquisite sense of the luxurious'; of simple human solidarity and cooperative endeavour; of a refined complexity of social existence; of a constantly maintained and renewed sense of affinity with natural things – any of these ideas, and a great many others too, may form the core and substance of a personal ideal. (p. 26)

He goes on:

> I think there can be no doubt that what I have been talking about falls within the region of the ethical. . . . Whether it falls within the region of the moral, however, is something that may be doubted. . . . I should first like to say something about this region of the ethical. It could also be characterized as a region in which there are truths which are incompatible with each other. There exist, that is to say, many profound general statements which are capable of capturing the ethical imagination in the same way as it may be captured by those ideal images of which I spoke. They often take the form of general descriptive statements about man and the world. They can be incorporated into a metaphysical system, or dramatized in a religious or historical myth. (p. 28)

Thus, Strawson clearly differentiates between the 'region of the ethical' and the sphere of morality. The region of the ethical embraces a wide variety of phenomena: ideologies, religions, myths, visions and images of all kinds. Many of these may capture the same ethical imagination at different times, yet they cannot be simply all put together to form a composite whole, and this: 'may be expressed by saying that the region of the ethical is the region where there are truths but no truth' (p. 29). Strawson gives the example of the encounter between Bertrand Russell and D.H. Lawrence, one representing the life of reasons, the other the life of instinct, where they failed to find common ground:

> The clash was a clash of two irreconcilable views of man, two irreconcilable attitudes. The spectator familiar with both may say: Russell is right; he tells the truth; he speaks for civilization. He may also say: Lawrence is right; he tells the truth; he speaks for life. The point is that he may say both things. It would be absurd to hope for a reconciliation of the two conflicting attitudes. It is not absurd to desire that both should exist in conflict.
>
> The region of the ethical, then, is a region of diverse, certainly incompatible and possibly practically conflicting ideal images or pictures of a human life, or of human life; and it is a region in which many such incompatible pictures may secure at least the imaginative, though doubtless not often the practical, allegiance of a single person. (p. 29)

But what then is morality? Strawson is not certain, but he offers one 'widely accepted' account, namely, that morality is the:

> rules or principles governing human behaviour which apply universally within a community or class. The class may be variously thought of as a definite social group or the human species as a whole or even the entire class of rational beings. It is not obvious how these contrasting conceptions, of diversity of ideal and of community of rule, are related to each other; and in fact, I think, the relationship is complicated. (p. 30)

Strawson is offering what has been called a 'highway code' view of morality; that is, the bare rules of honesty, refraining from harming others, etc., which make social life possible. However, there is no corresponding attempt to define the region of the ethical. Nor is there any attempt to characterize in broad terms the relationship between the two regions. The relationship is, as Strawson says many times, a very complicated one. But instead of tackling it, he avoids it, choosing instead to affirm his own belief in a society where a variety of ideals are tolerated and deploring totalitarian societies where they are not. In short, he affirms his own Liberalism. But at least some attempt must be made to state, if only crudely, what the relationship between morality and the 'sphere of the ethical' might be.

We might begin by examining a distinction that Strawson does not consider, between the nature and origin of moral rules on the one hand, and their justification on the other. We can dispense with Strawson's functional 'highway code' and substitute the notion of 'ordinary morality' based on the Wittgensteinian analysis outlined above. This complicates the matter slightly, since the Wittgensteinian insists on seeing moral rules, concepts, beliefs and practices as a single whole. However, rules and their justification can always be separated analytically. The inclination to see them as inseparable is countered by the fact that any given set of rules can be justified in a number of different ways.

Furthermore, while it is difficult and perhaps (as Peter Winch has argued) impossible to conceive of a society devoid of any moral rules, we can quite easily conceive of one possessed of a morality but devoid of associated justificatory beliefs. Indeed, we could construct an ideal case where a society has a morality that has simply grown out of its way of life and is entirely innocent of theory. We might then imagine an individual who, for some reason (perhaps inspired by his travels), wishes to change the way of life by changing moral behaviour. To convince others, and perhaps himself, of the need for change he must produce some theory or vision or other form of ethical belief to justify the new values as against the old. This in turn may provoke another, who, seeing this as an undesirable threat to his way of life, produces a rival theory which justifies the morality that already exists. Strawson's 'sphere of the ethical' embraces the whole range of beliefs and values – ideals, myths, religions and ideologies – all of which justify moral codes of different kinds. In the light of such beliefs existing rules may be justified; or they may be modified and reorganized; or they may be rejected and replaced by something else.

The idea that moral innovation can be conceived theoretically and then imposed upon practice is ruled out by the Wittgensteinian position. As we have seen, they argue that thinking beyond established morality is unintelligible, and that there can be no 'theories of goodness' (which, if taken to mean that universalist ethics are not philosophically viable, is not here doubted, but for the purposes of this part of the discussion it will be taken to mean that any substantive ethical theory is unintelligible simply because it is abstract). This view is partly correct and partly incorrect. The correctness can be seen by comparing 'ordinary morality' with abstract theory.

The notion of society is closely bound up with the notion of shared rules of conduct. Social life would be inconceivable without some version of such moral rules as not telling lies, stealing or breaking promises. These rules must be part of people's lives, figure in their judgements of each others' characters and regulate conduct in a more detailed way than could possibly be covered by a formal legal system, or subject to the whim of a Hobbesian sovereign. What matters is the detailed application of what stealing, keeping promises, etc. means in particular circumstances familiar to those belonging to a particular community. The reality of moral life is in human practices, and the articulation of the rules in a code always to some extent misses this. Artificially constructed codes are even more remote from reality, to the extent that as they stand without embodiment in practices they are virtually meaningless. The point is that any set of written rules can always be interpreted in many different ways, (otherwise the notion of 'working to rule' as a trade-union weapon would be absurd). Furthermore, it is in the detail that we learn morality, at our mother's knee, or perhaps across our father's; but either way it is not from books. Hare's theory of 'universality' may say something about the logic of moral judgements, but, as Bernard Williams implies, (in the passage quoted in the Introduction) it does not touch the reality.

Where the Wittgensteinian view is wrong is in its insistence on the unintelligibility of moral thinking beyond established practices. The new moral rules that may flow from such thinking may be deficient in meaning, in the sense that their abstraction makes their application necessarily uncertain, but they are not thereby unintelligible. This is not a trivial distinction, since the implication of characterizing something as unintelligible is that it is irredeemably so; whereas any abstract code can, over time, acquire a set of applications – though never a definitive one – and be embodied in practices. Thus, we may reject or modify our inherited morality in the light of reflection, and perhaps under the influence of some theory. Artificial codes may indeed, over time, become, so to speak, 'operationalized', mixing with or replacing traditional rules. But as such they are not a morality in themselves. Knowing *how* to be moral is not reducible to the ability to articulate a set of rules. Morality can exist independent of any articulation of its rules, let alone any theory or beliefs, to give it support; though no doubt one would be hard pressed to discover an example of such a completely independent morality. The important point is that it is possible in principle, and therefore while morality is arguably a necessary feature of any social life, theories or beliefs which justify or otherwise sustain it are not.

Popular morality does evolve over time, and many factors are involved. The implication of the Wittgensteinian view, that changes in ethical belief cannot influence this evolution, is inherently implausible. No doubt there were young Philosophical Radicals who deliberately went about making felicific calculations in the Benthamite manner and acting accordingly; and it could hardly be doubted that Bolshevik Marxism has had its impact on the morality of ordinary Russians. On the other hand, given that an abstract morality is open to an indefinite number of interpretations the notion of simply 'putting theory into practice' has little plausibility either. The reality would seem to be a complex interplay between ordinary morality and ethical belief with each continually modifying the other. Ethical beliefs (especially religious) may become to a greater or lesser extent embodied in practices, but become changed in the process; values and concepts may become detached from their original setting and become part of the moral consciousness of many who do not adhere to the original belief, as is often true of Christian values in the modern world. What constitutes ordinary morality at any given time or place may, therefore, comprise a mixture of values, beliefs and rules from various sources. But rarely, if ever, is ordinary morality constituted by some tightly integrated theory. It is rather a collection of applications giving rise to a set of intuitions, and capable of existing independently of some or all of the beliefs that attach to them. In consequence, the relationship between any given ethical belief, and the ordinary morality it seeks to influence, is always a complex one. This is the advantage of the ideal case which contrasts a pure ordinary morality of practice-based rules and quasi-descriptive concepts that are not bound together by any theory, with a pure theoretical construction with its pseudo-descriptive concepts and explanations. It is only in this abstract way that we can generalize about the relationship between ideology and ordinary morality.

II

An ideology belongs to the sphere of ethical belief, and as such always justifies one moral position as against another. It either justifies what exists or else some alternative. At the same time, ideology is parasitic upon ordinary morality, even where it seeks to replace it; and it is dependent in two clear and related senses. The first we have already discussed, which is that ideology has to be intelligible in terms of the prevailing morality, the limits of its intelligibility being set by the extent to which established moral concepts can be stretched. Its values must make sense to people in terms of those values they already possess; it must bridge the gap between what exists and what is proposed. In the ideal case people would not understand, let alone be influenced by an ideology unless it made moral sense to them. The ideologist must, so to speak, stay in touch with the moral understanding from which he seeks to depart; his ideas must be a plausible development of that understanding if they are to be comprehensible.

The second sense in which ideology is parasitic upon ordinary morality arises from the fact that ideology must not merely be comprehensible but must also be persuasive, and to achieve this it must engage the moral intuitions of those it seeks to influence. The morality we grew up with equips us with such intuitions, so that in most ordinary circumstances we 'know' directly what is right and wrong. These intuitions also operate in respect of theories. To take an obvious example: an individual is convinced of the truth of classical Utilitarian ethics, until the well-known case is put to him of the healthy person entering a hospital ward where each patient needs a different kind of transplant and where the greatest happiness of the greatest number is clearly best served by cutting up the healthy individual and distributing him around the ward. Now unless he is a blind fanatic, the Utilitarian will 'know' that, whatever his theory might say, this must be wrong, and that he must abandon his theory or modify it so that cutting up people is not seen as promoting the general good. To be persuasive an ideology must not run directly counter to people's deep-rooted moral attitudes. But they can be manipulated in various ways; one of which is to present the situation where action is needed as one where normal standards do not apply. Thus, the Irish terrorist who kills a British soldier will not admit to murder because he is 'on active service' in an 'army' (the Irish Republican Army or the Irish National Liberation Army) which is engaged in a 'war' where killing an 'enemy soldier' of the 'army of occupation' is a legitimate act; others killed are either 'civilian casualities' or else have been 'executed' for informing or other 'capital crimes'. The basic attitudes of ordinary morality are not being challenged here, but they are being taken account of by defining the situation in such a way that they do not apply.

However, the ideologist must not just avoid running directly counter to the intuitions of those he would influence, but must directly engage them. In the case of Republican cause in Northern Ireland the minority population feels itself to be discriminated against in a way that would not prevail if Ireland were politically united. Their case could be interpreted in terms of the denial of those civil rights enjoyed by other UK citizens; but a radical nationalist ideology offers a wider interpretation in terms of the denial of national rights and the inevitable oppression of a subject people by an imperialist power. In Weimar Germany, the horrors of defeat and economic collapse could be 'explained' by the Nazis in terms of betrayal and conspiracy by race-enemies. And for the misery and squalor created by early industrialization, socialists offered 'explanations' in terms of the evils of the capitalist system. In all these cases people 'knew' that something was wrong, that their world had become morally incoherent,[13] because their ordinary sense of right and wrong told them so quite independently of any theory. To be effective ideology must make use of such intuitions. It must explain why the world is morally incoherent, or else in what way a coherent world is threatened; and that explanation must be of such a kind that guarantees the efficacy of appropriate action that will create or preserve a world that will satisfy those prior intuitions. This is also true where the individual has no initial sense of moral incoherence and only acquires one when the ideologist says, 'see the world *this* way' and its moral inadequacy stands out; it is still a prior moral understanding that has to be engaged, and, if necessary, manipulated.

We might put this another way by saying that what the ideologist must do is to lock a set of pseudo-descriptive concepts onto the individual's prior set of quasi-descriptive ones, thereby converting a moral understanding into an ideological one. Quasi-descriptive concepts are the concepts of ordinary morality – honesty, cruelty, murder and the like – where, as the Wittgensteinians suggest, the descriptive and the evaluative are fused, so that in using them we both describe and evaluate at the same time. But while such concepts have conceptual links with each other they do not form part of an explanatory theory about human reality. Sometimes theories of this kind are said to be implicit, but this cannot be shown to be necessarily so. It is perfectly possible to imagine a morality without the benefit of theory, i.e. the ideal case, so that the relationship with theory can at best only be a contingent one; and if only one possible theory could be derived from a morality it would hardly be implicit, in which case an indefinite number of other theories would be consistent with it. Besides, moralities are never that rigid. Even within a closely knit community people differ over what is right or wrong in particular situations, and who is absolutely right is impossible to determine.

We are also, with quasi-descriptive concepts, more or less aware of their essentially evaluative nature. We know that telling lies is wrong, but telling 'white lies' is not so wrong. We know that justified killing is not murder, and that 'being cruel to be kind' is not true cruelty. This is very different in the case of ideological concepts, such as proletarian and bourgeois, Aryan and Jew, 'the people', 'rational government', a 'free society' and 'true democracy', all of which present themselves as wholly descriptive concepts and take their meaning from a purportedly objective account of the world. These are *pseudo*-descriptive concepts, for the very reason that they proclaim themselves to be what they are not. Thus, for ideology to take hold of an individual's mind the quasi-descriptive concepts of his prior moral outlook must be harnessed to a theoretical understanding of reality in terms of concepts whose ethical purpose is disguised. Good and evil thereby become implicit in the world, and the need for action is presented as growing directly out of the reality the individual faces. And this is perhaps part of the reason why, as with religion and myth, ideology motivates so powerfully.

III

Along with the development of a great diversity of actual moralities has been a parallel development of conflicting theories and beliefs associated with them. Religious beliefs and political beliefs, myths, doctrines and ideals of all sorts exist in profusion. All they have in common is that they seem to answer to a persistent need, albeit a contingent need, to give morality a particular content and a foundation. Whatever need or needs these beliefs do answer to – sustain social life, explain a confusing world, make sense of evil, give life meaning, facilitate group action, and perhaps others – they are deeply important to us. So much so that we require that they give a foundation to morality as deep-rooted and secure as human thought can conceive; that is, the moral order must be seen to grow directly out of reality itself, either natural or supernatural. But in the nature of things this is not possible and consequently all such beliefs, however they may be presented, must ultimately be sustained by faith.

Religions, myths and ideologies are all, in one way or another, concerned with determining, justifying and securing commitment to a morality. Religion has always sought to embrace the whole of human experience, including the morality of everyday life. Indeed, it was once held that common morality could not exist without religious sanction: John Locke would not extend toleration to atheists because they could have no obligation to keep promises or contracts, threatening the very existence of society;[14] many late Victorian intellectuals, like Matthew Arnold,[15] agonizing over the conflict between science and religion, emphasized the social necessity of religion even when they could no longer accept its truth. Ideologies, while they may embrace all aspects of social life, including personal relationships, tend to centre upon the political order, moralizing the political by evaluating actions, policies and institutions in terms of a moral order. But that moral order must be firmly embedded in reality, in the nature of things; a circumstance guaranteed by an appeal to what the community will accept as genuine knowledge of that reality. The ideologist must appear to be making a contribution to objective knowledge. But ideologies are not concerned with knowledge for its own sake. They are action-guiding theories which divide the world into good and evil, friend and enemy. They determine the believer's moral and political identity: whose side he is on, his place in the world, in the story, in the struggle, in history. Their function is to point the way, to arouse and above all to justify. They use every device to persuade and inflame, which is why they are so often decked out with analogy and metaphor, mythic dramas and utopian tableaux. These are necessary, for we no longer live in a world where within communities all share the same morality and the same beliefs, but in a more complex world where moralities overlap and systems of belief compete for adherents. There is a chaos of faiths, religious and ideological.

Morality is about rules. But in a confusing world the problem of by what rules we should conduct our lives, individually or collectively, is acute. It is argued by some that we all can be and ought to be moral self-legislators. But this is not only unrealistic in practice but logically doubtful; if the basis of morality is shared practices it hardly makes sense to say that everyone could, let alone should, be going their own way, playing a different game. (Such basically Kantian notions of absolute moral autonomy gain plausibility from the unspoken assumption that there is an absolute rational morality which all reasonable men will, upon reflection, approximate to.) Yet a total reliance upon traditional morality, mother's-knee morality, is in some ways equally unrealistic, particularly in a rapidly changing world. Morality grows and changes as people respond, with unavoidable creativity, to new situations. We cannot, collectively at least, simply shed our moral inheritance; at the same time we still have a large measure of free choice. Ethical belief bridges that gap, though in time beliefs may interpret traditional values out of existence and replace them. The sphere of ethical belief is a complex one of theories, religions, myths, ideologies, doctrines and ideals, and it operates at different levels. At the most comprehensive level is religion and ideology, either of which can embrace the other forms. To fix the position of ideology within the sphere of the ethical we need to distinguish it, if we can, from religion.

Ideology and religion

Ideology and religion have much in common. They are both ethical understandings of the world. They both offer a moral vision and are concerned to interpret the world in terms of that vision. Thus, when there is some great event a thousand pulpits bloom with sermons on the Christian significance of the crisis. So too the Marxist is overwhelmed with pamplets, articles, and speeches on the significance of the event. And not only great events: the death of a child, or the fate of a local strike have their significance for the Christian and the Marxist respectively.

This process of constantly applying the doctrine to new instances goes on against a vast background of solid interpretation with heavy treatises on the 'The Christian significance of the family', 'The role of the IMF in capitalist imperialism' and so on. However, this interpretation in the light of an ethical understanding is not seen as such by those who undertake it, but rather as describing the world correctly in an objectively true and factual way. But since religions and ideologies offer morally charged accounts of reality, those accounts are not compelling for the ethically neutral. They are only compelling for those who have faith.

Having so much in common it is not surprising that many have said that ideologies are religions, or that religions are ideologies. The point of this claim is often no more than to point up the similarities, without really addressing the question of whether the similarity does in fact amount to identity. Claims of this kind are often made with no more serious purpose than to denigrate either ideology or religion. Thus, Marxism is sometimes said to be a 'secular religion' in order to suggest dogmatism and even fanaticism. The claim that religions are ideologies sometimes has a serious theoretical purpose, but often the point is to dismiss religion as false and irrational belief (e.g. 'false consciousness'). In both cases the attempt to identify religion and ideology is frequently theoretically pointless and question-begging. On the other hand, the above account does suggest an identity unless we can show there to be significant differences.

What appears to be central to all religions, though usually absent from ideology, is a sense or concept of something divine; god or gods, a pattern or a process. The relation between man and man's world on the one hand, and the divine world on the other, may vary from Augustine's worlds apart to pantheistic integration. But religion is man's world conceived from the point of view of the divine. The obvious question is whether ideology also has such a defining conception.

Glib though it may sound, the ideological equivalent of the divine is the human. Just as different concepts of the divine issue in different religious understandings, so different concepts of man issue in different ideological understandings; each standing at the keystone of the arch of their respective understandings. Keystones, however, do not stand alone. Doctrine, in the case of religion, must spell out how man and man's world is and ought to be in relation to the divine; and in relation to man's true self, in the case of ideology. The framework of the understanding needs to be set out in such statements as 'God created the world', 'the Church is the body of Christ', 'all history is the history of class struggle', 'all men are created equal', and so on. These are not statements of fact, but, in Wittgenstein's sense, statements of grammar; they state the concepts, rules and principles of the understanding. This means that they are the 'given' in terms of which the world is judged, and not, as with plain factual claims, to be judged in relation to the world. Some, like all history being the history of class struggle, may appear to stand as empirical statements that could be investigated. But this is not the logic of their actual usage; within ideological thinking they are taken for granted. Besides, given their pseudo-descriptive nature, they could not be empirically investigated without giving them meanings that are quite different from those they have within the ideology.

Ideologists do not speak of themselves as developing doctrine or dogma; for one of the rules of the game, so to speak, is the presentation of belief as objective knowledge where demonstration is adequate and faith unnecessary. But ideologists do develop doctrine just as theologians do, only they call it 'theory'. Religions, or at least some of them, are perhaps more self-knowing in this respect. They may not go as far as Oscar Wilde's 'Religions die when they are proved to be true. / Science is the record of dead religions.' But they recognize the central role of faith and deem it a supreme virtue. Ideologists, on the other hand, persistently claim that their doctrines are theories in the academic sense; that is, objective and demonstrable. But as we have discussed at length above, the status of academic theories as objective knowledge depends upon their conforming to those criteria and satisfying those procedures which constitute those forms of understanding which are academic disciplines. In science, for example, the uniformity of nature, causality, prediction, experiment, etc., which are all interdefinable and mutually supporting, together constitute the scientific understanding. This framework of understanding is not regarded as 'true', for it contains no assertions of fact and embodies no substantive theories about the way the world is, but is neutral as between such theories; yet at the same time it guarantees the possibility that theories that do satisfy the appropriate criteria are factually descriptive, explanatory and potentially refutable. But in religion and ideology things are very different. Particular substantive doctrines of God, the church, prayer, salvation, etc., also interdefinable and mutually supporting, constitute the framework of understanding of a religion, without any higher framework to guarantee their objectivity or status as knowledge. Similarly with ideology. The theories of Marxism, Liberalism and others are not theories in the academic sense, whatever ideologists may claim, and have no higher framework in terms of which they may be judged (or disputes over revisionism or heresy may be settled): theory and understanding are conflated. This common feature of their logic distinguishes religion and ideology from academic understandings, together with their related characteristic of being forms of ethical understanding. What separates them is that while the central feature of a religious understanding is its concept of the divine, the central feature of an ideological understanding is its conception of human nature.

The theories of human nature which give rise to ideologies, or variants of ideologies, are legion. There are notions, not only of socialist, autonomous and race-determined man, but also of rational, or moral, or competitive, or cooperative man; he is not only homo sapiens but homo faber or homo ludens; he may be seen as essentially spiritual or material, body or soul, as God's creature (a just God, a rational God, a vengeful God, etc.) or as basically a pleasure/pain machine, or driven by passion, libido, aggression or ego; he may at birth be good or bad, perfectible or imperfectible, or merely a stranger in a meaningless universe, and his fate ultimately tragic or comic or romantic or absurd. Each of these views of man – and there are many more and many variations – has implications for the kind of society in which he can develop most fully. We may thus characterize the root conception of political ideology as: *this* is the nature of man, therefore *this* is the kind of society appropriate to his nature. From this basic proposition is inferred a moral obligation to create (or preserve or restore) that society. All the basic political ideals – freedom, equality, order, justice – can be interpreted in terms of this theoretical complex. But all this is implied in a basic conception of man from which the rest is deduced much in the manner of Natural Law. But either these deductions involve a logical fallacy, as Hume showed in the case of Natural Law, or the notion of man is morally loaded so that prescriptions can be inferred, though only at the price of abandoning the possibility of correspondence with reality. Either way, faith is involved; faith in a vision of human society and how to get there; faith in the values that that society embodies; faith in a conception of human nature that fits the good society; and faith that the theory that embodies all this constitutes a true and total account of human experience, past, present and future.

Apart from obvious similarities with religion here, there is also a clear overlap in certain religious conceptions of man upon which political beliefs are based. The political ideas of Aquinas, Calvin and others, we may wish to regard as religious *and* ideological. This raises semantic and classificatory problems, but not of an important kind; though they do raise the interesting question as to whether all ideologies are necessarily political ones, a question we will return to later. For the moment it is sufficient to note that while religion and ideology have certain common logical characteristics, they are, nevertheless, not the same thing.

Notes

1. R. M. Hare, *The Language of Morals*, (OUP, 1952); R. M. Hare, *Freedom and Reason*, (Oxford, 1963); R. M. Hare, *Moral Thinking*, (OUP, 1981). Hare's formal analysis of the nature of morality, his 'prescriptivism', was first fully set out in *The Language of Morals*. But although this position is still maintained in the later books his interest shifts progressively towards using it as a foundation for his own version of utilitarianism. It could well be argued that it is not logically possible to derive one from the other as Hare thinks, but there is not space here to discuss this. The concern here is with the pure prescriptivism; Hare's substantive moral views are merely mentioned in passing later in the chapter.
2. D. Z. Phillips and H. O. Mounce, *Moral Practices*, (RKP, 1970).
3. G. E. M. Anscombe, 'Modern moral philosophy', in *Philosophy*, XXXIII, reprinted in W. D. Hudson (ed.) *The Is–Ought Question*, (Macmillan, 1969); Philippa Foot, *Virtues and Vices*, (Blackwell, 1978); P. T. Geach, 'Good and evil', in *Analysis*, vol. 17, reprinted in Phillippa Foot, *Theories of Ethics*, (OUP, 1967).
4. W. D. Hudson, *The Is–Ought Question*, op. cit., p. 194.
5. Human flourishing is related to the notion of a human *telos*. P. T. Geach in *The Virtues*, (CUP, 1977), argues that human beings do have a *telos* upon which ethics can be based, but that we do not need to know what it is, (see p. 13 and elsewhere). But a teleological ethics without a *telos* would seem to be a 'Hamlet' with neither the prince nor any of his family. In *After Virtue*, (Duckworth, 1981), Alasdair MacIntyre pursues a similar line to a similarly disappointing conclusion, as we shall see in a later chapter.
6. R. W. Beardsmore, *Moral Reasoning*, (RKP, 1969); D. Z. Phillips and H. O. Mounce, op. cit., (RKP, 1970); Peter Winch, *Ethics and Action*, (RKP, 1972); subsequent references are to these editions.
7. W. D. Hudson, *Modern Moral Philosophy*, 2nd edn, (Macmillan, 1983), pp. 374–5.
8. A similar point is made by Winch, (op. cit), p. 55.
9. Ibid., Chapter 3.
10. R. M. Hare, *Moral Thinking*, op. cit; subsequent references are to this edition.
11. R. M. Hare, *Freedom and Reason*, op. cit, where Hare devotes the best part of Chapter 9, to 'fanaticism', by which he means such as Nazis and religious bigots. He also talks (e.g. pp. 114–5) of 'perverted ideals'. By the time of writing *Moral Thinking* Hare seems to have concluded that some of his best friends are 'fanatics'.
12. Peter Strawson, *Freedom and Resentment and other Essays*, (Methuen, 1974), pp. 26–44. Subsequent references are to this edition.
13. I owe the phrase 'morally incoherent world' to Mr Henry Tudor, although I use it with less discrimination than he does.
14. John Locke, *A Letter Concerning Toleration*, (Bobbs-Merrill, 1955).
15. See for example, Matthew Arnold, *Literature and Dogma*, (Smith, Elder & Co. 1873).

CHAPTER FIVE

HUMAN NATURE AND THE STRUCTURE OF IDEOLOGY

There is perhaps a certain obviousness about the suggestion that conceptions of human nature are at the heart of ideology. This is because political theory in the past has often been characterized in this way; so much so that Martin Hollis can casually caricature 'traditional political theory' thus:

1. Take about 2,000 hom.sap., dissect each into essence and accidents and discard the accidents.
2. Place essences in a large casserole, add socializing syrup and stew until conflict disappears.
3. Serve with a pinch of salt....the exact ingredients vary with the chef. In particular the magic socializing syrup varies with the analysis of human nature.[1]

Yet the suggestion is not the commonplace it might at first appear, and for several reasons. To begin with, it is far from common to equate ideology with traditional political theory. Hollis, for example, does not.[2] The most widely held view is that ideology is connected with mass politics, mass manipulation, propaganda and ultimately totalitarianism; very much features of the modern world, and in sharp contrast to 'legitimate' political theory resulting from the noble reflections of great minds. Marxists and traditional Conservatives are rather less inhibited about labelling past thought ideological, but then their views of ideology take little account of human nature. It was noted in Chapter 1 that accounts of ideology within political doctrines tend to analyse it in terms of its causes and its effects, and not its internal structure. They stress those features which tend to show rival beliefs to be dangerous and wrong, and not features that may be shared. Ideology is thus associated with totalitarianism or class oppression or uselessly abstract reasoning, while the structural similarities between what is deemed ideological and that which deems it so is, no doubt understandably, ignored. Again, sociological approaches to ideology concentrate on the social functions – such as expressing class interest or fostering group solidarity – which they are thought to perform irrespective of their content. Indeed, among all the various accounts and discussions of ideology considered in Chapter 1 (including the most recent philosophical studies) there is hardly a mention of human nature, and those that do mention it, like Corbett, proceed to ignore it in their subsequent analysis.

On the other hand, there have been various accounts of the role of conceptions of human nature in political theories, especially in recent years as the high tide of behavioural political science has ebbed, but where there is little mention of ideology. Hollis's book, quoted above, is one example. Others include two recent volumes of essays on the topic – *Human Nature in Politics* edited by Pennock and Chapman,[3] and *Politics and Human Nature* edited by Forbes and Smith[4] – where, in a total of 26 essays, ideology is hardly mentioned and nowhere is a substantial link made between conceptions of human nature and ideology as such.[5] And where the connection has been made, as it has by Alan Ryan, its nature has been mistaken, as we will see below. Thus, seeing conceptions of the nature of man as central to ideology is far from being a commonplace. But even if the connection were more widely asserted there would still be a need to analyse its nature, since if, as this work has sought to demonstrate, the nature of ideology is not properly understood, then the role of human nature within ideology will not be properly understood either.

We have, then, the suggestion that theories of human nature have a crucial role in ideology, but we have yet to see how and why they are the key structural element. The first task, however, is to say what we mean by an ideological conception of human nature, as distinct from other possible conceptions. When this has been done we can show the role of such conceptions within the formal structure of ideological theory.

Ideological and non-ideological conceptions of man

I

We might begin the process of isolating Ideological Man by considering two statements which appear to put the matter correctly, but which, upon closer examination, need to be qualified substantially.[6] The first is a comment by Isaiah Berlin:

> The ideas of every philosopher concerned with human affairs in the end rest on his conception of what man is and can be. To understand such thinkers, it is more important to grasp this central notion or image (which may be implicit, but determines their picture of the world) than even the most forceful arguments with which they defend their views and refute actual and possible objections.[7]

The quarrel with Berlin's remark lies in his use of the term 'philosopher'. The passage occurs in an essay on the thought of George Sorel, and since Berlin opens his essay by identifying Sorel with 'the other ideologists and prophets of the nineteenth century'[8] he is clearly using a different notion of philosophy than the one which informs this work. The philosophical and the ideological need to be distinguished.

In the above passage Berlin is using the term 'philosophy' in the very broad sense of general theorizing about the nature of the world and man's proper place within it. It is a very common use of the word (as in 'philosophy of life') and in itself unobjectionable. But it is much too vague a notion to be of use in analysing the nature of general theorizing. For this purpose a much stricter and narrower conception of philosophy as an academic discipline is needed. As we saw in Chapter 2, the concept of an academic discipline depends crucially on the idea of a decision-procedure by means of which disputes between rival claims to knowledge can be conclusively settled. In the case of philosophy, disputes are settled by an appeal to logic, in the broad sense of the rules of meaning implicit in the way we talk. To this view there is a fairly obvious objection that philosophers are permanently at loggerheads and nothing is ever settled; and that this is manifested in the continuing controversies over empiricism and rationalism, idealism and materialism, determinism and free will, and other such endless debates. To answer these objections it is necessary to distinguish between broad conceptions or pictures on the one hand, and particular arguments on the other. Any general conception of ultimate reality or how the mind works or the nature of moral obligation, must have supporting arguments to justify its acceptance. These particular arguments may be refuted or otherwise shown to be inadequate. But this does not necessarily destroy the general conception; and it is quite reasonable to maintain belief in the picture while searching for fresh arguments or reworking old ones. From time to time certain sets of arguments hold the field for a period, so that the matter seems settled in favour of one particular general conception. But rival conceptions tend to reappear eventually with new arguments to support them, and so the process goes on. It is the business of the philosopher to challenge accepted arguments and generate new ones, and the philosophical enterprise will continue so long as people possess intellectual ingenuity and creativity. Now this may seem depressingly inconclusive, not to say pointless. Yet there is progress of a sort, and there is an accumulation of knowledge, and the decision-procedure does operate. The point is that it operates at the level of arguments and not at the level of general conceptions, at least not directly; we know for example that Plato's world of Forms cannot be sustained by his argument from the universality of concepts. Particular arguments are refuted, distinctions are established, and the realm of possibility is thereby narrowed.

If this account of philosophy is correct, and if as argued earlier disputes over fundamental values cannot, in principle, be settled, then it follows that such disputes cannot form part of philosophical debate, and the determination of values cannot fall within the scope of academic philosophy. On this basis the distinction between philosophy and ideology becomes clear. A moral evaluation of the world is central to an ideology and is implicit in all its concepts and statements. No matter how seemingly factual ideological statements may be they are in reality evaluations and behave logically as evaluations. Consequently, disputes between rival ideological 'descriptions' (that is, pseudo-descriptions), unlike philosophical disputes, cannot, in principle, be settled.

An ideological concept of man embodies the values of its ideology; it is a pseudo-descriptive concept from which moral prescriptions may be legitimately drawn. A non-ideological concept, on the other hand, embodies no such values and implies no such prescriptions. It might be argued that any concept of man will have moral implications of some sort. But this is doubtful. An incontrovertible truth about our essential humanness is our common mortality; but while it is open to anyone to read any amount of moral significance into this fact, the fact in itself has no *necessary* implications for how we ought to live our lives. Similarly, a fuller conception of man may be such that no moral implications follow of necessity from it.

At this point we might consider the second pronouncement on the role of theories of human nature, one which, on the face of it, is a corrective to Berlin's. Alan Ryan writes:

> Our images of human nature are centrally important ideological phenomena, for the evident reason that what distinguishes ideology from a merely random string of moral and political imperatives is the way it incorporates the validating assumptions of those imperatives. The assumption that these imperatives – whether taken for granted, defended desperately, or pressed for the first time – have their roots in 'human nature' is one main condition of their very intelligibility.[9]

Ryan makes this statement in the context of a discussion of Hobbes and Rousseau, both of whom he takes to be ideologists. But there are significant differences between them which, though Ryan does not draw attention to them, his analysis nevertheless makes clear. With Hobbes's 'secular, mechanical, naturalistic approach to human nature, we are left with absolutely no forbidden actions, no intrinsically wicked behaviour' (ibid., p. 13).

For Hobbes, all human action is ultimately reducible to physics, and the natural laws which govern it are in themselves no more morally significant than the laws of planetary motion. Hobbes's ideas generally do not have positive moral force, and Ryan does not claim that they do. But Rousseau is a very different matter. His concern is a moral concern, provoked by his disgust with contemporary society as morally degenerate and alienating. Ryan summarizes Rousseau's view thus:

> The depravity of society and the arbitrariness of social convention create an obsession with personal prestige that is utterly self-destructive. . . . Civilization is a condition in which we lose touch with ourselves.
>
> (ibid., pp. 18 and 16)

Thus, on Ryan's own account of Hobbes and Rousseau they would seem to have two very different kinds of theory. However, this difference is not recognized by Ryan who treats them as being theories of the same kind, as equally factual and equally capable of being true or false. Values are not a determining feature, or even, it seems, an important feature of his view of ideology.

This is confirmed in Ryan's treatment of James and John Stuart Mill in his paper 'Two concepts of politics and democracy'.[10] Here again he treats these two accounts of politics and democracy as rival factual accounts, and differences of values, though mentioned, are only incidental. But what we have with James and J. S. Mill are two alternative visions of the proper ends of society which arise from differences of values. Of course, James Mill shared with Bentham a conception of human nature that has certain similarities with that of Hobbes. But Hobbes did not regard peace or security, or indeed anything else, as intrinsically moral goods; we are, so to speak, simply programmed to pursue them, and we are certainly under no moral obligation to work for the peace and security of others. For Bentham and James Mill, however, pleasure, individual happiness and above all the happiness of mankind are intrinsic and absolute goods. They were not thoroughgoing nominalists in this matter as Hobbes was.

Like Bentham and the Mills, Rousseau possessed a moral vision which is inseparable from his seemingly factual assertions. But this is not true of Hobbes. We might put the matter another way by saying that Hobbes's ideas are open to criticism and refutation, empirical or logical, in a way that Rousseau's are not. Observation and experiment could, for example, be relevant to many of Hobbes's important assertions: cases of social breakdown in the absence of government, or of states where sovereignty is divided between institutions, or of suicides that seem perfectly reasonable could all be adduced as evidence for or against his claims, while, in principle if not in practice, an experimental state of nature could be set up to see if and how men might escape from it. But it is difficult to see what arguments, empirical or logical, could be used to refute or confirm Rousseau's belief that modern society is corrupting and alienating, or that unless men live according to laws which they themselves (or rather their better selves) have agreed to then they are slaves and are being denied their true humanity.

Values play no part in Ryan's account of the conceptions of human nature that he says are central to ideological thought, and he clearly does not see ideology as any kind of ethical understanding. Consequently the nature of ideology eludes him. As we have just seen with Hobbes and Rousseau, he cannot distinguish between the ideological and the non-ideological. Furthermore, he cannot explain the nature of ideological differences. This is clear from his discussion of James and John Stuart Mill, where he argues that it is not possible to reconcile their views of man and politics, but cannot say why.[11] But an adequate explanation is possible in terms of pseudo-description and incommensurability arising from differing values. These features are central to ideology's logical distinctiveness and to any ideological conception of man. By ignoring the ethical content, or at least its implications, Ryan cannot comprehend ideology as a distinctive way of thinking. In his ' "Normal science" or political ideology?' he writes: 'To analyse what is merely ideological we enquire into the origins of the ideologist, or ask whose interests are served by putting forward the doctrine in question.'[12]

But as we saw in Chapter 1, defining ideology in terms of expressions of class or group interest cannot be the basis of a coherent theory; and in accepting this account Ryan effectively denies ideology's logical autonomy. Finally, Ryan fails to see the necessarily metaphysical status of Ideological Man. In his discussion of Hobbes and Rousseau, he points out that in the seventeenth century the nature of lead was a seemingly insoluble mystery, but one which over time has been solved, and by the same token the nature of man may be similarly revealed to us in the future.[13] But the ethical content of ideological conceptions of man, which Ryan ignores, makes them, like all ideological concepts, pseudo-descriptive and non-referring. Consequently, Ideological Man is incorrigibly metaphysical. And the academic pursuit of an ideological account of man which is also a true account, that Ryan seems to think is possible, is doomed not only to failure but to hopeless confusion.

II

Failure to distinguish between moral and non-moral conceptions of human nature or to understand the significance of any ethical content, is the abiding weakness of most accounts of the role of human nature in political theorizing. Neither Pennock and Chapman nor Forbes and Smith make the necessary distinction; and both their volumes are conceived as contributing to the ultimate aim of discovering the true and ethically significant conception of man, as their respective introductions make clear.[14] In the second essay of the latter volume Graeme Duncan attempts to show how this is to be done. Although admitting that there are 'no commonly agreed criteria for appraising political beliefs, including beliefs about human nature,[15] Duncan nevertheless insists that they can be objectively assessed according to empirical evidence, logical analysis and moral considerations which amount in practice to whether the consequences of a theory are 'nice or nasty' (p. 15). The kind of empirical evidence he has in mind includes what he calls: 'laws of human nature or of human psychology, or the laws or imperatives governing all (complex) societies' (ibid.)

But even on the doubtful assumption that such laws existed and we knew what they were, they could not decisively refute or confirm the kind of conception of men where (as Duncan himself observes in a moment of insight, p. 14) their moral and 'factual' components are inseparable. The ethical content of such theories puts them beyond the reach of empirical evidence and makes them necessarily metaphysical. The appeal to logic is, on the other hand, more promising in that gross contradiction is undoubtedly damning for any theory. But it would be naive to suppose that all theories of human nature are flawed in this way except the one true one. Besides, the kinds of questions Duncan has in mind under this heading concern such matters as the compatibility of values, which tend not to admit of the kind of straightforward answers he aspires to. But much the most important criteria by which Duncan proposes to judge theories of human nature are moral.

Unfortunately, in order to fulfil his evaluatory purposes Duncan needs a moral viewpoint which is objective and absolute: but this he neither has, nor, apparently, aspires to possess. In the end, what his moral criteria boil down to is personal preferences. He tells us that 'personal preferences will certainly influence interpretations of the ideals and values of others' (p. 16) and goes on to give examples of theories he rejects because of his own preferences. But this is the very opposite of objective evaluation. Indeed, that everyone does evaluate according to preferences, with no independent way of choosing between preferences, is precisely the problem and not a solution to it. Thus, Duncan's attempt to devise objective means of choosing between ideological conceptions of man only succeeds in suggesting the futility of the project as an academic exercise. It also implies, conversely, that an attempt, however sophisticated, to create an objective theory of man possessed of moral significance, will only generate ideology and not overcome it. This can be illustrated by the work of Martin Hollis.

Martin Hollis's book *Models of Man*[16] is specifically concerned with the role of conceptions of human nature in social scientific explanations of human action. He insists that such conceptions are necessarily implicit in any social scientific theory, and that despite claims that the assumptions of traditional political theory (caricatured in the passage quoted at the beginning of this chapter) are dead, they are in fact:

> buried in the roots of the very theories which purport to reject them and they still act as premises for metaphysical systems with implications for social ethics. There is no dispensing with a model of man.... Every social theory needs a metaphysic ... in which a model of man and a method of science complement each other. There is no shirking question of quasi-fact, of normative analysis and of praxis. (p. 5)

What Hollis is arguing is that all the elements of traditional political theory, including values, are necessarily part, though often an unacknowledged part, of any substantial social scientific theory.

This is a large and bold claim, and one which contradicts what has been said earlier by insisting on the impossibility of a morally neutral conception of man. However, when Hollis comes to make good this claim he does so in terms of the much weaker claim that the acceptance of a certain concept of man may rule out other conceptions along with their moral implications. But no one would wish to deny this. It may be true, for example, that if Hobbes's account of human nature is a correct one then the kind of anarchistic society envisaged by Godwin is an impossibility; but this of itself does not make Hobbes's account a morally-charged one, and could not be evidence for Hollis's larger claim that no conception of man can be neutral.

It was noted earlier that Hollis draws a sharp distinction between traditional political theory and ideology, but in terms of the present analysis, what Hollis is trying to establish is that ideology is inseparable from social science because all social scientific theories imply a conception of man and such conceptions cannot be morally neutral. There are, in fact, three cases which Hollis fails to distinguish : there is the intrinsically moral and therefore ideological; there is the neutral conception that indirectly rules out certain moral possibilities (as with Hobbes); and there is the neutral conception which is used ideologically. Hollis can only make his larger claim by subsuming the last two under the first. An excellent example of the ideological use of an otherwise neutral concept is the use made of the Darwinian account of human evolution by Spencer, Kropotkin and others. In this case the neutral concept and its ideological use are clearly separate; but the distinction is less obvious where the neutral concept and its ideological use occur in the same writer's work. A good example is B. F. Skinner. As Leslie Stevenson points out in his *Seven Theories of Human Nature*,[17] the concepts Skinner uses in his psychological work are unimpeachably scientific, and this is quite separate from his social (that is, ideological) writings such as *Beyond Freedom and Dignity* and the novel *Walden Two*[18] where he sets out his ideas on how, given the nature of man as revealed in his psychology, society ought to be governed. There is, then, a distinction to be made between Ideological Man and a neutral conception of man, even though the latter may be turned into an ideological conception. This transmutation into Ideological Man is accomplished by addressing to the neutral conception the question, 'What are the moral and practical implications of this conception?' But the important point here is that there are no inevitable answers to this question. Such answers as are arrived at merely reflect the prior values of those who do the asking, however much they may insist they are inherent in man. Hence the varieties of Social Darwinism. By contrast, Ideological Man by birth, so to speak, has his values built into him, and is designed to furnish a particular set of moral and social implications dictated by the values of his creator.

Hollis's failure to recognize these distinctions turns out to be highly convenient for his overall purposes, which are clearly ideological. He wishes to argue, in effect, that since a morally charged conception of man is a necessary feature of social science it had better be the right one, one that is objective, philosophically sound and has the right moral content. He writes:

> The book's constructive attempt is to find a metaphysic for the rational social self. The conclusions are strictly to do with making the actions of Autonomous Man a subject for science. (p. 19)

His account begins with an analysis of the polar opposites: Plastic Man (that is, wholly subject to and explained by causal laws, sociological or psychological) and Autonomous Man (who acts for reasons which are not causes and which are self-explanatory). His own account embraces both. In somewhat Kantian fashion he argues that:

> the actor is autonomous when he is rational and plastic when he is not (p. 183) ... rational action is its own explanation and ... departures from it have a causal explanation. (p. 130)

But being rational is not, for Hollis, simply a matter of having reasons because it makes a difference to the explanation of the action 'whether it was done for good or for bad reasons' (ibid.). When we are being lazy, ignorant, stupid or otherwise not using the very best reasons possible then, apparently, we are behaving according to causal laws and not being fully human. Even just doing what seems best in the circumstances is not good enough, for Hollis insists upon the strictest possible interpretation of 'rationality':

> He has good reason if he acts in his ultimate interests. His ultimate interests derive from what he essentially is (p. 101) ... autonomous action is equated with fully rational action [and] ... that plainly prevents our regarding action as rational, merely because the agent desires to do it or believes that it is appropriate. (p. 137)

Unfortunately, Hollis cannot tell us what man's ultimate interests are. Indeed, he admits that 'we often cannot judge where reason lies' (p. 160), and that 'ultimate reasons are hard to come by' (p. 137).

This is a very strange thesis. Quite apart from the difficulties of regarding any reasons as caused or causal, the problems of dividing reasons between those that are caused and those that are not on the basis of their quality as reasons would seem to be insuperable, especially if Hollis cannot be sure which reasons are the good ones. It is rather like a man who claims anyone can levitate if their reasons are good enough, of whom one is inclined to ask how the force of gravity can tell the good reasons from the bad ones so that it knows when not to operate. However, the important point in the present context is the nature of the concept of man that Hollis is offering to social science. It is in fact an ideological concept, one that has its values built into it. The argument turns on the meaning given to the term 'rationality'. Hollis writes:

What starts as a search for an active model of man leads first to a demand for actions which are self-explanatory because fully rational, thence to an account of rationality in terms of real interests, thence into ethics and finally to that ancient problem about the nature of the Good Society. Yet it should come as no surprise that questions in ethics and politics attend an analysis of human nature. We cannot know what is rational, without deciding what is best. (p. 137)

'Rationality' is not, therefore, a neutral concept (as it certainly can be), but is defined in terms of what is good for Man; that is, it is a pseudo-descriptive concept. It is through exercising this 'rationality' that men can achieve the Good Society, where the ends of every occupant of every social role can be rational ends (p. 186), where each can identify with his social role and so do his duty rationally (p. 106), and where everyone can be fully rational and fully autonomous and thereby fulfil their essential human nature.

With his concept of man, Hollis has the foundation of a complete ideological position. He has a set of values expressed in a pseudo-descriptive conceptual framework, with concepts such as 'man', 'Good Society', 'rational', 'autonomous', 'self-expression', 'role' and 'duty'; and including 'ideology' which, we are told: 'can now be assigned to the superstructure and explained as products of a socio-economic base, only insofar as they are false. True consciousness is its own explanation' (p. 160).

He also has the outline of an ideal society in which, presumably, all will think clearly and ideology will be eliminated. There are, however, some elements missing. We are not given a systematic evaluation of the present world, or any account of how we arrived at it, or any instructions as to how we might arrive at the ideal society. But these things might be said to be implicit in what he does say and in the form of social science he advocates. Criticism of the present world is implied in the extent to which it falls short of the ideal, and is explained to some degree by the prevalance of false reasoning, while the proper future course must lie in man's improved self-understanding and the cultivation of right reason. The fleshing out of these points must, of course, be the function of Hollisian social science. Hollis believes he is providing an objective and rational foundation for the social sciences, but the ideological nature of his concept of man is not a possible basis for any kind of objective study. Any social science that was built on his concept could be no more than an elaboration of his ideological position, in the same way that Marxist social science is an extension of Marxism.

Hollis's conception of human nature contains the seeds of a fully developed ideology, and this indicates the central importance of such conceptions to this kind of thinking. Precisely what their role is and how the other elements of ideology relate to it, and to each other, we must now examine more closely.

The structure of ideology

In the last several chapters we have discussed or touched upon a number of elements and characteristics of ideology, and it is now time to show how they relate together to form a coherent whole; a process that should indicate whether anything more is needed to provide a complete picture. This may be approached by attempting to make good the claim of the last two sections which has accorded particular importance to ideological conceptions of man, as being in some way central to or definitive of ideology.

It is the fusion of fact and value, of description and evaluation, and the consequence of this fusing, that gives ideology its particular logical character. Values have to be embodied in the objective world, and an ideology's concept of man is central to this process. On the one side, the values of an ideology are concerned with what is good or bad for man as such, and so must stem directly from that ideology's account of essential human nature. On the other hand, that same concept of man must play the central role in the ideology's explanation of the world, for what it basically explains is why the world is the way it is for man as such, and that explanation must be cast in terms of man's realization or failure to realize his potentialities. It is therefore in the concept of man that the factual and evaluative sides of ideology are brought together, and through which the values come to pervade the whole of the theory. Therefore, this value/theory combination determines both the prescriptions of the ideology and its conception of the good society, since both involve a notion of what is humanly possible derived from the explanatory theory, and a notion of what is good and right which are an expression of the values. The ideology's concept of man therefore shapes and unifies the entire system of ideas.[19]

I

Ideological man is first of all a bearer of values, the standard of good and bad. Ideologies have to have such a concept of man because they deal in solutions of human problems in absolute terms, and not with the temporary or local. The claims of ideology are universal claims. They are concerned with mankind as such; with the ills of mankind and the good of mankind. What constitutes human good and ill depends upon how human nature is conceived, and is expressed as a set of values. To evaluate the world in terms of a particular set of values is necessarily to understand the world in terms of a particular concept of man in which these values are implicit. Such values are what we take to be good for man, what answers to his needs, releases his potentialities or at least enables him to be at his best. For the religious believer the ultimate source of values is the Divine ('God is good', 'God is love', etc.), whereas ideology takes its starting point as man so defined that the values are built into the definition; man becomes the foundation of values, the sources of their certainty and justification. If, for example, essential humanness is conceived in terms of rationality, then whatever is deemed rational is good for man and whatever irrational bad; if freedom is a value it is because people cannot express their full humanity without it; and if order and authority are values it is because men need them to be at their best.

Armed with this kind of morally-loaded, value-infused conception of human nature one can begin to evaluate the world. Rousseau, for example, directly applied a moralized conception of man to produce his sweeping condemnation of contemporary society: 'Man is born free; and everywhere he is in chains'.[20] By which he meant that freedom is part of man's essential nature, in the sense that man must be free to make moral choices and live according to his own rules, otherwise, as happens to be the case in most societies, his humanity is denied and he is effectively a 'slave'.[21] Similarly, though less dramatically, John Locke in his *Second Treatise on Government*,[22] gives us an account of essential man as being possessed of certain natural rights which are an immediate yardstick for evaluating governments, dividing those that respect and protect their citizen's rights, and are therefore good, from those that deny or threaten those rights and which are therefore tyrannous and bad. Or yet again, in Marx's 'Paris manuscripts'[23] we have a picture of essential man as alienated and oppressed when the product of his labour is appropriated by another, so that all societies based on such appropriation, as all class-divided societies are, must necessarily be condemned as dehumanizing.

However, a pseudo-descriptive concept of man provides only the basis of an evaluatory framework. A Marxist evaluation of capitalism, for example, is more than a simple condemnation based on the extent of alienation and misery it creates, but also takes into account such matters as its contribution (much praised by Marx) to the development of productive forces. Ideological man, therefore, needs to be filled out with a wider social theory, an essential part of which must be some conception of the good society. Any evaluatory system implies a 'best possible', which in turn becomes a standard against which we can measure our present or any other social circumstances; although ideologies vary in the degree to which they make this explicit. Indeed, the good society is implicit in any ideological notion of man, and may be viewed as a direct development from, and even an extension of, the ideology's account of human nature. Conception of man, evaluation and the social ideal form a continuum. The good society embodies the values implicit in the ideology's conception of human nature, while what is bad for man, equally implicit in that conception, is eliminated or minimized. Thus, if man is essentially rational, and the rational is the good and the good is the rational, then the good society will be a wholly rational one; or if equality is essential for men to flourish then the good society will be based upon equality, and inequality will be banished.

On the other hand, the idea that all ideologies have a conception of an ideal society is not to say that such conceptions are necessarily utopian. Many ideological positions take pride in being 'realistic' and condemn any kind of utopian thinking. 'Utopia' has implications of individual and social perfection, which anti-utopians tend to regard as ridiculous. Nevertheless all ideologies, conservative as well as radical, have some notion of the ideal or best possible society. Besides, the distinction between what is utopian and what is realistic is open to some question, if not 'tendentious and misleading' as Arblaster and Lukes insist.[24] They are surely correct in arguing that:

> the distinction between realism and utopianism is itself a misleading and value-loaded, indeed polemical distinction, serving to conceal the value premises from which it is made [p. 10]. ... Realists are not to be distinguished from those thinkers

commonly regarded as utopians by their having *no* general principles or *no* general idea of what society should be like – although it is often implied that just such a distinction can be drawn.

Traditionalist conservatives, organizing technocrats, dogmatic and pragmatic liberals and piecemeal social reformers – although they attack socialists, anarchists and other radicals for attempting to produce blueprints of the desired future society (which very few of the latter do in any detailed way) – are only able to do so by reference to rival conceptions of the good society. The anti-utopians are apt to claim, nevertheless, that their approach to politics is radically different from that of those they see as utopians. The latter are said to be dogmatic, doctrinaire, and inflexible, while they are naturally flexible and realistic. . . . But there seems no reason to accept this trite contrast. It is not self-evident that Burke is less dogmatic in his commitment to tradition, or Oakeshott to his belief in limited government, or Hayek to 'true individualism', or Lipset and Riesman in their commitment to the fundamental excellence of American democracy than is Condorcet in his commitment to the possibility of unlimited human perfection, or Lenin in his commitment to communism, or Proudhon or Kropotkin in their devotion to the anarchist ideal.[25]

Thus, whether it be acknowledged or not, every ideological position has at least an implicit conception of the good or best possible society.

The ideal society is one which by definition cannot be improved; or, more accurately, is possessed of a framework that cannot be improved. Ideological positions, like those of Condorcet or J.S. Mill or Popper or even Marx, which have some kind of open-ended belief in progress, are clearly not advocating any Plato-like static perfection. For them the good society is not something that can be described in any detail, since the detail can and should change. What matters is the framework. The important thing for Mill and Condorcet is a society where changes of the right kind are possible and encouraged; for Popper it is where change is pragmatic and piecemeal; for Marx it is where the obstacles to man's free creativity have been removed (the coming of Communist society, Marx believed, would mean the end of 'prehistory'[26] and the beginning of truly human history). But whether it be the details of relationships or institutions or a broader framework within which change can take place, something has to be fixed and permanent. It is the justification of that fixity and permanence that is problematic. Given the flux of human history it is evident that for any aspect of society to be unchanging it must speak to some permanent human need or potential or aspiration. Or, put another way, it must relate to essential human nature. Herbert Spencer once wrote: 'The co-existence of the perfect man and the imperfect society is impossible'.[27]

Not all ideologists would wish to put the matter in this way; but there must be some necessary link between the good society and human nature. Unless the good society is particularly suited to essential man then it will not work, or at least could not be permanent. In which case there must be a society which suits human nature better. Hence, no picture of an ideal society can stand on its own without an associated conception of human nature to guarantee its possibility and its permanence. Indeed, a conception of an ideal society may be understood as an extension of a conception of man. Certainly without such a conception no picture of an ideal society can make sense.

II

However, ideologies are more than just evaluatory and visionary. They also have to explain and prescribe. A conception of man by which we may measure what is good or bad in present society and picture the best possible society for man is not in itself enough, since evaluations or ideas cannot explain anything. Ideological man must also be at the centre of a descriptive and explanatory framework that must explain our present world and show how we might achieve (or preserve) the best possible one. Ideological theories purport to explain the whole of the human condition, or all of it that is significant, but being essentially practical systems of ideas their inevitable centre of attention is the relationship between our present world and the ideal, including the relationship of identity (as, for example, with Hegel). That is, they explain the relationship between the actual and the possible; or why the world fulfils, or more usually why it falls short of, the ideal. Thus, if property and social hierarchy are evils which distort and dehumanize human existence then how can it be that we live in societies which are characterized precisely by property and social hierarchy?; or again, if racial mixing and the non-observance of racial hierarchies are the great obstacles to mankind's advance, then why are such evils unchecked?; or yet again, if the present world is the best of all possible worlds then why are some discontented or bent on its destruction? In other words, how has the present world, with its ills or its blessings, come about?

However, there is a sense in which it is not the case that ideologists are all seeking to explain the same world, for 'the present world' means different things to different ideologies. It would be more accurate to say that what is described and explained is the 'state of the world' the 'condition we are in'. Ideology describes and explains what is good and bad in the world and why the actual is or is not the ideal; whether and why the present state of affairs is morally coherent or incoherent. This is because the world that an ideological theory explains is not the world as such but the world as evaluated, and what is explained is what is deemed significant in terms of the values of the ideology and its version of ideological man. Of course, for the ideologist the world-as-evaluated simply is the objective world, and his ideological man none other than all of us. But to the non-believer, the ideologist occupies a world of his own, a theoretical construct which, in the manner of a Kuhnian paradigm, he cannot step outside.

Ideological man is central to ideological description and explanation in several ways. The ideal world is the social expression of the values man is thought to embody, values which also determine the nature of the world-as-evaluated. In addition, all the concepts with which these worlds are described and the relationship between them explained are pseudo-descriptive and therefore carry the values that are derived from the ideology's concept of human nature. (It is perhaps worth noting that ideological theories are more or less complex and the explanatory power of their concepts of man are more or less direct. In Marxism – the most complex of ideological theories – explanatory concepts such as 'surplus value' and the 'dialectic' put some distance between the Marxian concept of man and the world to be explained; whereas in Liberalism there is a more direct relationship between rational man and an irrational world.) Furthermore, the actual content of the explanations must relate to how people are constituted. For the Nazi, race is the crucial feature of human nature and he explains the state of the world in terms of race, with the present being a critical phase in the world-historical struggle between Aryan and Jew. But what for the Nazi explains all, for the Liberal and Marxist explains nothing whatsoever. For the Marxist the principal explanatory category is social class; but behind class is the notion of property, which by definition systematically distorts the relationship between man and the world he has created. Thus, ideological man, as the standard of good and bad, is the source of what must be explained, while at the same time, is an essential part of the explanation.

It is the value content of ideological description and explanation that makes it possible to infer prescriptions from what purport to be factual accounts of the world. What is prescribed is the ideal and how to reach, or defend, that ideal. Much attention is paid to the prescriptive element of ideology since it is that aspect which, one might say, engages directly with the actual world. The detail of social and political action is understood and justified in terms of moving from the present to the ideal, or transforming a morally incoherent world into a coherent one, or preserving a coherent one from disintegration. Ideological explanations explain what is good and bad in the world and ideological prescriptions prescribe the promotion of the good and the elimination of the bad; such explanations and prescriptions are therefore closely linked by values. But they are also linked in other ways.

One of the functions of ideological theory must be to guarantee the efficacy of the prescriptions in closing the gap between what is and what ought to be. Explanation and prescription are linked in the sense that, often as not, the solution is implicit in the explanation. If man's ills flow from some great lack (liberty, equality, discipline, education, national self-determination or whatever human nature is deemed to need), then making good that lack is self-evidently part or all of the solution. On a more practical level, the nature of man must determine what solutions are possible and permissible. For example, education is not a possible solution to the Nazi's problems, for, given the nature of man, it is futile; only struggle will suffice. For Kant, the 'republican constitution' could be brought about by violent revolution, but as a means it was not for him permissible. Then again, the explanation of society's ills may be in terms of social forces, which in turn are related to human nature; in which case solutions may well involve the harnessing and exploitation or directing of those very forces (which, for example, is to some extent true of Marx, especially as interpreted by Engels, and of Herbert Spencer).

Finally, explanation and prescription are closely related in two further ways. Ideological theory identifies what is good or ill for man; what conduces to, and is an obstacle to, the good society; and this implies the identification of friends and enemies. Enemies are those who constitute the obstacles or threats – Jews, the ruling class, tyrants, bigots or the ignorant mass – and who must be overcome. But the power of enemies alone cannot account for why the truth held by the ideologist and his adherents is not common property. Christians traditionally explain this in terms of sin. Liberals have the simplest explanation, namely ignorance (although totalitarian propaganda is now a secondary source). Marx developed an elaborate theory of ideology, while Hitler attributed wrong thinking to the pervasive influence of Jewish thought. In both of these cases the solution, whether the overcoming of enemies or the spread of right thinking, is implicit in the explanation.

Thus, the conception of man is both the centre of the value-system and the centre of the theoretical explanation of the world, the fusion of which is what makes ideology logically special. One might say that ideology consists of two interlocking spheres: with, on the one side, a value-laden conception of man, an evaluation of the world and an ideal society forming one unity; and a conception of man as actuality and potentiality, an explanatory theory and practical prescriptions forming another unity. It is through ideological man that the two are fused together to form an ideological theory which can both explain and evaluate the world at the same time. Ideological man is the linchpin of the ideological structure, 'a hyphen that joins, a buckle that fastens' the values and the facts; although in the process the facts become pseudo-facts and disparate elements are transformed into a logically homogeneous system of ideas.

But the elements of ideological man that make this possible are the very elements that prevent him from corresponding to ordinary empirical humanity as he is supposed to do. Ideological man is a theoretical construct. Just as is the atom; and like the atom he is posited in order to explain. Neither are observable; but the unobservability of ideological man is not a practical matter (we have no problems with the limitations of instruments), but flows from the value elements of his composition. These make ideological man incorrigibly metaphysical and incapable of corresponding to people actually in the world. Furthermore, by infusing these values through the whole ideological structure, ideological man renders all of that structure both ethical and metaphysical. This is because the ethical content removes the apparently factual and explanatory out of the sphere of what may be observed, tested or otherwise deemed true or false. Consequently, ideological theory cannot have a real grip on the world. It is not concerned with explanation, prediction or truth in any objective, academic sense, but with practice. Ideological theory, therefore, embraces, links and unifies present actuality with the future that is possible and desired. One might say that, being centrally concerned with the practical, ideology is necessarily preoccupied with the present and its transformation into a possible future. But ultimately all ideologies address the human condition as such; it deals in universals. It must therefore embrace the whole of human experience, past, present and to come.

III

Clearly, if an ideology explains the present and predicts the future in terms of man's ultimate nature and needs, then it must be able to explain the past, explain how we came by our present condition, in the same terms. Not all ideologists have quite seen the need to do this, as Jeremy Bentham's 'considerable disdain for history'[28] testifies. It is certainly true that the past and its explanation will mean more to a Marxist or a Burkean Conservative than a philosophical radical, but, nevertheless, explanations of the past must be possible. Ideological man is universal man, not some phenomenon of the present age. Thus Bentham's lack of interest in the past can be seen as a personal idiosyncrasy. No less a Benthamite than James Mill had a clear Utilitarian version of history, developed in his monumental *History of India*, which is perfectly consistent with the rest of Benthamite philosophy.[29] Thus, it is fair to conclude that an acccount of the past is necessarily at least derivable from all ideological positions. However, the result is necessarily an ideological past and not an historical past, being no more an objective account than is the ideological account of the present. The present from an ideological point of view is 'the condition we are in', and the past is how we got into this condition; that is, where mankind went wrong or what it did right. It is a selective and distorted view of the past, a moralized view of the past. The ideological past is a function of the ideological present; it is an understanding of the past in terms of our present problems and preoccupations. The past is merely the preamble to the present; that is, the earlier part of the story which will ultimately lead to the good society as the happy ending.

Talk of stories is suggestive of myth. Myths play an important role in political beliefs. However,before looking at their relations to ideology we need to be clear about just what they are. 'Myth' is a much misused term, often used as a term of abuse to denigrate any idea deemed to be false (as, for example, is Gilbert Ryle's characterization of the Cartesian theory of mind as the 'myth of the ghost in the machine')[30] Properly understood, a myth is a story which has significance for the lives of those who believe it to be true. Archetypal examples are the stories of the gods of the Ancient Greeks, which defined their religious beliefs, duties and way of life, and explained mysterious aspects of the human and physical world. Like ideology myths purport to be true, and explanatory and have moral significance. Myths, of course, are only called 'myths' by those who do not believe them (much like ideology); for the believer they are simply the truth (witness the controversy provoked by the book *The Myth of God Incarnate* and the response, *The Truth of God Incarnate*).[31]

But myths can also be said to have a role in political life, and there are political myths of various kinds. Henry Tudor's account of political myth[32] suggests that there are essentially two kinds, which he calls 'foundation myths' and 'eschatological myths', and which might be said to correspond to religious myths of creation and the end of the world. For the Russian Communist, for example, there is the foundation myth of the Bolshevik Revolution, which is a simplified version of actual events excluding whatever might detract from its contemporary significance (such as the role of Trotsky), which explains the creation of the Soviet state in such a way as to bring out its moral significance; that is, the values the state stands for and which present and future Soviet citizens must live up to, as is set out in the preamble to the Soviet constitution.[33] Other examples include the American Founding Fathers, the World Communist Revolution, the Anarcho-Syndicalist General Strike, Mao Tse Tung's 'Long March' and so on. Myths of this kind have an important place, though only a contingent one, in ideological thinking. They might be said to be a significant structural element in some, though not all, ideologies; as well as no doubt being important in the psychology of ideological adherence. However, it can be argued that myth plays a much larger role in ideology than this suggests.

This wider role is indicated by ideology's tendency to mythologize the past, to turn it into a story with moral significance. But this is true not only of an aspect of history, but the whole of significant time, past, present, and future; that is, to see the present as one chapter (though perhaps the climactic one) of an unfolding story. In other words, in a fully developed ideology foundation myths and eschatological myths are merely end-pieces of a larger mythological structure. The model here is also religious. Jewish and Christian myths of creation and the end of the world, for example, enclose the story of man in a cosmic struggle of good and evil.[34] What is peculiar about such myths of universal history, unlike other types of myth, is that the believer is necessarily part of the story, is an actor in the drama; there are no neutrals, one has to make a choice between good and evil. Such myths may be characterized as participatory myths. That myths of this kind play a major role in ideological thinking is easily demonstrated. For the Marxist all history is the history of the class struggle and one must take one's stand with the oppressors or the oppressed. Similarly for the Nazi, belief entails commitment to the racial struggle. Liberalism is more complex with many different versions of and attitudes to history. But Liberals are normally committed to the concept of progress and see history as in some sense a struggle between the forces of darkness and enlightenment, although the concrete enemies change from time to time: the traditional ones are priests and kings as, for example, with Condorcet; for J.S. Mill it is the mass mind; for modern Liberals it is totalitarianism and bureaucracy. In all these universal dramas the central character is Man, oppressed, alienated, the victim of class, foreign or racial oppression.

It is with such an archetypal man that the adherent can identify. The adherent therefore knows where he stands in the world, can gauge his moral status, knows who his enemies and comrades are, has a sense of direction, knows what part he has to play, knows his social, moral and political identity. However, this is to start to stray into speculation about what, psychologically, ideology does for us and our need for it, which will be touched upon in the closing chapter. Sufficient for the moment to say that it would appear that a participatory myth is an inevitable feature of a fully developed ideology, and that this completes the set of structural elements, and of features bound together by the concept of man.

The structure of ideology may, therefore, be summarized in the following way. Ideology develops conceptions of human nature in which observable aspects of humanity (rationality, competitiveness, sociability, creativity, etc.) are compounded with particular sets of values. Ideological man is the resultant theoretical construct, which is then used to both evaluate and explain the world as we know it. An ideological conception of man on its own can tell us broadly what is good and bad in the world; but for a fuller and more accurate evaluation it needs to be supplemented with a conception of the good society. An ideology's notion of the good society is usually little more than the extension or filling out of its conception of man; it is the values inherent in that conception made, so to speak, social flesh. But with such a conception it can be shown just how far the present world lives up to, or, more usually, falls short of the ideal. And just how this living up to or falling short is to be explained also involves the same concept of man; only this time extended and filled out into a wider theoretical framework that explains where we are in relation to the ideal, why we are where we are, and how the gap can be closed or prevented from widening. The process of explanation necessarily involves the uniting of past, present and future into a unified whole, which can then be aesthetically shaped into a universal myth, both explaining the world and making moral sense of it.

Kant's political ideas as an example of ideology

The structure of ideology outlined in the previous section might be illustrated with any number of examples. However, it is Kant's thought that will be considered. Kant did not set out his political ideas in a major work on the subject, though he did have a coherent and individual view which is worth studying. But more importantly, Kant is among the greatest as well as the most fastidious of philosophers, so that showing him in certain aspects of his thought to be an ideologist – that is, a confuser of logical categories, a speculative metaphysician and maker of myths – is particularly telling and instructive.

I

Kant did not accept the conventional view of his age that it was reason as such that differentiated man from the animals. Insofar as reason was, in Hume's phrase, 'the slave of the passions' then it was simply a superior piece of equipment to that possessed by other animals for the satisfying of their needs, the difference being merely one of degree. As they pursued their interests and sought to satisfy their needs, men belonged to the same 'phenomenal' world governed by cause and effect as other creatures. What genuinely made men special, and qualitatively different from the animals, was their capacity for moral choice. This meant that men were capable of acting for moral reasons alone, independently of their needs and desires, and in so doing step outside that realm of necessity shared with the animals and into the realm of freedom. It was precisely when they did act for moral reasons alone, in spite of what their needs and interests dictated, that men were fully rational, fully free and fully human.

Freedom was, therefore, a condition of fully developed humanity. But what Kant meant by 'freedom' was conformity to the moral law, which, being completely rational, was equally binding upon all rational beings. We remain free because the law we have to follow is precisely that law which, as rational beings, we give ourselves. We are free because in moral matters we are self-determining; we legislate our own moral law. But since the moral law is wholly rational, it will be the same law for all; it is both our own universal. The very fact that we are capable of such rationality in itself confers a special dignity upon man as a universal legislator, giving him intrinsic and absolute worth, since 'Rational nature exists as an end in itself'.[35] And since the rational being is ruled only by his own laws he is truly autonomous, and autonomy is 'the ground of the dignity of human nature and of every rational nature' (p. 97). Kant conceived of all rational beings, human or otherwise, as potentially members of a 'kingdom of ends', since all are subject to the same self-imposed moral laws. The foundation of this system of universal laws is what Kant called 'the supreme principle of morality' (p. 57), which is his 'categorical imperative' in its various formulations. This first of all enjoins us to act only according to those maxims we would willingly see as universal laws; it then requires that we treat each and every human being as an end and never merely as a means; and finally, it demands that in determining those maxims that will guide our actions we should do so as though we were legislating for a kingdom of such ends (pp. 67, 91 and 95). Whether these three amount to the same thing, as Kant believed, may be doubted. However, the important point is that the categorical imperative provides the basis of a rational moral life. If we lived up to its demands we would always act unselfishly according to self-imposed universal principles, always treating others with respect as autonomous beings possessed of dignity and worth, and as fellow members of a kingdom of ends. This is the basis of a morality all men could live by, irrespective of their social circumstances.

However, this analysis also has implications for man's social and political life. While even a slave has some scope for moral choice, and therefore for living according to universal principles, nevertheless, the life of a slave or serf is not consistent with the dignity of man as an autonomous moral being. Following Rousseau, whom he much admired, Kant believed that his status as a moral being gives man fundamental rights, and in particular a right of freedom. Men must have freedom in order to make moral choices and thereby live as fully rational and fully human beings. It is not sufficient to live an outwardly good life because constrained to do so by law, like the man Plato describes in the Myth of Er.[36] The genuinely good and fully human life must be freely chosen; and all men, even the depraved,[37] must have the opportunity to chose, even though they may choose wrongly. Furthermore, the demand of the moral law that men be treated as ends and not means (that is, the second formulation of the categorical imperative) implies that all men must be treated equally (i.e. equality of opportunity and equality before the law).[38]

The good society, therefore, is one where all men are treated equally and all possess the maximum freedom consistent with good order. But 'good order' requires coercive laws, and Kant's problem, as with Rousseau, is how coercive laws can be justified if men are to be free. J.G. Murphy writes:

> Kant quite clearly believes that freedom does not stand in need of any positive justification, for it is good in itself. Rather it is coercion, bad in itself, that must be defended ... coercion is justified only in so far as it is used to prevent invasions against freedom. Freedom itself is the only value which can be used to limit freedom, for the use of any other value (e.g. utility) would undermine the ultimate status of the value of freedom.[39]

Men have a right to be free to pursue their own ends. But this inevitably will bring men into conflict, and the purpose of civil society is to ensure justice between conflicting claims. Kant writes:

> Justice is … the aggregate of those conditions under which the will of one person can be conjoined with the will of another in accordance with universal law. … Hence the universal law of justice is: act externally in such a way that the free use of your will is compatible with the freedom of everyone according to a universal law.[40]

Thus, for Kant, coercion is justified if it is used as a 'hindrance to a *hindrance of freedom*'; that is, freedom may be limited only for the sake of greater freedom (p. 134).

The kind of civil society that embodies these ideals is what Kant called 'Republican'; by which he meant a system of government with a sovereign representative assembly based on a franchise limited to the independent and propertied (pp. 29, 78 and 100–1). Though he is vague about just what institutions, procedures and franchise his ideal government should have, Kant is none the less clear that: 'the *republican* constitution is the only one which does complete justice to the rights of man' (p. 112; see also p. 99). Without a representative system a government cannot: 'accord with the concept of right … and without it, despotism and violence will result, no matter what kind of constitution is in force' (p. 102).

In the *Critique of Pure Reason* of 1781 he wrote of a Republican constitution:

> A constitution allowing *the greatest possible human freedom* in accordance with laws by which *the freedom of each is made to be consistent with that of all others* – I do not speak of the greatest happiness, for this will follow of itself – is at any rate a necessary idea, which may be taken as fundamental not only in first projecting a constitution but in all its laws.[41]

Kant regarded this as an ideal, like Plato's *Republic*, to which all societies should aspire and approximate to as far as possible. He believed it to be not only the society most conducive to happiness but also one where, because men exercised their reason to its fullest extent, they would become increasingly rational and therefore increasingly good. He goes on:

> The more legislation and government are brought into harmony with the above idea, the rarer would punishments become, and it is therefore quite rational to maintain, as Plato does, that in a perfect state no punishments whatsoever would be required. This perfect state may never, indeed, come into being; none the less this does not affect the rightfulness of the idea, which, in order to bring the legal organization of mankind ever nearer to its greatest possible perfection, advances this maxim as an archetype.
> (Ibid.)

This was the kind of government appropriate universally to rational creatures. The principles underlying it and the kind of laws it ought to enact are universal principles. As an ideal, Kant believed it was 'our duty to enter a constitution of this kind' (p. 187); that is, to make the ideal of a 'kingdom of ends', referred to in the third version of the categorical imperative, as far as possible a human reality. This involved both striving to bring about a Republican constitution by peaceful means, but also striving to bring about permanent universal peace as a necessary condition of the ideal society being permanent and universal, since war is the 'destroyer of everything good' (p. 187) and states with republican constitutions are 'incapable of bellicosity' (p. 184). And although Kant did not believe a Republican world-government was feasible, he did believe that a league of such states was both possible and, eventually, would be created (pp. 104–5). For history is the history of freedom, and progress towards universal freedom was, even if delayed, an inevitability (p. 184).

Contemporary society fell well short of Kant's ideals. His criticisms of it are often more by implication than direct, but they are clear enough for all that. Living in an absolutist authoritarian state marked by hereditary privilege and the absence of civil liberties, Kant's advocacy of republican government, equality of opportunity and maximum political freedom was criticism enough. More generally, we have just seen that in the good society men will be happier and more moral; there will be greater obedience to the laws, more honesty, charity and greater sense of honour, and generally less conflict and violence (pp. 187–8). This is because as a result of their freedom they will have developed into mature rational beings. But in the meantime: 'mankind groans under the burden of evils which, in its inexperience, it inflicts upon itself'.[42] It would therefore seem to follow that in contemporary society an absence of freedom stunts that development and is responsible for much unhappiness and immorality. Again, Kant's ideal future is characterized by permanent international peace, which will only come about when all governments are Republican. Unfortunately:

> the world's present rulers have no money to spare for educational institutions or indeed for anything which concerns the world's best interests (for everything has already been calculated out in advance for the next war). (p. 51)

To the objection of the 'supposedly clever stateman' who says that all this is unrealistic because you have to take men as they are, Kant replies:

> But 'as they are' ought to read 'as we have *made them* by unjust coercion, by treacherous designs'.... For that is why they are intransigent and inclined to rebellion, and why regrettable consequences ensue if discipline is relaxed in the slightest. (p. 178)

What modern man needs, Kant believed, is not discipline but enlightenment.

In his essay *What is Enlightenment?* (1784) Kant defines 'enlightenment' in terms of maturity. It is essentially thinking for oneself and not relying on others. Unfortunately, because of laziness or cowardice, too many people allow others to do their thinking for them, and this is exploited by those in power who argue that such independent thinking is highly dangerous. In a later work he argues that paternal government is the 'greatest conceivable *despotism*' (p. 74). This is at least part of the reason why men are less free than they might be. But although Kant admitted that he did not live in an enlightened age, it was nevertheless, an age of enlightenment in the sense that enlightenment was spreading (p. 58). Mankind was moving in the right direction and the trend could not be reversed.

Kant's confidence that mankind was moving towards an ideal future was based on more than an increase in general rationality through tolerance and education. He also believed that human progress was guaranteed by nature. In his *Idea for a Universal History with a Cosmopolitan Purpose* (1784) he wrote:

The history of the human race as a whole can be regarded as the realization of a hidden plan of nature to bring about an internally – and for this purpose also externally – perfect political constitution as the only possible state within which all natural capacities of mankind can be developed completely. (p. 50)

The good society (or rather, the good societies in a state of organized international peace; i.e. the 'external' political constitution) is all part of nature's plan, which is 'hidden' in the sense that its aim is attained by roundabout, even perverse, means. The means, implanted in man by nature, is what Kant calls man's 'social unsociability'. Man is naturally a social animal, while at the same time his behaviour displays a strong bias towards the anti-social: he is ambitious, egocentric and aggressive. But while these lead to conflict, crime, tyranny and war, they also, ultimately lead to their opposites. For the horrors of crime and civil strife force men to create orderly societies with laws and institutions, and eventually to recognize the need to live within a rational legal order based on the principles of freedom (pp. 44–5). Much progress, Kant believed, had been made along these lines; though much still remained to be done in domestic politics and even more in international politics. Here states were in a state of nature in relation to each other. But in time the horrors of war would teach men the same lesson. Without an international order progress and security were threatened by continual preparations for war. But Kant had no doubt that in the end: 'the highest purposes of nature, a universal *cosmopolitan existence*' (p. 51) will be realized.

But although this end is inevitable, Kant is somewhat ambiguous about exactly how it will be realized. Sometimes it seems that the growth of a general enlightenment will be sufficient, while at others man appears to be entirely dependent on the appearance of enlightened rulers, but at yet other times it seems that it will be providence alone, working not through men's rationality so much as the evil side of their nature to force men to do things in their own interests that they would not otherwise do. Hence, on the prescriptive side of Kant's theory there is often an air of inconsistency about some of the things he says. For example, he repeatedly insists in all his political writings that resistance to established rulers, however bad, is wrong (e.g. pp. 81–2), while at the same time he is openly enthusiastic about the achievements of the French Revolution as a major step in human progress (pp. 182–3). All of this perhaps reflects a deeper uncertainty about the nature of man, and in particular his capacity for evil. From this point of view the theory of man's social unsociability might be seen less as a solution to the question of man's nature as a restatement of the problem. There is, as Howard Williams suggests: 'a fundamental tension in Kant's philosophy which manifests itself in a dualistic view of man as rational and yet capable of radical evil'.[43]

This generates a certain doubt as to whether man's capacity for evil will, in true Liberal progressive manner, be eliminated by the spread of enlightenment, or whether what Kant sometimes calls in his more Augustinian moments 'the depravity of human nature' (e.g. p. 103) will make the ultimate good society (a combination of the ideal republic, the kingdom of ends referred to in the categorical imperative, and the religious ideal of the kingdom of God on earth)[44] a practical impossibility. This ambiguity has important implications. However, for present purposes, it is sufficient to note this possible element of inconsistency within what is otherwise a clear and fully worked out theory of human nature, and the good society that is appropriate to that nature.

II

This account of Kant's political thought, though no more than an outline, is sufficient to demonstrate its ideological character. To begin with, Kant holds certain values which are embodied in his conception of man and inform his account of the world, and which are the basis of his ideal society. His principal values are rationality and individual freedom which he contrives to intertwine logically with each other, and with his notions of moral good and human nature. Thus, men are only fully human when they are free, and only fully free when they rationally pursue the moral good. Other values – such as republican government, equality, tolerance and peace – play a supportive rule, to be understood in terms of the conditions under which man can be at his free, rational, moral best. Altogether, these values define a society in which humanity can flourish and develop itself to the full. The good society in turn becomes a standard by which we measure existing societies. Where freedom is denied, men's development is stunted, they are prone to crime and to unhappiness, and the majority remain immature and fail to reach their full moral stature. Men have a clear moral duty to work to transform the present world into the ideal one, for the enlightenment and freedom of mankind.

Kant's version of ideological man is thus the bearer of values that find expression in an evaluation of the contemporary world and are the foundation of the future one. It is also the foundation and the focus of a wider explanatory theory that embraces all of reality. Kantian metaphysics divides that reality into two spheres and places man at their juncture. On the one side is the sphere of 'phenomena', which is the perceived physical world governed by causal necessity. On the other side is the 'noumenal' sphere, which is both the unknowable world on the 'thing-in-itself' behind perception and also (although how they are connected Kant never makes clear) of freedom and reason. Either can determine man's behaviour. But the moral good lies in the extent to which man chooses to accept the promptings of the noumenal world (i.e. do his moral duty). The whole of reality is apparently so constructed as to give man every capacity and incentive to live up to his full moral potential; he is 'secretly guided by the wisdom of nature' (p. 48).

Nature had laid down man's telos, and has so formed him that he is compelled to pursue his own perfection. The working out of this process through time, from man's barbaric state to the achievement of his telos, is the connecting thread of history. History is the story of man's climb from barbarism to the perfection which is his ultimate destiny; and it is a story in which we can all participate. It is substantive philosophy of history; or, put another way, it is speculative metaphysics and grand myth. Thus, Kant's values are not merely built into his definition of man, but pervade all reality to the extent that the good society appears to be the culmination of that reality. Kant's account of the human condition insists that we occupy a thoroughly moralized universe. The noumenal world has superior moral standing to the phenomenal, while nature is infused with moral purpose, is designed as a setting for man and imparts to him his telos together with the impulses that, over time, will compel him to fulfil it. Thus, 'noumena' and 'phenomena', 'nature' and 'history' are all pseudo-descriptive concepts, as much as the more obviously moral ones: 'freedom', 'autonomy', 'tyranny' and 'war'. Thus, Kant's values are embodied in nature and above all in man, so that the good society is 'natural' in the Aristotelian sense of what is needed for man to fully develop himself and fulfil his telos.

However, before finally deciding on Kant's status as an ideologist there is a possible set of objections that should be considered. Someone might argue that there are certain aspects of Kant's thought where he did no more than follow the common beliefs of his age – God's providence, human perfectibility, a benign and man-orientated nature, etc. – which seemed reasonable to most educated people of his time but somewhat implausible today. These eighteenth-century assumptions, compounded by a doubtful metaphysics, account for the ideological content of Kant's thought. They can be easily dispensed with, especially since Kant only accorded them the status of Ideas of Reason. This leaves us with a rational core which is as philosophically sound now as it was then; a coherent moral and political philosophy fit for modern man.[45]

The first thing that might be said about these objections is that one cannot simply dismiss as dross those ideas of a thinker one finds to be inconvenient. The ideas of Kant that we find implausible today are not optional extras but are integral to his thought. But even if we could dispense with Kant's eighteenth-century assumptions and doubtful metaphysics, what remained – the supposed rational core – would be just as ideological as the original. We would still be left with a moral ideology pointing towards a political one. At its absolute bare minimum, we have a particular conception of man whose nature demands a certain way of life which is morally desirable. Man's humanity resides in his moral rationality which must have freedom to be exercised. The good society is one which recognizes man's moral autonomy and consequent right to freedom, (though today our assumptions make it self-evident that this must mean democracy – which Kant abhorred). This is the classical ideological formula: a conception of man with particular values defined into it, from which can be inferred a good society in which those values form the principles of social organization. Only if it could be demonstrated that this conception was grounded in reality and that the values, because inherent, were logically superior to any others, might Kant's political ideas avoid being properly classified as ideological.

But in fact there is nothing in Kant's substantive ethical theory that logically compels assent. His values and ideals may be attractive, but this is not to give them the logical status Kant and his followers attributed to them. Despite Kant's great, and deserved, reputation as a moral philosopher they are no more rational than any other values and ideals some of which may be equally attractive. The foundation of his substantive ethics is the categorical imperative, the first formulation of which is an empty formula (the Nazi, for example, can consistently will that all Aryans persecute all Jews[44]), from which the other two versions, which do have content, simply do not follow. Treating all with dignity and legislating for a kingdom of ends, however desirable they may be as ideals, have no higher logical status than any other statements of value. It simply does not follow that because human beings are rational, or capable of moral choice, every single one of them has infinite worth or right to political freedom. In fact in Kant both 'freedom' and 'reason' are pseudo-descriptive terms reflecting his own values rather than any standard usage.

This is fairly obviously the case with 'freedom', since for him being free means conforming to the moral law as he defines it; but 'reason' is equally a carrier of Kantian values. The concept of 'rationality' in Kant is not an objective one. It is used pseudo-descriptively: associated with the moral, with the superior noumenal world and identified with God and the angels. Kant does not use it in the everyday sense as a means to work out mundane problems (in which case one way of robbing a bank may be more rational than another), but rather as the instrument of man's moral purpose. Like Aristotle, the rational life is the morally good life. And it is Kant's account of reason which is central to his definition of human nature. But his use of 'man', 'freedom', and 'reason', are arbitrary usages, not demonstrably better than anyone else's. They reflect his values which have no solid foundation in the sense that they grow from the categorical imperative, where the first formulation is empty and the others, because they do not follow from it, are merely assertions. Thus, there is no basis for assuming that Kant's substantive ethical theory is superior than any other, and consequently no further reason to accord his political thinking any special philosophical status.

Kant's political thought fulfils all the criteria for ideology developed in previous chapters. Thus, we have a value-loaded conception of man, a pseudo-descriptive vocabulary, an ideal society, explanations, prescriptions and a participatory historical myth; that is, all the ingredients of a fully developed ideological position. And Kant is, therefore, demonstrably a confuser of categories, a speculative metaphysician and a maker of myth; in other words, an ideologist.

Notes

1. Martin Hollis, *Models of Man*, (CUP, 1977), p. 1.
2. See ibid., p. 160 where ideology is seen as resulting from socio-economic causes.
3. J.R. Pennock and J.W. Chapman (eds), *Human Nature in Politics*, (New York UP, 1977).
4. I. Forbes and S. Smith (eds), *Politics and Human Nature*, (Frances Pinter, 1983).
5. The only discussion of ideology in either book is by J. Chapman in Pennock and Chapman, op. cit., pp. 308–13, where it is associated with irrationalism and rationalization of interests, and is distinguished from 'great political theories' (p. 310). Human nature does not enter into the discussion of the internal nature of ideologies.
6. Both these statements might be described as unelaborated insights, since both were made in passing and neither has been worked up into a general theory.
7. Isaiah Berlin, 'George Sorel' in *Against the Current*, (OUP, 1981), p. 298.
8. Ibid., p. 296.
9. Alan Ryan, 'The nature of human nature in Hobbes and Rousseau' in J. Benthall (ed.) *The Limits of Human Nature*, (Allen Lane, 1973), p. 3. Subsequent page references are to this edition.

10. Alan Ryan, 'Two concepts of politics and democracy; James and John Stuart Mill', in Martin Fleisher (ed), *Machiavelli and the Nature of Political Thought*, (Croom Helm, 1973), pp. 76–113.
11. Ibid., p. 180: 'My own view is that in the end such an attempt runs into so many difficulties as to render the revised account incoherent, but there is no simple proof of this point'. C.f. Christopher J. Berry, *Human Nature*, Issues in Political Theory Series, (Macmillan, 1986). This excellent book was available too late to be taken proper account of in the present work. It too emphasizes the descriptive/prescriptive duality of theories of human nature, but no attempt is made to explain how the logic of this duality works. Consequently, Berry, like Ryan, fails to distinguish between moral and non-moral theories and lumps in Hobbes with the rest.
12. Alan Ryan, '"Normal" science or political ideology?' in Peter Laslett *et al.* (eds), *Philosophy, Politics and Society*, fourth series, (Blackwell, 1972), p. 87.
13. Alan Ryan, 'The nature of human nature in Hobbes and Rousseau', op. cit., p. 5.
14. See Pennock and Chapman, op. cit., p. 14; and Forbes and Smith, op. cit., p. 4.
15. Graeme Duncan, 'Political theory and human nature' in Forbes and Smith, op. cit., p. 15. Subsequent page references are to this edition.
16. Martin Hollis, *Models of Man*, op. cit., Subsequent page references are to this edition.
17. Leslie Stevenson, *Seven Theories of Human Nature*, (OUP, 1974), Chapter 8, pp. 91–9. See also W. Stafford, 'Utopianism and human nature', in Forbes and Smith, op. cit. pp. 68–85.
18. B.F. Skinner, *Beyond Freedom and Dignity*, (Penguin, 1973); and *Walden Two*, (2nd edn), (Macmillan, New York, 1976).
19. C.f. Ian Forbes's list of components of political theory in Forbes and Smith, op. cit., pp. 21–2. Significantly, there is no mention of values and therefore no element that binds the components together in any necessary way. C.f. also Graeme Duncan's remark that views of human nature 'do not occupy an identical place in each political theory' (ibid., p. 11), which misses the point entirely.
20. Jean-Jacques Rousseau, 'The social contract', in *The Social Contract and Discourses*, (Dent (Everyman), 1973), p. 165.
21. See Howard Williams, *Kant's Political Philosophy*, (Blackwell, 1983), for a quite different interpretation.
22. John Locke, *Two Treatises of Government*, Peter Laslett, (ed.), (Mentor, 1965), pp. 305–477.
23. Karl Marx, *Economic and Philosophic Manuscripts*, (Lawrence & Wishart, 1973).
24. Anthony Arblaster and Steven Lukes, (eds), *The Good Society*, (Methuen, 1971), p. 2.
25. Ibid., pp. 10, 6 and 7.
26. Karl Marx, Preface to 'A contribution to a critique of political economy' in L.S. Feuer (ed.), *Marx and Engels: Basic Writings on Politics and Philosophy*, (Fontana, 1969), p. 85.
27. Herbert Spencer, *The Data of Ethics*, (1907), p. 241. Quoted in Frederick Copleston, *A History of Philosophy*, vol. 8, pt 1, (Doubleday, New York, 1967), p. 160.
28. James Steintrager, *Bentham*, (Allen & Unwin, 1977), p. 14.
29. Ely Halevy writes: 'It can indeed be said that the idea of a philosophy of history is totally foreign to Bentham's thought. It is, on the other hand, fundamental to James Mill. . . . Mill lamented that philosophers had not yet succeeded in agreeing on the rules suitable for determining the principal degrees of civilization, and his *History of India* . . . was perhaps, for the most part, an attempt to define the notions of civilization and progress, by reference to a particular example. James Mill laid down the principle that a nation is civilized to the precise extent to which *utility* is the object of all its efforts'. *The Growth of Philosophical Radicalism*, (Faber, 1972), pp. 273–4, See also J.W. Burrow, *Evolution and Society*, (CUP, 1966), pp. 28–9, 42–9.
30. Gilbert Ryle, *The Concept of Mind*, (Penguin, 1963), p. 10.
31. John Hicks (ed.), *The Myth of God Incarnate*, (SCM 1977); and Michael Green (ed.), *The Truth of God Incarnate*, (Hodder & Stoughton, 1977).
32. Henry Tudor, *Political Myth*, (Pall Mall Press, 1972).

33. See S. Finer (ed.), *Five Constitutions*, (Penguin, 1979), pp. 146–8.
34. There are many versions of the Christian view of history, but the traditional view comes from St Augustine. One might compare the religious 'participatory myth' with, for example, Bernard Shaw's remark of 1897: 'Socialism wins its disciples by presenting civilization as a popular melodrama, or as a Pilgrim's Progress through suffering, trial and combat against the powers of evil to the bar of poetic justice with paradise beyond'. (Quoted in Henry Pelling, *Origins of the Labour Party*, 2nd edn, (OUP, 1965), p. 217.)
35. Immanuel Kant, 'Groundwork of the metaphysic of morals', in H.J. Paton (ed.), *The Moral Law*, (Hutchinson, 1948), p. 91. Subsequent page references are to this edition.
36. Plato, *The Republic*, (trans. F.M. Cornford), (OUP, 1941), p. 357.
37. Although as Pierre Hassner points out in L. Strauss and J. Cropsey (eds), *History of Political Philosophy*, (2nd edn), (Chicago UP, 1981), p. 562, this was a view Kant had to come round to.
38. H. Reiss (ed.), *Kant's Political Writings*, (OUP, 1971), pp. 75–6. Subsequent page references are to this edition.
39. J.G. Murphy, *Kant: The Philosophy of Right*, (Macmillan, 1970), p. 109.
40. Immanuel Kant, *The Metaphysical Elements of Justice*, (trans. J. Ladd), (Bobbs Merrill, 1965), pp. 34–5.
41. Immanuel Kant, *Critique of Pure Reason*, (trans. Norman Kemp-Smith), (Macmillan, 1933), p. 312.
42. Immanuel Kant, *On History*, Lewis White Beck (ed.), (Bobbs Merrill, 1963), p. 62.
43. Howard Williams, *Kant's Political Philosophy*, (Blackwell 1983), p. viii.
44. See ibid., pp. 266–8 where Williams argues that the account of a universal church, set out in 'Religion within the limits of reason alone', represents Kant's ultimate vision of the good society.
45. This is roughly the position of Stanley Benn and R.S. Peters, in *Social Principles and the Democratic State*, (Allen & Unwin, 1959).
46. The point is made by Alasdair MacIntyre in *A Short History of Ethics*, (RKP, 1966), pp. 197–8.

CHAPTER SIX

OBJECTIONS AND REFINEMENTS

The conception of ideology developed over the last four chapters is no doubt open to many objections. Three objections, however, are worth considering in detail. This is partly because they are important in themselves and need to be replied to, and also because in answering them we may refine and extend our understanding of ideology.

Ideology and 'academic political theory'

The first objection concerns the place of ideology within the wider field of political theorizing. In *The Nature of Political Theory*[1] David Miller and Larry Siedentop present what is perhaps a standard view of the relationship between traditional political theory and ideology. They write:

> Political theory is, therefore, an essentially mixed mode of thought. It not only embraces deductive argument and empircal theory, but combines these with normative concerns . . . so acquiring a practical, action-guiding character. (p. 1)

This combination of elements can, on their account, constitute objective knowledge because it is subject to the different truth criteria appropriate to each of these elements (pp. 11-12); hence Siedentop calls it 'academic political theory' (p. 53). The contrast they draw is with ideology, which is concerned with 'defending or propagating the interests of particular social groups or classes' (p. 1). The distinction here appears not to be any matter of structure or content but, in somewhat Aristotelian manner, a difference between proper and degenerate forms of the same things, one being objective and the other biased. If such a distinction were sustained it would put the present analysis at risk. But there are a number of reasons, that have already been discussed at length, for taking this to be a false dichotomy. As we saw in the opening chapter, class or group bias cannot be an adequate basis for a theory of ideology, while the logical and structural features that do provide such a basis do not support a distinction between ideology and traditional political theory of the kind Miller and Siedentop want to make. We cannot separate the facts from the values in a way that would allow their separate truth criteria to be applied; and even if we could, we have no truth criteria applicable to the values. However, Miller and Siedentop develop a number of arguments not answered by the previous discussion which need more detailed consideration.

What Miller and Siedentop attempt to do is to update and strengthen the defence of political theory offered by John Plamenatz (to whose memory their book is dedicated) in his article 'The uses of political theory' and elsewhere.[2] To do this they criticize Plamenatz's account in an attempt to eliminate what they take to be the unnecessary positivist elements in his work. Plamenatz accepted the current positivist wisdom that there are only three types of theoretical activity in relation to politics: conceptual analysis (i.e. political philosophy); empirical theory (i.e. political science), and normative theory (i.e. 'political theory' in its traditional meaning). But whereas the positivists would only allow the first two to be legitimate academic activities, and doubting the validity of the third, Plamenatz sought to defend political theory as legitimate by insisting on its intellectual rigour and the need for academically acceptable criteria, though without specifying precisely what these should be. Plamenatz's error, according to Miller and Siedentop, was to concede that political philosophy and empirical theory were value-free and quite independent of normative theory. This, they insist, demotes political theory to the status of 'poor relation' (p. 12) and deprives it of 'the requisite intellectual credentials' (p. 9).

The positivist objection to political theory is that its value content and prescriptivity rule out any possibility of objective knowledge, and Plamenatz does not really answer the point. Perhaps the obvious answer to the positivists is to argue for or assume the possibility of an absolute ethics. But Plamenatz does not take this line and neither do Miller and Siedentop, although they correctly understand that Plamenatz's demand for greater rigour is not enough. They have the quite different strategy of denying the validity of any alleged divisions between political theory and either empirical theory or political philosophy that are based on ethical content. They insist that, in fact, ethical content pervades all three, and that there can be no fundamental division between them in content or method. The three form a continuum: 'the boundaries drawn between these three forms of intellectual activity are conventional in character, representing a convenient academic division of labour, but no clear-cut differences of method' (p. 12).

The implication is that the unchallenged academic respectability of political philosophy and empirical theory is transferred to political theory, thereby giving it the academic status that Plamenatz wished to confer on it without succeeding.

The first and obvious point to make is that even if all these claims to continuity were demonstrably true they would still not establish the objectivity and academic credibility of political theory. All it would do would be to cast doubt upon the objectivity and academic credibility of political philosophy and empirical method. But these claims are not true, at least not on the arguments presented by Miller and Siedentop. The crucial question is the pervasiveness of values. They base their claim that empirical theory is necessarily value-laden upon two arguments that are equally thin. The first is Charles Taylor's notion of 'value-slope';[3] that is, social scientific theories may not be directly prescriptive, but indirectly favour one view of the world by ruling out another. But, as we saw when discussing Hollis, this will not do. To take a moral example, if 'Hume's law' is true then Natural Law is not, but this does not make 'Hume's law' value-laden; it would be a bit like saying that because Vesuvius destroyed a Roman city it therefore had an anti-Roman bias – it just does not follow.[4] Their second point is that in social science a given body of evidence may be accommodated by more than one theory, and there may be no empirical way of deciding between the rival theories. The choice, therefore, must be on other than empirical grounds, and it is here that value considerations operate. But then even if a choice must be made (and it is not made clear why, or by whom, or for what purpose), these non-empirical grounds need not be moral or political; it could be on the basis of simplicity or elegance as in physical science. Besides, it is not claimed that all social scientific theories are in this situation. It is therefore difficult to see how this can support a claim that all social scientific theories are value-laden. Nevertheless, it is upon the basis of what are at best two rather shabby arguments that Miller and Siedentop conclude:

> Taking these two observations together, we are led to the conclusion that the theoretical position adopted by a social scientist must be value-related, inasmuch as it supports a political standpoint of a particular kind. (p. 11)

But this is an unwarranted leap that will not support the contention that there is no clear division between empirical theory and political theory.

The case for the necessary value-ladenness of political philosophy is equally unconvincing. Their argument is based upon what they take to be the nature of political concepts and how the philosopher responds to them:

> The concepts used in political argument are typically contestable concepts, in the sense that each may be interpreted in a variety of incompatible ways without manifest absurdity. Such contests cannot be resolved by formal means ... establishing a preferred meaning for such a term involves engaging in substantive political argument, bringing forward both empirical evidence and moral principle to justify the general perspective to which the preferred meaning corresponds. (p. 10)

From this Miller and Siedentop conclude that political philosophy is value-laden; that it employs both moral and empirical criteria to reach its conclusions; and that the difference between political philosophy and political theory consists 'at most in a difference of emphasis' (p. 10). However, these arguments do not bear serious examination. In the first place, there is no reason why the philosopher dealing with contested concepts need go beyond analysing their different meanings and relating them to political beliefs, and good reason why he should not go further.[5] Miller and Siedentop quite rightly point out that such disputes cannot be settled by formal means, and that they 'can only be resolved by taking up and defending a political standpoint' (p. 14). But such a resolution could not be an objective academic resolution, and it therefore cannot be the business of the philosopher to attempt it, since he is restricted to 'formal means' and to the ideal of objectivity. It is solely a matter for ideologists and their adherents to defend their 'preferred meanings'. Secondly, not all political concepts, as Miller and Siedentop imply, are 'essentially contestable': 'democracy' is, but 'constitution' is not. However, the situation is not quite this clear-cut. The account of pseudo-description in Chapter 2 suggests three possible types of political concept in this respect: (a) the intrinsically pseudo-descriptive (i.e. 'essentially contested'); (b) the ethically neutral, and (c) those otherwise neutral concepts that have been drawn into an ideological theory and invested with ethical significance (such as the Marxist concept of the 'state'), and therefore have had, so to speak, pseudo-description thrust upon them.

It is the business of political philosophers to point out logical distinctions of this kind, but not to take sides in ideological conflict by defending their own versions of ethically-loaded terms. It is significant that in the passage just quoted 'empirical evidence and moral principle' only come into play when philosophers are justifying their 'preferred meanings'. But it is precisely when philosophers attempt this kind of justification that they cease to be doing philosophy and begin engaging in the quite different activity of political theory or ideology. Thus, political philosophy can be clearly distinguished from political theory, both in terms of ethical content and methodology; and the same is true of empirical theory. Miller and Siedentop's idea of a continuum must, therefore, fall; and, on their own criteria, must lack the 'requisite intellectual credentials' for academic status. What then of their view of ideology?

What, for Miller and Siedentop, distinguishes ideology from political theory is that ideology expresses class or group interests (p. 1), and has an economic basis (p. 2), which makes it systematically biased in a way that they believe 'academic political theory' is not. But we saw in Chapter 1 that the expression of class or group interests canot be a satisfactory basis for ideology, while the economic theory of ideology was also shown not to be viable. It is logic alone that can determine what is and what is not ideology, and ideology as it is analysed in the present work embraces all that Miller and Siedentop would count as academic political theory. In fact they seem somewhat unsure themselves. On the one hand, they count Liberalism as an ideology (p. 4), while giving the status of political theory to Rawls's *Theory of Justice* and Nozick's *Anarchy, State and Utopia*, both recognized as belonging to the Liberal tradition. Indeed, if the central arguments of this work are correct then 'academic political theory' is a contradiction in terms.

It is not particularly difficult to see how Miller and Siedentop have fallen into these errors. Much of what passes for empirical theory and political philosophy is indeed value-laden and connected (logically connected) with one or other ideological position. Marxian sociology is the most obvious example in social science, while much of what is accepted as political philosophy is concerned with the determination of values and is bound up with Liberal beliefs. Many standard works of political philosophy are in fact works of Liberal political theory,[6] such as D.D. Raphael's *Problems of Political Philosophy*, in which, for example, a discussion of the concept of 'democracy' merely consists of a rather idealized description of the British Constitution from a Liberal point of view.[7] We have noted that it is characteristic of ideology to influence the apparently factual through the process of pseudo-description, thereby giving to the disparate sources of any particular ideological theory a certain homogeneity based on values. Miller and Siedentop have observed theorizing that has been influenced by ideology and jumped to the wrong conclusion that all empirical theory and political philosophy must be like this. At the same time it could be said that they are particularly prone to this mistake in that they share Plamenatz's conviction that human beings need 'practical philosophy' and they are clearly attracted to political theory's 'practical, action-guiding character' (p. 1):

> political theory is associated with a more active impulse than either 'the study of political thought' or 'doing political philosophy'. It involves, at least implicitly, the assumption that shaping social and political concepts is also, in the longer run, shaping social and political institutions. (p. 2)

What they do not seem to recognize is that the existence of a human need for objective political theory does not guarantee that such a thing is possible; we might say that there is an acute human need to be able to predict the consequences of our actions, but unhappily reality is not such as to make this possible either. In the end all Miller and Siedentop are doing is attempting to invest ideology with an academic status it does not and could not have. This is not to say, however, that the creation of ideology is necessarily a waste of time (any more than the creation of art is a waste of time). But that is another argument.

Positions and traditions

The second objection is the essentialist argument that a political doctrine is first and foremost a set of principles, and that various theories of man and society may be used to justify them at various times, but it is the principles that are essential while the theories are not. This may be said of Conservatism or Socialism or some other doctrines, but it is most often and most readily said of Liberalism, which can stand for the rest. The argument might be used against the present analysis in one of two ways: either the analysis is basically wrong, or the analysis is correct but does not apply to Liberalism which is, in consequence, not an ideology.

For this objection to hold water at least three things must obtain. First, there has to be a single core of principles to which all recognized Liberal thinkers subscribe. This means that such thinkers must share the same values, and that terms like 'freedom', 'reason' and 'justice' must have the same meaning for all. Secondly, this set of principles must be sufficiently clear-cut to enable anyone to identify who is and who is not a Liberal. Thirdly, it must be possible to separate these principles from the various theories of man and society that are used in their support. In fact none of these conditions can be met.

In the history of Liberal thought there are many instances where theorists have differed profoundly over principle. Usually the differences are masked by the process of using the same words in different ways. But sometimes they have been quite open. Competition, for example, has been an important value for various Liberal thinkers from Bentham to von Hayek.[8] For Herbert Spencer competition was the means by which man and society reached ever-higher stages of civilization;[9] while for Leonard Hobhouse competition was anathema because quite incompatible with 'harmony' which was the highest human good and only achievable through cooperation.[10] However, differences of principle that turn on differences of usage are much more common. Freedom is one such case. Bentham, for example, believed a man to be free when he could pursue his own self-interest without hindrance; while for Kant man was not free at all when pursuing his self-interest, but only when acting according to some self-imposed moral rule *against* his self-interest. These conceptions of freedom are closely bound up, as we have seen, with different theories of rationality and what it is to be human. This was also true of the radically different views of the proper extent of state activity put forward by T.H. Green and such contemporaries as Herbert Spencer.[11] A more recent example is the very different notions of justice entertained by John Rawls and Robert Nozick.[12] Many more examples could be cited, but the point need not be laboured.

Nor, if the point has been well made, will it require elaborate demonstration to show that the boundaries of Liberal thought are uncertain and controversial. It is sufficient to point to examples of thinkers deemed Liberals by some but not by others, including such diverse figures as Rousseau, Hegel, Edmund Burke and R.H. Tawney. For example, John Plamenatz in his *Readings from Liberal Writers*[13] writes: 'It is not often claimed for Rousseau and Hegel that they were liberal philosophers, and I am not now concerned to argue that they were' (p. 25). But he goes on to insist that Edmund Burke was a Liberal (p. 36), and to include passages from R.H. Tawney among his essential Liberal texts. Burke and Tawney are more often claimed by other ideologies than as a Liberal[14] while Hegel is more problematic. He is often claimed as a Conservative; but a passage of his is included in J.S. Schapiro's, *Liberalism: its Meaning and History*;[15] while he is clearly not regarded as a Liberal by E.K. Bramsted and K.J. Melhuish in their *Western Liberalism*.[16] The idea that Liberalism is essentially a set of fixed principles, to which everything else is secondary, must be rejected.[17]

However, there is another version of essentialism that can be considered briefly, which takes the opposite course of locating the essence of Liberalism in theories of human nature rather than principles. This case is most forcefully put, and in great detail by G.F. Gaus in his book *The Modern Liberal Theory of Man*.[18] Gaus writes:

> The account of the modern Liberal tradition defended in this book might be called 'essentialist' in the sense that it asserts that the essence of modern liberalism is a particular theory of human nature. (p. 9)

This theory, he claims, is shared by all modern Liberals and underpins their various, though broadly similar, political proposals. However, 'Modern Liberalism' is not to be equated with 'contemporary Liberalism', nor with the 'new Liberalism' of the turn of the century. In fact Gaus ends up confining his concept to only six thinkers: J.S. Mill, T.H. Green, L.T. Hobhouse, John Dewey, Bernard Bosanquet and John Rawls.

There may be something to be said for linking these thinkers in terms of certain shared features of their thought, but to insist that they all share the same conception of man is to overstate the case greatly. Gaus himself notes that:

> we are struck by the tremendous diversity of ethical and metaphysical views that 'new

liberals' have put forward to support their prescriptions ... utilitarianism, idealism (and the common good), harmony, instrumentalism and the social contract all have been offered as the basis for a revised liberalism. (p. 1)

But clearly, these thinkers could only be said to share the same concept of man if these wider theoretical frameworks have no bearing on the matter, which is hardly plausible. To take just one example, J.S. Mill was an atheist who believed an individual could develop himself on his own, while for T.H. Green we are all manifestations of the divine consciousness and none of us can develop ourselves in isolation but only as part of a wider moral community. To say, therefore, that Mill and Green have the same concept of man is absurd. Even less plausible is his contention that the ethical beliefs of modern liberals have no bearing on the matter either. He writes:

if the theory of human nature is so central, one may wonder if my account of modern liberalism allows any significant political role for modern liberals' ethical theories. ... Well, it must be acknowledged that the main thrust of my account is that, indeed, they are not of central importance ... modern liberals very often argue in support of liberty, democracy and economic proposals *directly on the basis of their theory of human nature, with little or no reference to their formal ethical theories.* (p. 272)

But this is naive. Gaus simply treats terms such as 'growth', 'harmony', 'development', 'happiness', 'democracy', 'liberty' and above all 'man' as simply factual terms, as purely descriptive (as does Ryan, as we noted earlier). These theories are not factual, nor the concepts simply descriptive, but are the vehicles for expressing the ethical beliefs of their respective authors.[19]

The 'modern liberal theory of man' which Gaus puts forward is in fact his own construction. It is a pastiche achieved by selecting and arranging points and arguments from his six thinkers; and by emphasizing similarities and ignoring differences, sometimes at the cost of some vigorous Procrustean stretching:

by positing additional psychological dynamics or by reconceptualizing notions like private property ... Bosanquet can quite consistently embrace the modern liberal theory of man. (p. 235)

In spite of such contortions Gaus's theory of man is not tightly drawn, but is a rather broad elaboration of the view that the development of the individual is bound up with the development of others. But putting a hand in that bag one could just as easily pull out a Socialist or Anarchist (or Hegelian or Marxist for that matter) as a Liberal. Furthermore, Gaus admits that modern Liberals embrace a variety of not always compatible political prescriptions, and that if these all relate to the same concept of man then the relationship can only be a 'loose' one. Nevertheless, he insists that these 'loose' connections amount to good philosophy and not 'mere ideology' (p. 5).

But ideology is precisely what all this is. And this is not because of loose connections or baggy concepts, but because of its ethical content. Even though Gaus may indeed be identifying similar features in the work of his six thinkers, the 'modern liberal theory of man' is still his construction, and one that expresses his own ideological viewpoint. This is especially apparent when he adds his own points to it (e.g. p. 182), and when, even more suprisingly, he criticizes one or other of his six for straying away from it (e.g. p. 72). The idea that the individual can only develop in conditions of political freedom, and where all are equally free, and that denial of this freedom inevitably leads to 'behavioural pathologies' (pp. 135–9), is not a factual theory but a set of ethical beliefs. Like most ideologists, Gaus believes himself to be dealing with the objective facts of human existence, when in reality he is articulating his own moral vision of the world.

Thus, the essentialist objection, whatever its form, does not appear to stand up to examination. However, the disposal of this objection throws up another. If ideologies have no fixed core, then how can we say that, for example, Bentham, Kant, Spencer, Hobhouse and Nozick all belong to the same Liberal ideology? In the absence of an essence, what holds the disparate ideas together as one set of political beliefs? An adequate answer to these questions will necessitate some further refinement of the conception of ideology so far developed. But first we need to say something about the way in which ideologies produce different versions.

It is inevitable that, over time, ideologies develop and evolve. The world changes and an ideology must be kept up-to-date to maintain its claim to truth and relevance. But those who undertake such updating may be inspired by different things: by the course of events or the mood of the times, by new intellectual developments or trends, or by differences of background or experience. Herbert Spencer and T.H. Green both aspired to modernize Liberal thinking in the mid-nineteenth century. But what impressed Spencer was the development of biological science, and he sought to show the significance of evolutionary theory as underpinning the truth of classical Liberalism. T.H. Green, on the other hand, was moved by quite different considerations. His concern (partly at least influenced by his religious background) was with the social evils attendant upon unregulated capitalism. As a result, Spencer saw a diminishing role of the state, an extension of *laissez faire* and the triumph of individualism, while Green desired an increased need for state intervention to limit *laissez faire* and assert the responsibility of the community. These constituted two new and different versions of Liberalism, involving important differences in values, and having two quite different conceptions of man and society. It is such deeper concerns that also underly those differences mentioned earlier, between Kant and Bentham over the nature of freedom, between Spencer and Hobhouse over the importance of competition, and between Rawls and Nozick over the nature of justice. Within a successful ideology there will be many developments of this kind, some of which may be successful in attracting support and some not. Theorists are always liable to go off in different directions and end up with several versions of the ideology that are funamentally at odds with each other.

There are no rules governing the direction in which ideologies evolve. They respond to their times. Consequently, it makes more sense to think of ideologies in terms of traditions of thought, each composed of a number of variations or positions, rather than a fixed core of essential doctrine. An ideological tradition has more in common with a tradition of painting or novel-writing than with the development of an academic discipline, in that different positions may be linked to others in the tradition by a variety of connections in a highly complex pattern.

Each thinker contributes to the tradition, while at the same time his system of ideas is autonomous, with its own set of basic elements – conception of human nature, vocabulary, and the rest – some of which may be shared by other positions within the tradition, while other elements may be incompatible or incommensurable. Nor can there be any authoritative human direction of the process. There are no popes in ideology (the nearest equivalent was perhaps the 'Moscow line' which was authoritative within Marxism–Leninism for a while), and anyone is free to develop their own version.

What the main line of development might be is largely a retrospective judgement, which itself may, from time to time, be revised. It just so happened that T.H. Green articulated what many other Liberals were coming to feel, and the future lay with his revised Liberalism, rather than Spencer's. The development of ideologies is, so to speak, practice-led in response to current need. We might say that a kind of evolutionary law of survival of the best-adapted operates, to the extent that, of the various ideological positions available, some will gain adherents, grow and develop, while others will not. When a theorist feels that his inherited beliefs are no longer adequate to the times and need revision, then anything is possible, even including the absorption of values hitherto regarded as alien to the tradition. This, of course, is to create another variation or position. It may fall on deaf ears and wither, or inspire a sect, or it may attract wide support and be followed by other variants. The need of the time may dictate that successful variants are closer to other ideological traditions than rival positions might be, which may lead to further internal strains and incommensurabilities.

At least some of the problems of analysing ideology have arisen from taking the tradition, or some conception of the essence of the tradition, as the appropriate unit of analysis. But this is highly misleading, for traditions are vague and elusive entities, whose exact content and boundaries are uncertain and controversial. It is only in analysing the individual position that the structure and logic of ideology will be clearly revealed; while at the same time the position will have a variety of loose, though important, connections with other positions within the tradition of thought.

Ideological evolution is governed by no laws; and this is because of ideology's peculiar logic. The possibilities of reinterpretation and adaption lie in the almost infinite flexibility of ideological language. Concepts in academic discourse, and the theories which sustain them, are all to some degree adaptable; but in science and other intellectual disciplines there are controls and limits to flexibility which are bound up with the relationship between assertion on the one hand, and evidence or some other test of validity on the other. But ideological concepts, because of their value-content, are non-referring, and consequently there is no control provided by fact or evidence, and no authoritative test which can be appealed to in case of doubt. This being so, almost anything is possible. New values may be introduced or old ones reordered; words can be given new meanings; new theories can turn established arguments on their head; the wrong course of action can suddenly become the prescribed course. If an ideologist feels compelled to develop doctrine in conflict with established versions then only his own creativity need limit him.

Hence the problem of establishing the boundaries of a tradition. How is the identity of an ideological tradition of thought to be determined; who belongs and who does not? How do ideologies hang together? How (to return to the earlier question) can Kant, Bentham, Hobhouse and the rest, all be Liberals when their beliefs and values were so different? The identity of a tradition is not determined by any logical process, but rather a combination of contingent factors, including consciousness of the tradition, use of traditional themes and vocabulary, reference to revered thinkers of the past, the theorist's own identification with the tradition, and ultimately the recognition of other Liberals. This latter may not be forthcoming, or it may come from some but not others. This helps to account for the fuzziness of the edges, for there is no definitive means of establishing who are the genuine contributors to the development of the doctrine. Which ideas constitute the mainstream, and where it is going, is often only apparent at some point in the future; and even then the judgement must be provisional and may be disputed, since it is essentially an ideological judgement.

It is sometimes assumed that the question of who can be included as an authentic theorist of Liberalism or Marxism or whatever can be determined objectively, academically. But the difficulties of doing this are insuperable. We might imagine that Liberalism has, let us say, seventeen essential elements; how are we then to assess the thinker who has only twelve or ten or eight or six? The problem would be difficult enough if we could in fact isolate a set of essential Liberal doctrines, but as we have seen not even this can be done. It is Liberals alone who can decide who is and is not a Liberal and different groups may disagree; they may disagree amongst themselves; and the majority opinion may change over time. The same is true of any ideology. Since Marxism has a more identifiable doctrine it might be thought that such problems should not arise. But this is not so. Edward Bernstein regarded himself as a Marxist, but most Marxists have not accepted his own evaluation and exclude him from their ranks. Even Engels is regarded by some as a contributor and by others as a distorter of Marx's thought; while, more recently, some have sought to exclude the likes of Marcuse and other Frankfurt School theorists from the list of the genuine Marxist thinkers. It all boils down to what the body of believers will accept at a given time. This is a judgement over which there is often disagreement. It is often a practical matter, as to what is thought to be relevant or plausible, or what fits in with the mood of the time; and may change for just the same reasons. In short, there is no objective test of ideological identity. The independent observer can do no more than express an opinion.

In dealing with the essentialist objection it has been necessary to develop a more complex and flexible notion of ideology. Dealing with the next objection opens up a wider conception still.

Neo-Aristotelianism and the range of ideology

Another important objection to the present analysis is inherent in what has been called 'neo-Aristotelian' ethics (the phrase is W.D. Hudson's),[20] as most vigorously expressed in A.C. MacIntyre's widely read and widely admired book *After Virtue*.[21] A consideration of this work suggests that a wider conception of ideology is needed.

I

MacIntyre's thesis may be stated roughly thus. The modern world is morally and culturally degenerate, and modern man has lost his sense of identity and sense of purpose. Part cause and part reflection of this state of affairs is the collapse of moral thought (both everyday and in philosophy) into a meaningless subjectivism. We still use a traditional moral vocabulary, but it has no real meaning for us because the traditional framework or context of thought within which it was developed, and from which it derived its meaning, has been lost. He writes:

> modern moral utterance and practice can only be understood as a series of fragmented survivals from an older past and that the insoluble problems which they have generated for modern moral theorists will remain insoluble until this is well understood. (pp. 104–5)

What we use this vocabulary for today is manipulating each other; and we do so because the language of morality is more efffective than the language of personal preference, so that 'It is your duty' is more compelling that 'I want you to'. Indeed, we live in a manipulative world, governed and persuaded as we are by an endless array of bureaucrats, technocrats, 'experts' and 'therapists' who employ a technical–rational mode of thinking which in reality is pseudo-scientific and ignore the real nature of human beings. All this is shrouded in ideology which reassures us that everything is for our own good. So effective and benumbing have these forces of modernity become, MacIntyre believes, that we are already living in 'the new dark age' (p. 245) without even being aware of it.

MacIntyre contrasts the modern condition with a happier past when morality did cohere and did make sense because the framework that sustained it was in place. This framework may be called 'Aristotelian' because it was Aristotle who first laid bare its logic. It has three elements. First, there is man-as-he-happens-to-be; that is, untutored human nature. Secondly, there is man-as-he-could-be-if-he-realized-his-essential-nature; that, if man fulfils his 'telos'. Finally, there are the values to be adhered to and the virtues to be cultivated if the individual is to progress from the first to the second. There were several versions of these elements, both classical and Christian, during the millenium in which this framework remained in place. But in the seventeenth century the whole Aristotelian system came under attack. Aristotelian metaphysics and science were rejected along with the whole apparatus of essences, potentialities and teleology; and since Aristotelian ethics was bound up with these notions, it too fell under the general condemnation. Consequently, from the eighteenth century various thinkers, including Hume, Kant and Kierkegaard, all attempted to put morality on new foundations. But all such attempts were doomed to failure because they only had two of Aristotle's elements to work with: man-as-he-happens-to-be and moral prescription. What they lacked was the concept of a telos, the fulfilment of the human essence, which gives coherence and meaning to the other elements. The ultimate consequence of their inevitable failure has been the moral and cultural emptiness of the modern world.

In somewhat Hegelian fashion, MacIntyre takes philosophy, especially moral philosophy, as summing up the age in which it is written (each moral theory, he thinks, implies a sociology and vice versa). The moral philosophy of the modern world is Emotivism: that is, the view that moral utterances only express personal preferences and are essentially persuasive in purpose. But the nature of Emotivism has been misunderstood. It is not, as it has always been assumed to be, a theory about the *meaning* of expressions, but in reality is a theory about their *use*. It tells us how people today actually use the moral vocabulary, which is to manipulate each other. With this interpretation, Emotivism is made to embrace Neitzschean ethics, Existentialism, Hare's Prescriptivism and other modern theories, on the grounds that they all reduce morality to personal preference. This reflects the reality of moral life today, where, devoid of objective moral purpose or criteria for moral judgement, modern man is the victim of bureaucrats and 'experts' who claim to know what is good for him.

What MacIntyre is in fact doing is telling a story of how Western civilization went wrong and lost its way, through the loss of a sense of the essence and telos of man, and of the cultivation of the virtues which that way of thinking sustained. He is deeply pessimistic about the prospects of recovery. But he does have a tiny sliver of optimism based on the possibilities of practice and community. Practices, in MacIntyre's sense of the term, are complex activities like art or agriculture or sport which have their own internal goods, vigorously and healthily debated within a tradition, which provide a basis for identifying virtues and cultivating them. What is needed to bind these practices together into a coherent way of life is a conception of the good for man as such. Another essential condition of a coherent moral life for man is an adequate sense of community, which is difficult to achieve in the modern world where it is constantly undermined by the dominant culture of liberal individualism. However, it is only through the: 'construction of local forms of community within which civility and the intellectual and moral life can be sustained through the new dark ages which are already upon us' (p. 245), that there is hope that civilization might be rebuilt. It is the one small glimmer of hope in MacIntyre's otherwise entirely bleak picture.

II

In terms of the present analysis *After Virtue* bears all the marks of a work of ideology. But this cannot simply be asserted, since MacIntyre directly attacks many of the assumptions upon which this present work is based. Clearly, if MacIntyre is correct then the present analysis falls, and indeed will be seen as just another example of modern man's fragmented consciousness. MacIntyre's case has to be shown to be fatally flawed before it can be shown to be ideological.

After Virtue is indeed a much flawed book. Its sweeping generalizations, unsupported assumptions and clear inconsistencies go well beyond the allowances normally made for a book of this scope. To take just two of many examples: the assertion that we live in an emotivist age and use moral language mainly for manipulation begs countless questions and ignores the evidence of common experience. Secondly, debates over ends and values within practices are taken as being healthy and right, but when the practices are politics and philosophy MacIntyre regards such disagreement as a sign of deep malaise. However, in relation to the present work one aspect of the central thesis deserves particular attention. MacIntyre's picture of modern man lost in a cultural and moral desert involves large value-assumptions, as does the view that all this stems from certain seventeenth- and eighteenth-century thinkers finding Aristotelian teleology difficult to swallow. Such grand evaluations would be difficult to justify even if MacIntyre could show that 'Hume's law' was false and merely a manifestation of the collapse of coherent moral thinking. Nevertheless, there are two points which MacIntyre must establish if his case is to have any plausibility. He must show that the fact–value dichotomy is false, and he must also show that man does indeed have a telos. If these points cannot be established then his work has little defence against the charge that it is ideological.

MacIntyre's main case against the absolute separation of fact and value relies on what can be called the good man/good farmer argument (p. 55). This view makes use of the fact that the statement 'X is a good farmer' can be cashed out in purely factual terms: 'X looks after his animals, obtains good yields, maintains the soil' and so on; from which it can be argued that there is no good reason why similar factual criteria cannot be found for the judgement 'X is a good man'. But this view rests upon a confusion. 'X is a good farmer' is a technical evaluation related to function, much as we call a watch a 'good watch' if it performs its function of keeping accurate time. But moral evaluation is not the same as technical evaluation. Men as such do not have a function. The technical use of 'good' in relation to man only makes sense within the context of certain specific practices, such as farming or medicine or war, which have recognized ends. It does not make sense for life in general.[22] Furthermore, for MacIntyre's argument here to be comprehensible, let alone true or false, he must demonstrate that human life does have an overall purpose or telos, a purpose that can be specified and demonstrated in purely factual non-evaluative terms. But this task MacIntyre fails to perform.

Despite the vital importance of a conception of man's telos to MacIntyre's whole thesis, the nearest he comes to offering one is when he says that 'the good life for man is the life spent in seeking the good life for man' (p. 204). But this strange and admittedly 'provisional conclusion' is self-defeating, if only because presumably knowing what is good for man we no longer need to search for it, so that finding it deprives us of it. But it will not even do to be going on with, since it could hardly bear the weight MacIntyre needs to place on it. It is difficult to see how it could sustain a social ethics, or express that sociability which is essential to MacIntyre's conception of human nature. Nor is it clear that it could justify the cultivation of all the desirable virtues. Still less could it justify MacIntyres's wholesale condemnation of the modern world, particularly since the pursuit of the good of man has been at least as vigorous over the last two centuries as at any previous time, even though, according to MacIntyre, this is just the time that civilization has been going steadily downhill. Thus, 'life spent in seeking for the good life' is not much use even as a provisional telos, and would have to be very different from the ultimate telos, whatever that might be. MacIntyre cannot so much as make a guess at what the ultimate telos could be like, and this undermines his entire case. He is in no position to maintain that only a teleological ethics is viable, or that the fact–value dichotomy is a fallacy, or that the moral vocabulary has lost its meaning in the moral world. Even less is he in a position to reject the present analysis which would characterize *After Virtue* as a work of ideology.

After Virtue has all the features of an ideological position, although not all of them are fully developed. It purports to offer a factual and explanatory theory about the human world, which in reality is an ethical evaluation of that world. Past, present and future are turned into a moral story in which forces of oppression and (much weaker) forces of good are at work, and man's present predicament is explained. All is couched in a morally charged language, where, for example, 'bureaucracy', 'therapist' and 'expert' denote bad things, while 'community', 'practice' and 'tradition' (properly understood) denote good things. But on two vital points MacIntyre is not wholly explicit: the nature of the good society and the nature of man. However, we can infer a number of things about each with some confidence.

Modern man has an alienated and fragmented consciousness and lacks a sense of moral community; the restoration of both are essential to his nature and would presumably be accomplished in the good society. However, MacIntyre is less interested in showing how the good society could be organized than in the problem of restoring to man a coherent moral life within a genuine community. This has the implication that if this could be achieved then the good society and an appropriate political theory would flow from it (all modern political tradition being exhausted, p. 244). A necessary condition of this is that man must put his thinking straight. The pervasive influence of spurious technical–rational reasoning is a central feature of MacIntyre's condemnation of the modern world. It appears that MacIntyre believes that a key element in man's restoration is the recovery or development of true reasoning; that is, a form of reasoning which overcomes the false dichotomies of fact and value, and of individual and society, and enables man to come to a true understanding of himself (the model here would seem to be Hegel). Clearly, the concept of rationality is central to MacIntyre's concept of man (as we have seen above with Bentham and Kant and with Hollis). Unfortunately, MacIntyre does not tell us what his concept of rationality is. Perhaps this is difficult to do in the absence of a theory of man's telos. Nevertheless, he does promise an account (p. 242), in a later book which has so far not appeared. Thus, there are good grounds for characterizing *After Virtue* as a work of ideology, even though not an entirely complete one.

III

MacIntyre's thesis is interesting as an ideological position, but perhaps more interesting for what it might suggest about ideology as such. That MacIntyre offers us moral prescriptions rather than political ones, with only the implication that the fulfilment of the first would lead to the second, suggests that we could classify *After Virtue* as primarily a work of moral rather than political ideology, and that this might be true of other ideological positions. This suggests that the concept of ideology may be further developed along one of two possible lines. The first is that moral ideology is the core concept and that a political ideology is only an extension of a moral ideology; or secondly, that the moral and the political are, or can be, two distinct forms of ideology.

The first of these suggestions has a certain initial plausibility. We have seen in the case of Kant, for example, a political ideology (a variety of Liberalism) that is simply an extension of a moral ideology, so that for Kant, as Paul Hassner points out:

> In principle, politics is simply the application of that legal doctrine whose theory is morality. Any conflict between politics and morality is to be resolved by the pure subordination of the former to the latter.[23]

And similar cases could perhaps be made for a number of other political thinkers such as Aristotle or Bentham. But the idea is much less plausible in respect of other thinkers, such as Rousseau or Hegel, and it is difficult to see what Marxism or National Socialism would amount to without their political dimensions. It seems reasonable, then, to suppose that there are at least two forms of ideology, the moral and the political; with perhaps, as MacIntyre suggests, the logic of the former having been explored by Aristotle. There are a number of possible examples of purely moral ideologies among the Hellenistic 'philosophies' (notably Epicurianism) and perhaps back to Socrates, which might or might not have provided the basis of a political ideology (again we might follow MacIntyre, this time in his *A Short History of Ethics*, where he argues that all ethical theories imply a conception of man).[24] Perhaps the most interesting case in this context is Existentialism, which while displaying many features here identified with ideology, nevertheless appears at such a distance from politics that the notion of an Existentialist state or political party seems absurd.

IV

There are many varieties of existentialist thought and some fundamental differences between major existentialist thinkers, some of whom will not even accept the title 'existentialist'.[25] Nevertheless, some generalizations are possible which will be sufficient for present purposes.

All versions of Existentialism begin with an analysis of 'existence', taken as that form of being peculiar to man. This means not creating abstract theories but analysing man as a concrete reality by concentrating on his individual uniqueness, his 'wholeness' as a willing and feeling as well as a thinking being, his 'finitude' and awareness of death, the 'facticity' or 'givenness' of his individual existence; and, most importantly, his capacity for 'transcendence', for transforming himself from whatever he is at the moment to some future state. This latter characteristic of man's existence means that every individual has the capacity to make of himself whatever he likes; he is free to create his own being and is unavoidably responsible for what he makes of himself. This has certain implications for how men should live. John Macquarrie writes:[26]

> By the very way humanity is constituted, one is driven to talk of a 'true' humanity (and presumably also of a 'false' humanity). For if man is not a nature or essence that is simply given, but rather 'makes' himself what he becomes by his own deeds and decisions, then it would seem that he can either become what it is in him to become, or fail to become it. . . . Man must decide who he will be, and more than this, each individual must decide the question for himself. Each one's existence is his own, characterized by a unique 'mineness'. There is no universal pattern of a genuine humanity that can be imposed on all or to which all must conform. Indeed, to impose such a pattern would mean to destroy the possibility of a genuinely human existence for the persons concerned. They become truly themselves only to the extent that they freely choose themselves. (p. 161)

Existentialists use the terms 'authentic' and 'inauthentic' to denote an individual's proper use or ill use of his freedom and power. Macquarrie continues:

> Existence is authentic to the extent that the existent has taken possession of himself and, shall we say, has moulded himself in his own image. Inauthentic existence, on the other hand, is moulded by external influences, whether these be circumstances, moral codes, political or ecclesiastical authorities, or whatever. (ibid., p. 162–3)

The central value here is the individual's freedom and power to determine his own destiny, the exercise of free choice being more important than the content of that choice. On the other hand, as Macquarrie points out, 'no major existentialist philosopher has taught that everything is permitted' (ibid., p. 162) and adds that in his view the concept of existence itself suggests the general 'direction of human fulfilment' (ibid., p. 164) which presumably rules out such choices as being a murderous dictator, a master criminal or whatever else we think undesirable; and it certainly rules out the decision to be a conformist. This is a general problem with Existentialist ethics which is dealt with by a variety of means (usually involving the introduction of some principle from outside Existentialism, but that need not concern us here). But however it is dealt with, the starting point is a value-laden and therefore pseudo-descriptive conception of man and the human condition by means of which the world and the individual's circumstances can be evaluated.

Each significant Existentialist thinker has developed these basic ideas in their own way, but we may take Sartre as representative.[27] Whereas, for example, Heidegger took man's existence to be his essence, Sartre took the more radical view that man's existence precedes his essence (p. 438), thereby taking much of what other thinkers had regarded as man's 'facticity' to be the individual's own responsibility, including his genetic endowment, his social circumstances and his psychological make up. Consequently theories, such as those of Freud, purporting to explain human behaviour are deemed worthless (p. 40). What does explain human behavior) is human choice; we are inescapably 'condemned to be free' (p. 439), though people go to endless lengths to escape the anguish of freedom (p. 44); that is, to deny to themselves their own responsibility for what they do. This self-deception is what Sartre calls 'bad faith' (*mauvaise foi*), and it is only by learning to live without it, and by rejecting all moral codes and making one's own choices that one can live, as far as it is possible,[28] honestly and authentically. He writes:

> My freedom is the unique foundation of values and *nothing*, absolutely nothing, justifies me in adopting this or that particular value, this or that particular scale of values.... My freedom is anguished at being the foundation of values while itself without foundation. (p. 38)[29]

There is nothing comfortable about a life of freedom, since one must live with perpetual anguish and uncertainty. Not even other people are any consolation, since our relationships are marred by our ceaseless, frustrated desire to have power over them.[30] Human reality is 'by nature an unhappy consciousness with no possibility of surpassing its unhappy state' (p. 90). The only consolation is the awareness of living an authentic existence.

Other Existentialists have different though similar analyses of the human condition. Some put greater stress on the individual's relationship with fellow human beings, or with nature; while others emphasize the particular threat of modern society to individual freedom. These accounts each have their different conceptual schemes, with concepts such as 'mass man' (Jaspers), 'Being-towards-death' (Heidegger) and 'superman' (Neitzsche), by which the world can be evaluated and the means to the 'good life' prescribed. At first sight at least, there is something odd about Existentialists prescribing anything beyond the injunction to exercise one's freedom. But as suggested earlier, 'philosophers of existence' never stop there, but have additional values beyond the self-conscious exercise of freedom,[31] which they recommend in order to assist the individual in working out his unique salvation. For Existentialists the 'good life' is not, of course, equated with the good society, nor even 'good' in the sense of 'happy'; it is the life that is 'authentic'. Whether this is achieved through Kierkegaard's 'leap of faith', Nietzsche's 'will to power', Heidegger's reordering one's life in the face of death, or whatever else Existentialist philosophers recommend, it will not be comfortable and it will be individual rather than collective.

Being concerned with personal and not group salvation, Existentialism has little to say about politics and society. And this remains true despite the fact that Heidegger joined the Nazis (albeit briefly), and that Sartre became a Communist. Both can be seen, as with Kierkegaard's Christianity, as an existential choice or 'leap of faith'; that is, not dictated by their Existentialism,[32] nor a choice their admirers have necessarily felt any need to follow. Possibly connected with the lack of a collectivist dimension is the lack of any consistent Existentialist view of history. Existentialist analysis can always encompass the past in the sense of dealing with individual biography; but, apart from a tendency to reject views of progress, the need to deal with society or mankind as a whole has not been universally felt. Kierkegaard had nothing to say on the matter,[33] while Heidegger saw history in terms of decline,[34] a view shared with Nietzsche who had added on his revival of the classical conception of eternal recurrence. But none, as in political ideology, see mankind as having a destiny to which the individual might contribute. It is the individual's destiny alone that has significance.

Thus, we have in Existentialism a doctrine of personal salvation that has most of the structural elements previously identified as ideological. We have a conception of human nature and a theory of the human condition which embodies certain values, expressed in a pseudo-descriptive vocabulary, by means of which the individual can evaluate his immediate and his historical circumstances. He can determine whether his actions, his lifestyle and his relations with others are authentic; whether he is a member of a genuine community; whether he is a victim of modern mass society and so on. And having assessed his life he can seek in Existentialist writings guidance on reordering and living it more honestly in the light of Existentialist ideals of human fulfilment. All that are 'missing', in the sense of not being universal features, are the political and historical (in the sense of a history of society or mankind) dimensions. From which it is reasonable to conclude that Existentialism is not a political, but some form of moral, ideology.

V

If Existentialism is some form of moral ideology then we have established two kinds, the moral and the political. This prompts the question as to whether there might be more, perhaps many more. Could there be, or potentially be, a different form of ideology for every variety of human activitity: a farming ideology, a sexual ideology, a sport ideology? Indeed it sometimes seems that this is just what we do have. But there has to be some limit, if not in principle at least in practice. There are two problems. The first is that not all practices are amenable (realistically amenable) to the notion that they may be the means by which humanity might achieve fulfilment. This might be possible in the case of art, but hardly so in the case of, say, bricklaying. The second problem is subsumption. It would, for example, be difficult to conceive of an economic ideology that would not be subsumed under some wider political ideology. An interesting case here is education, where both subsumption and non-subsumption seem possible: that is, educational theory as an extension of political ideology, or as an independent educational ideology. However, for present purposes it is sufficient to say that confining ideology to politics appears to be too narrow, and that other forms of ideology seem both possible and actual.

Notes

1. David Miller and Larry Siedentop (eds), *The Nature of Political Theory*, (OUP, 1983). Subsequent page references are to this edition.
2. John Plamenatz, 'The uses of political theory' in Anthony Quinton (ed), *Political Philosophy*, (OUP, 1967).
3. Charles Taylor, 'Neutrality in political science', in P. Laslett and W.G. Runciman (eds), *Philosophy, Politics and Society*, 3rd series, (Blackwell, 1967).
4. It is a kind of reasoning that assumes the meaning of something is determined by what effect it has; a type of reasoning discussed and dismissed in Chapter 1. C.f. Gordon Graham, *Politics in its Place*, (OUP, 1986), where Graham uses a version of the value-slope argument in attempting to make a related case for the legitimacy of the substantive discussion of values in political philosophy. This is followed up with an

argument of yet greater poverty. He maintains that the pursuit of values is part of political philosophy as conceived by such as Locke, Rousseau and Mill and that to deny that it is a proper part is to ignore the subject 'as it really is' (p. 5). But such a question-begging approach would rule out all kinds of innovation in philosophy and given an authority to tradition more appropriate to the tenth than the twentieth century.

5. Anthony Quinton makes a similar point when he writes: 'Opposing ideologists try to pre-empt words like *liberty, justice* and *democracy* for the type of political arrangement they favour. The political philosopher can keep himself from being embroiled only if he confines himself to articulating the way in which different ideological groups use the terms in which they proclaim their ideals.' In Anthony Quinton (ed.), *Political Philosophy*, (OUP, 1967), p. 14.

6. See again the list of texts referred to in note 47 on p. 25.

7. D. D. Raphael, *Problems of Political Philosophy*, 2nd edn, (Macmillan, 1976), Chapter 6.

8. See Jeremy Bentham, 'Rationale of reward' in *The Works of Jeremy Bentham*, 11 vols, Edinburgh, 1838–43, (reissued Russell & Russell, New York, 1962), vol. II, pp. 189–266, for a passionate defence of competition. For Hayek see, for example: Frederick von Hayek, *The Road to Serfdom*, (RKP, 1944), pp. 27ff.

9. For Spencer, competition is the necessary condition of evolution through natural selection and therefore the basis of all his social and political writings.

10. See for example: L. T. Hobhouse, *Liberalism*, (OUP, 1941).

11. For Green see especially: T. H. Green, *Lectures on the Principles of Political Obligation*, (Longman, 1963). For Spencer see, for example, the title essay of: Herbert Spencer, *Man Versus the State*, (Penguin, 1969).

12. John Rawls, *A Theory of Justice*, (OUP, 1972). Robert Nozick, *Anarchy, State and Utopia*, (Blackwell, 1974).

13. John Plamenatz (ed.), *Readings from Liberal Writers*, (Allen & Unwin, 1965). Subsequent page references are to this edition.

14. All books on Conservative thought see Burke as the father of modern Conservatism; while on the left, social democrats and radical socialists dispute over which of them has the best claim to Tawney's ideas. See, for example, Tony Benn's Preface to R.H. Tawney, *The Attack and Other Papers*, (Spokesman, 1981).

15. J. S. Schapiro (ed.), *Liberalism, Its Meaning and History*, (Van Nostrand, 1958), pp. 166–7.

16. E. K. Bramsted and K. J. Melhuish (eds), *Western Liberalism*, (Longman, 1978). Several references to Hegel clearly indicate that the editors do not regard him as a Liberal.

17. C.f. David Manning, *Liberalism*, (Dent, 1976). But while Manning insists upon the 'error of essentialism' (p. 60) the uncertain status of his own 'symbolic form of Liberalism' (see p. 143) gives rise to the suspicion that he is reviving under another name what he has earlier rejected. There is a similar ambiguity to be found in John Gray, *Liberalism*, (Open UP, 1986). In his Introduction (pp. ix–xi) Gray speaks of Liberalism's 'vast internal variety and complexity' and of its having 'no single nature or essence'; yet at the same time he speaks of a 'single tradition' with 'variations on a small set of distinctive themes'.

18. G. F. Gaus, *The Modern Liberal Theory of Man*, (Croom Helm, 1983). Subsequent page references are to this edition.

19. C.f. Hare's charge against Rawls that he fails to realize the normative implications of the terms he is using, in R.M. Hare, 'Rawls' theory of justice', in Norman-Daniels, (ed.), *Reading Rawls* (Blackwell, 1975), pp. 81–107.

20. W. D. Hudson, *Modern Moral Philosophy*, 2nd edn, (Macmillan, 1983), Ch. 7.

21. Alasdair MacIntyre, *After Virtue*, (Duckworth, 1981). There is a 2nd edn (1985), but this adds nothing relevant to the present discussion.

22. For a fuller account of the weaknesses of the good farmer/good man argument see R. W. Beardsmore, *Moral Reasoning*, (RKP, 1969), pp. 18ff.; and D. Z. Phillips and H. O. Mounce, *Moral Practices*, (RKP, 1970), pp. 51–3.

23. L. Strauss and J. Cropsey (eds), *History of Political Philosophy*, (Chicago UP, 1981), p. 567.

24. Alasdair MacIntyre, *A Short History of Ethics*, (RKP, 1967), p. 268.
25. The gulf between religious and atheistical existentialists is perhaps the best known division, but there are others. Heidegger is among those who have rejected the 'existentialist' label while Sartre has declared it 'meaningless'.
26. John Macquarrie, *Existentialism*, (Penguin, 1973). Since Professor Macquarrie is a distinguished Existentialist theologian this work may be taken as both an account of Existentialism and an expression of Extentialist thought. Subsequent page references are to this edition.
27. Sartre is representative of Existentialism in two works: Jean-Paul Sartre, *Being and Nothingness*, translated by Hazel Barnes, (Methuen, 1958); subsequent page references are to this edition; and John-Paul Sartre, *Existentialism and Humanism*, translated by Philip Mairet, (Eyre Methuen, 1948). Sartre's later adoption of Marxism involved the abandonment of many of the doctrines set out in these works, and arguably meant an abandonment of Existentialism altogether.
28. See *Being and Nothingness*, pp. 62–7 where Sartre doubts the possibility of complete sincerity, and later speaks of good faith and sincerity as 'ideals' (p. 69). But see the footnote on p. 70 where he appears to offer the possibility that we can 'radically escape bad faith'.
29. However, somewhat at odds with this Sartre came to argue that in choosing one's own essence one must choose as though one is 'thereby at the same time a legislator deciding for the whole of mankind' (*Existentialism and Humanism*, op. cit., p. 30). This very Kantian principle does not appear to arise from Sartre's or any other Existentialist analysis.
30. Hence the most famous line in Sartre's entire literary output: 'Hell is other people', from his play *No Exit*.
31. Even Sartre, the nearest to relying upon justification by free choice alone, would not accept the free decision to become a bourgeois conformist as morally acceptable.
32. This is a contentious matter about which critics disagree. In the case of Heidegger he did have a notion about nations being able at some point in their history to choose their destiny, just as the individual can. So a case can be made for seeing some connection between his ideas and his association with National Socialism. On the other hand, it is doubtful to what extent his ideas about national destiny can be reconciled with his otherwise strong individualism;
    The case of Sartre is more complex. It might seem that the Existentialism of *Being and Nothingness* must flatly contradict any conceivable variety of Marxism; for the reason, amongst others, that Sartre's absolute insistence that nothing determines the self, not even psychological make-up let alone social circumstances, renders the need for social revolution to give men freedom unnecessary and irrelevant. However, Sartre himself did not see it like that and attempted to synthesize Existentialism and Marxism in his *Critique of Dialectical Reason*, vol. 1, trans. Alan Sheridan-Smith, (New Left Books, 1976), and also *Search for a Method*, trans. Hazel Barnes, (Alfred Knopf, 1963). But this is a notoriously obscure and unconvincing work which Sartre never completed.
33 Except, that is, for expressing the conventional Christian view of the Incarnation being the most important event in human history.
34. See for example, Martin Heidegger, *An Introduction to Metaphysics*, trans. Ralph Manheim, (Anchor Books, 1961), p. 130.

CHAPTER SEVEN

THE PLACE OF IDEOLOGY

It has hitherto been tempting to regard the concept of ideology as more trouble than it is worth. Its use invariably obscures more than it illuminates and arouses passions in an area where there is already passion enough. And even if we can approach the subject with detachment we find that behind the muddle of controversy is what seems a mystery that cannot be solved. We are faced with sets of ideas so multi-purpose and multi-faceted – with values, historical generalizations, technical recommendations, ideal societies, explanations, moral prescriptions, myths and much else besides – that it does not seem possible that there could by any unifying principle or logical coherence. However, it has been the burden of this work that the concept has to be persisted with; that the controversy it generates is a measure of its significance; that a logical unity can indeed be found; and that, whatever its limitations, ideology occupies an important place in human thought.

The question of precisely what place ideology does have in our thinking can be understood in two quite different ways. On the one hand, we may take the question as a formal one and address it in terms of ideology's logical character: its constituent elements and how they fit together; how it relates to, and is distinguished from, other forms of thought; and so on. In other words, we can ask what area it occupies in the geography of human thought. But, on the other hand, the place of ideology might be interpreted in terms of an altogether different set of questions, concerned with such matters as how important ideology is to us and to what extent is it necessary; what needs it satisfies that it should be so pervasive; and just how far we could manage without it. Questions of this second type are the more problematic. It is not obvious that there can be clear answers to them, and still less that the methods used to deal with the first kind of question are at all appropriate to the second. Yet the latter questions are sufficiently important and intriguing to risk a few speculative suggestions; that is, once the formal questions have been settled.

Ideology on the map

I

The nature of ideology is a mystery that requires two keys: one to unlock its logic, the other its structure. At first sight ideology appears to contain an incoherent mixture of different kinds of thinking, and in particular an improper cohabitation of the moral and the factual. But it is precisely the illicit union of fact and value that is essential to ideology's distinctiveness as a form of thought. It is achieved during the formation of theory, at the stage when concepts are linked together to form a conceptual framework. Within any form of understanding, or individual theory, concepts are connected into a network by being defined in terms of each other. In ideology, and other forms of ethical belief, value concepts are used to define factual ones which in turn can be used to define further concepts. The outcome of this process of pseudo-description (as it might be called) is a vocabulary imbued with the values of the ideology, so that all its descriptions, explanations and accounts of the world are expressions of those values. In this way a certain logical homogeneity and a unified moral vision are simultaneously imparted to all elements of the ideology. The resultant picture of the world may appear to be objective, and yet at the same time it makes clear to the believer, without apparent logical violence, what is good and bad and where his duty lies.

But, for this logical consistency and the reassuring belief that true value is firmly anchored in reality, there is a price. The union of fact and value is an illicit one in that it produces a kind of thought that is not what it seems, that does not fulfil its promises in an honest fashion. Ideological pictures of the world can have no truth, they only deal in pseudo-descriptions and pseudo-explanations which cannot, because of their ethical content, correspond to any reality. Deriving prescriptions is possible only because values are artificially built into the picture in the first place. Furthermore, it is the ethical content of ideologies that make them incommensurable; their differing pictures of the world are absolute and self-enclosed and unable to enter a dialogue with each other. The nature of ideology ensures that they cannot be consistent; in Strawson's terms they form a world of truths that cannot be systematized into a world of truth.[1] Each ideological position, like each religious sect (and each work of art – there are parallels here with aesthetic understanding), has its own understanding of the world, its own moral vision, and therefore its own answers to questions of what we should do and how we should live. This contrasts with academic disciplines, where a framework of understanding exists that is quite separate from any theories that manifest that understanding, and which provides a neutral context within which rivalries between theories can be decisively settled in a way that guarantees all successful theories are (despite Kuhn's assertions about science) ultimately consistent with each other and can claim, in the absence of a viable challenge, the status of knowledge. Ideologies have no such common framework; in each case the theory doubles up as the understanding. Nor do they respect any one else's framework, but freely appropriate the conclusions of other forms of understanding for their own purposes. Yet, however illegitimate ideology's claim to knowledge might be, it nevertheless does possess the logical consistency and moral unity that fusing fact and value bestows.

The theory of pseudo-description broadly establishes ideology's logical identity as a form of ethical belief. What it does not do is to determine what the essential elements of ideology are and how they relate to each other; they remain separate and in need of a further principle of unity. This further principle is the centrality of a conception of human nature, a theory of man, which gives to ideology its characteristic structure, and, incidentally, differentiates ideology (albeit imperfectly) from other forms of ethical belief, notably religion. Ideological man, so to speak, carries the ideological world upon his shoulders. If it were possible (which it is not) to subtract from an ideology its conception of man, then what would be left would just be a collection of elements, which, despite a certain consistency, would not touch each other and could not form a whole. Ideological man ties all the parts together into a system of ideas: he unites fact and value, explanation and evaluation, and guarantees the rightness and permanence of the ideal society envisaged, as well as the means of reaching it. To view the world ideologically is not necessarily to view it politically, for education or art or the moral life may be adequate vehicles for the fulfilment of certain ideals; but it is necessary to view it in terms of an interdefined set of morally charged categories which centre upon a particular conception of man.

II

Philosophers used to employ the image of a 'map of knowledge' to show what forms of knowledge there were, their nature and how they related to each other. Ideology would have no place on such a map. But we might imagine a wider concept of a map of *understanding* that embraced all the forms of knowledge, together with religion, art, practice and other forms of understanding the world that can be shown to be distinctive. On this map ideology would have a place, though a subordinate one. It belongs firmly in the sphere of acting and living in the world. This is a wide and complex sphere which is concerned with our actions, individual and collective; with our plans and projects, hopes and expectations; with what we can do and what we ought to do. To understand the world in terms of practice is to conceive of everything in terms of human purposes. The philosophy that embodies the practical understanding, reducing all other forms of thought to the practical level, is Pragmatism; and although its limitations as a philosophy are great, it does reproduce at a more sophisticated level a process we all engage in at least for much of the time. The categories of such an understanding include means and ends, actions and decisions, utility, efficacy and right. The sphere of practice is the sphere of choice, of reasons and justifications, of morality and of ideals, of technique and tradition. With almost any action, whether buying a pair of shoes or declaring war, we are faced with alternatives between which we must choose. Even doing nothing involves some kind of decision; we cannot escape choosing. This is not always easy and we seek guidance to aid our deliberations. Such guidance may be moral or technical or in the form of information or the wisdom of experience or homely maxims, according to the particular need. But if the need is of a more general kind concerning how to conduct one's life, or how a society can organize itself, or what aims humanity should pursue, then a comprehensive vision is needed which perhaps only religions and ideologies are sufficiently wide-ranging to satisfy.

Thus, in the sphere of practice ideology shares with religion a special place by virtue of its comprehensiveness. To deliberate effectively there are three things we need to know: the facts of the situation; what will be effective; and what is right and wrong. Different kinds of theory can cater for these different aspects – academic, technical and moral; it is only ideology and religion which seek to answer them all. Ethical belief not only answers to all these needs, it puts them in context of a unified vision with overall values and aims, a *weltanschauung*. It puts everything into perspective and tells us what is significant. Like Pragmatism, it subordinates everything to its practical vision, including all we take to be independent knowledge. But as we have seen, this is where ideology has to make false claims. The logic of ideology is such that what appear to be factual accounts of the world, together with all the descriptions and explanations within and flowing out of these accounts, are in reality disguised evaluations. On the map of understanding, ideology occupies a place alongside religion that is wholly within the sphere of practical understanding and wholly within the subsphere of the ethical. Apart from certain similarities with religious thought, ideology has a quite distinctive structure and logic, combining a whole range of elements into what is first and last an ethical understanding.

However, it is a peculiarity of ideology that it is constitutionally incapable of accepting such an assessment of its place, since each ideology by its nature aspires to be more than what it is, or what it can be. It necessarily makes claims to absolute truth, to academic status, and to a moral certainty that it cannot sustain. It sees itself as, so to speak, the interconnection between multiple worlds of sense, between the factual and the moral, the theoretical and the practical, the spiritual and the secular, the academic and the everyday. It disdains self-knowledge and demands sovereignty at the minimum, accepting no independent assessment of its claims. More often than not it demands a kind of imperium, each seeing itself in the manner of medieval theology as 'the queen of the sciences', as that which can pronounce authoritatively on the rest, presuming to pass judgement upon, to evaluate and explain, anything and everything of any kind of significance in human existence. It aspires to subsume all truth within itself, to be the true intellectual system of the universe. Ideology shares with religion the belief that scholarly truth is a mundane truth, a subordinate truth, that must be judged against the higher truth of the moral purpose of the world and the destiny of man. Ideologies and religions offer, when necessary, their own versions of history, philosophy, social and physical science or whatever else is deemed of practical significance.[2] Yet it will allow none of these things to test or to conflict with its own truth.

Ideology can only flourish by pretending to be what it is not, by arrogating to itself an intellectual authority it cannot possess, and by claiming certainties that are not there to be had. To this degree it is a false and misleading form of thought.

But this raises an obvious question. If ideology really is such a faulty mode of thought, why does it persist? Do we turn to it to provide the best answers we can find in the absence of something better? Or does it answer some deeper human need? In other words, can we live without it?

Do we need ideology?

Virtually all theoretical discussions of ideology portray it as an illegitimate manner of thinking which has to be exposed. As we have seen, Conservatives, Liberals and Marxists each in their different ways regard it as an evil to be rooted out. The present work, while it has not gone that far, has, nevertheless, insisted that ideology is an inherently defective mode of thought. Yet ideology has been a persistent feature of human experience and continues to be so. It provokes the question as to whether we need ideology, or at least some form of ethical belief; or whether, as some still maintain about religion, we will, so to speak, grow out of it. This is probably an unanswerable question, and certainly not a philosophical one; predicting the future and speculative psychology are both best left to ideologists. Nevertheless, some general points may be made concerning the role and importance of ideology in our thinking that might cast further light upon the subject.

The Conservative, Liberal and Marxist assessments of ideology need not be taken at face value. In each case they use 'ideology' in a pseudo-descriptive way that expresses their own values, so that we need not dismiss ideology as a radical evil on their testimony. This is equally true of much that passes for political philosophy and political science, but which in fact is ideologically inspired. But where ideology is not condemned as an evil it is still condemned for being, in a factual sense, untrue. Most accounts leave it at that, taking it as self-evident that if it is false then it is ipso facto bad; man, the assumption is, must live by truth alone.[3] But it might be questioned whether in fact man can live by truth alone; could ordinary human life as we know it proceed in the complete absence of ethical belief? Can we operate effectively in the world without some conception or image of ourselves that tells us our place in it, where we stand in the order of things? Isaiah Berlin writes:

> In the end, men choose between ultimate values; they choose as they do because their life and thought are determined by fundamental moral categories and concepts that are, at any rate over large stretches of time and space, a part of their being and thought and sense of their own identity; part of what makes them human.[4]

This suggests that what it is that ideology provides, the thing we need, is a sense of moral and political identity.

This needs further clarification. The term 'identity' has several meanings and shades of meaning. In the oldest sense it means sameness: in logic A = A has the same meaning as 'A is identical with A'. But in everyday language we use it with varying degrees of looseness: 'identical twins', 'identity of interests' and so on. Later, around two centuries ago, a new set of meanings developed which were concerned with the individual self; that is, with a person's identity, who the person is. At the mundane level a person may identify himself by reference to certain simple facts: John Smith, white, male, working class, English, of such and such address, occupation, religion and similar details. These are the sorts of things that might go into a bureaucrat's file and go along with such items as identity cards and the like. But this in itself suggests that we can go more deeply into a person's identity, who that person really is beyond the official facts. There is of course an old metaphysical problem about the self that can be expressed in the ancient philosophical categories of substance (i.e. that which persists through time) and accident (that which does not persist and is therefore inessential). What is it of the self, if anything, that does persist: in what sense, if any, am I the same person I was as a child? Less abstractly, though no less metaphysically, we speak of the 'essential self' or 'true self' that is behind the public data and is implied in such locutions as 'who am I?', 'being in search of himself' and 'identity crisis'. This kind of thinking might be said to be a legacy of Romanticism with its insistence on the uniqueness of every individual.

But the notion of 'true identity' has outgrown that assumption, so that like 'freedom' or 'democracy' it has become a whore of a concept, there to be used by any theory in the intellectual vicinity. Thus, a person's essential identity might be conceived in terms of a God-given soul, beneath the social layers of John Smith, white, male, working-class Englishman; or, at the other extreme, those social layers (or relationships) may be conceived as onion-like, which, if stripped away, would leave nothing left of John Smith. There are many more such theories, deterministic theories and voluntaristic theories; though on the whole the twentieth century has tended to favour the onion end of the spectrum. But without stepping into this morass we might say that most of us regard some, though not all, of the groupings that form our social identity as part of our essential identity – our sex or nationality, or perhaps our class or religion or occupation – some of which we choose and some not. Some may regard one such feature as overwhelmingly important in their lives – the IRA gunman his Irishness, the feminist her sex, the racist his race – and there is much room here for variation and choice.

A further step towards the metaphysical is taken when we make the move from the identity of the individual to the identity of the group. We may indeed conceive of group identity in terms of flat facts – 'a minor Christian sect of northern Sudan' or whatever – but we easily slip beyond the reach of the empirical. This is even more dubious than with individuals. At least when we speak of an individual we know we have a definite entity in mind; but with national identity, or black or female or class identity this is not always clear. National identity obviously has some relationship with the older notion of national character, though this is itself a somewhat doubtful idea, and there seems no equivalent to such modern constructions as the nation 'in search of its identity' or suffering 'an identity crisis'.[5] On the other hand, the transition from individual to group identity can come about in two ways that seem reasonable enough. One is through the locution 'I identify with' an individual or group or cause. Secondly, and not necessarily connected with the onion thesis, there is the idea that the individual's identity must in some way be bound up with group membership: nationality, sex, race, religion, family and the rest.

The important thing from the point of view of our purpose here is the relationship between identity and action. My understanding of my identity has implications for what I do, how I conduct myself. The mundane dimensions of our identity – as husbands, sisters, parents, motorists, gang members, citizens, hockey players, Yorkshiremen, bank clerks, etc. – are roles which imply expectations, rules and conventions about what is appropriate behaviour. These often have some kind of moral force since they imply duties, as parents, for example, or as citizens; though not necessarily. There is a spectrum that runs from moral to neutral to immoral, as in the following:

I am a doctor; there is a sick person needing help; therefore...

I am a park attendant; there is a beer can on the grass; therefore...

I am a prostitute; there is a customer; therefore...

I am a paederast; there is a juicy young boy; therefore...

Thus, the rules that roles imply are rules of appropriate behaviour that may or may not be moral. But when we pass beyond the mundane to an 'essential self', a metaphysical identity, this is inevitably an ethical conception which does imply moral rules.

To look for one's 'essential self', one's 'true identity', is necessarily to try to penetrate beyond the surface of everyday reality. This may be to escape from it or to find an underpinning for it: to give one's life a new meaning and direction, or to give a deeper meaning to the life we have. But whichever it is we must go beyond direct experience. We may do this for either or both of what seem to be two quite contrary reasons: either to discover our own uniqueness, our separateness from others, or to find our true relation to others. These two are in fact complementary, for it is when we know who we are that we know where we belong. And it is knowing who and what we are that gives us our orientation in the world. It is a necessary prelude to answering the question: what shall we do and how shall we live?

We may pursue our metaphysical identity somewhat in the spirit of Rousseau searching for the nature and duty of man as such, independent of social roles, beneath the corrupting overlay of the sophisticated society he despised. Or we may seek to understand the 'true identity' of the groupings we belong to – class, sex, race, nationality, etc. – in the sense of what does it *mean* to be black? or working class? or German? or a woman?; and to determine which of these is the truly significant one. For a Northern Ireland republican his Irishness is his true identity and his British citizenship an alien imposition; for some it is class identity that outweighs all others, while for others still, sexual or racial or religious identity may be candidates for overriding significance. But significance in relation to what? It is significant in relation to how we live our lives and how we conceive our humanity. These identities have varying degreees of significance in relation to the various practices in which we engage: politics, education, family life, earning a living, and so on. But also these identities are significant in relation to what we take to be our essential humanity. Thus, for example, groups who deem themselves to be oppressed, such as blacks or women or working class, see their liberation as the key to the liberation of humanity as a whole; and indeed often see their race or class or sex as in some way representative of humanity at its best. Their human identity is expressed *through* their group identity. For to take one group identity as all-important, as more fundamental than the rest, is to imply somthing about the nature of man, about human needs and what is important in human life, about what we should do and how we should live. It is to manifest an ethical understanding of the world.

But not all of us have the intellectual ability or originality or emotional stamina to create such an understanding unique to ourselves. Besides, part of the point of such an understanding is that it is shared. It is plainly one of the functions that ethical belief has that it gives a sense of membership, of belonging. Eric Fromm writes:

> This identity with nature, clan, religion, gives the individual security. He belongs to, is rooted in a structuralized whole in which he has an unquestionable place. He may suffer from hunger, or suppression, but he does not suffer from the worst of all pains – complete aloneness and doubt.[6]

But ethical belief also provides a sense of common purpose and gives expression to the felt need of many to do and to create what is right and what is just. Ideology, like religion, can satisfy these needs. But this is not to follow Fromm and others to the extent of assuming that these are absolute human needs that grow out of man's fundamental nature. These needs may be less or non-existent in some; and that they are the needs of anyone at all may be historically temporary. It is not necessary to define man as needing ideology, *homo ideologicus*, in the way man used to be defined as a being needing to believe in God, in order to establish that ideology has an important part in human thinking. (It would hardly be appropriate to set up another theory of man when the futility of this exercise, in terms of establishing demonstrable truth, has been so much insisted upon.) The purpose here is not to offer any insight into the essence of human nature but merely to show the logical possibility of a particular kind of understanding of the world that individuals may choose to adopt, and, at best, to show that it is comprehensible that such a choice is widely made.[7]

Whatever its logical limitations, adherence to an ideology is not as unreasonable as is often claimed (usually by those who do not recognize their own ideological beliefs as ideological). Ideology provides a total understanding of the world – as total as needs be – that for the believer is satisfying. In order to act in the world we need to be able to make sense of it, both causal sense of it and moral sense of it. We need a total understanding that is not fragmented but forms a factual–ethical continuum, and this is just what ideology offers. Few of us would opt to live in a bare cell. We humanize the world, anthropomorphize reality, in terms of what we understand ourselves to be. We create sense and must, for the sake of sanity, create envelopes of sense that give meaning to our life as such. We do this through creating ethical beliefs such as religion and ideology, which give us an understanding of who and what we are, and thereby orientate us in the world. That they make the world make sense to us is more important than the satisfaction of formal principles of logical coherence or falsifiability (and after all, do not the academics who insist upon these principles disagree about everything?), much like the practical problem-facing engineer for whom what is known to work is infinitely more important than what some abstract theory says should work. And if an ideology is congenial to our instinctive outlook, appears to fit the facts, provides plausible explanations and seems to cohere with what we think it right, then it is perhaps better to accept it than be crippled Hamlet-like by doubt (which is in any case a luxury of the privileged).

Ideology is a kind of practical understanding, and by making a certain sort of sense of the world it facilitates our living and acting together in it. That ideology may be logically doubtful, that rival beliefs seem to shout uncomprehendingly at each other, that clashes of belief undoubtedly generate bitterness and dangerous conflict, do not seem to outweigh its advantages. This is perhaps because the demands of practice are too immediate, and cannot wait while we philosophize, even if that philosophizing might produce something worthwhile, instead of digging a deeper scepticism. We must solve the political crises and educate the generations that are before us, using whatever practical principles seem most sound. In the end we all have to live in the world and we must make the best sense of it we can.

Notes

1. See Chapter 4, pp. 78–81.
2. Many examples may be cited. Every ideology has a special account of its own relation to one or other of the disciplines (Liberalism is true philosophy, Marxism is true social science, and so on) and all tamper with history. Many make more general claims, so that for the Nazi there is true Aryan science and philosophy and false Jewish science and philosophy; while many Marxists have sought to set the physical sciences on the right track, from Engels' *Dialectics of Nature*, through Lysenkian genetics to ideological objections to quantum mechanics. The map of understanding is always distorted, and every ideology (rather like every kind of map projection) has its own set of distortions.
3. A notable exception to this, as discussed in Chapter 1, is D.J. Manning and T.J. Robinson's *The Place of Ideology in Political Life*, (Croom Helm, 1985), where it is argued that, far from being an evil that must be eradicated, ideology is constitutive of political life. Manning and Robinson are making an important point, but they go too far. A curious but essential feature of ideology is that ideologists and believers must not be aware that their thought is ideological; what they believe must for them be a true account of the world (just as with myth: once the believer becomes conscious that what he believes is mythical it loses its power, it is no longer a myth in the true sense). But if this is true (as Manning and Robinson would probably accept) then their notion of politics is vulnerable to a serious objection. There must be something very peculiar about so vital a human activity as politics if it is dependent upon a form of thinking of such a kind that if people only knew what they were doing they could not carry on. If ideology really is constitutive of political life, and ideology depends upon people being unaware of the nature of their thinking, then politics would have to cease if people did gain awareness. This is so peculiar a consequence of Manning and Robinson's view as to suggest that their theory is either false or in need of drastic revision.
4. Isaiah Berlin, *Four Essays on Liberty*, (OUP, 1969), pp. 171–2. Berlin is not here using

'choose' in its usual sense, as Hare is when he speaks of the individual choosing his moral principles. Berlin's meaning is more indirect, as for example it might be said that in the modern world 'men choose to live in independent states'. It is not meant in this case that people actually sat down and made such a choice, but rather that a situation or way of life prevails when things could be otherwise.

5. See W.J.M. Mackenzie, *Political Identity*, (Penguin, 1978), especially Chapter 3. However, this book is not a very good guide to the topic in general, and Mackenzie comes to no very significant conclusion.

6. Erich Fromm, *Fear of Freedom*, (RKP, 1960), pp. 28–9.

7. It might be thought that these disclaimers are less than honest and that a particular picture of human nature and the human condition does underly this work, making it just another ideological view of things. This objection has some force, in that a certain view of man and his situation is implied in this analysis. It is one that is perhaps suggestive of the old Babel myth (Genesis, Bk, 11), although with some modifications. In this case man is, so to speak, a compulsive Babel-maker: a constructor of systems of thought that strive to touch Heaven to the extent of aspiring to a God-like understanding of reality, seeing everything in its true place within a moral universe. But the price of building these towers (which in the nature of things fall far short of their claims and their aspirations) is a mankind divided by mutual and dangerous incomprehensions. However, the charge of ideologizing, and perhaps the charge of disingenuousness, is met by two points. First, there is no claim to universal truth; but rather the observation of a state of things that may or may not be temporary. A single set of beliefs, and a consequent mutual understanding, may eventually rule us all. In the second place, nothing in the nature of a moral imperative necessarily follows from this picture of man. If people found it convincing, no doubt some would believe that it clearly pointed to the necessity of tolerance and other Liberal values. But others might equally argue that it is precisely such Liberal values which have given us our violent, divided world, and that the sooner a single vision (whatever it might be) is imposed on the whole human race the better.

BIBLIOGRAPHY

This bibliography contains all the books and articles referred to in the text.

Action, H.B., *The Illusion of the Epoch*, (RKP, 1972).

Anscombe, G.E.M., 'Modern moral philosophy', in W.D. Hudson (ed.), *The Is–Ought Question*, (Macmillan, 1969).

Arblaster, A. and Lukes, S., (eds), *The Good Society*, (Methuen, 1971).

Arendt, H., *Origins of Totalitarianism*, (3rd edn), (Allen & Unwin, 1966).

Arnold, M., *Literature and Dogma*, (Smith, Elder & Co., 1873).

Aristotle, *Ethics*, (Penguin, 1955).

Barker, E., *Political Thought in England from Herbert Spencer to the Present Day*, (Williams and Norgate, 1915).

Barker, E., *Principles of Social and Political Theory*, (OUP, 1952).

Barnes, B., *T.S. Kuhn and Social Science*, (Macmillan, 1982).

Barry, N., *An Introduction to Modern Political Theory*, (Macmillan, 1981).

Beardsmore, R.W., *Moral Reasoning*, (RKP, 1969).

Benn, A., Preface to R.H. Tawney, *The Attack and Other Papers*, (Spokesman, 1981).

Benn, S. and Peters, R.S., *Social Principles and the Democratic State*, (Allen & Unwin, 1959).

Bentham, J., 'Rationale of reward', in *The Works of Jeremy Bentham*, vol II, (Russell & Russell, New York, 1962).

Berlin, I., *Four Essays on Liberty*, (OUP, 1969).

Berlin, I., 'George Sorel', in *Against the Current*, (OUP, 1981).

Berry, C., *Human Nature*, (Macmillan, 1986).

Bramstead, E.K. and Melhuish, K.J. (eds), *Western Libralism*, (Longman, 1978).

Brown, R., *Explanation in Social Science*, (RKP, 1963).

Burke, E., 'A letter to the Sheriffs of Bristol', in B.H. Hill (ed.), *Edmund Burke on Government, Politics and Society*, (Fontana, 1975).

Burke, E., *Reflections on the Revolution in France*, (Penguin, 1969).

Burrow, J.W., *Evolution and Society*, (CUP, 1966).

Butterfield, H., *The Whig Interpretation of History*, (Pelican Books, 1973).

Chapman, J.W. and Pennock, J.R., (eds), *Human Nature in Politics*, (New York University Press, 1977).

Cohen, B., *Educational Thought*, (Macmillan, 1969).

Cohen, G.A., *Karl Marx's Theory of History: a Defence*, (OUP, 1978).

Condorcet, A.–N. de, *Sketch for a Historical Picture of the Progress of the Human Mind*. (New York, 1955).

Copleston, F., *A History of Philosophy*, vol. 8, pt 1, (Doubleday, New York, 1967).

Corbett, P., *Ideologies*, (Hutchinson, 1965).

Cornforth, M., *Communism and Philosophy*, (Lawrence & Wishart, 1980).

Crick, B., *In Defence of Politics*, (Penguin, 1964).

Duncan, G., 'Political theory and human nature', in I. Forbes and S. Smith (eds), *Politics and Human Nature*, (Frances Pinter, 1983).

Engels, F., *Dialectics of Nature*, (Lawrence & Wishart, 1941).
Engels, F., *Anti-Duhring*, (Lawrence & Wishart, 1975).
Engels, F., Letter to Conrad Schmidt, 27 Oct. 1890, in L.S. Feuer (ed.), *Marx and Engels: Basic Writings on Politics and Philosophy*, (Fontana, 1969).
Engels, F., Letter to Franz Mehring, 14 July 1893, in L.S. Feuer (ed.), *Marx and Engels: Basic Writings on Politics and Philosophy*, (Fontana, 1969).
Eulau, H., *The Behavioural Persuasion in Politics*, (Random House, 1966).
Field, G.C., *Political Theory*, (Methuen, 1956).
Finer, S., (ed.), *Five Constitutions*, (Penguin, 1979).
Foot, P., *Virtues and Vices*, (Basil Blackwell, 1978).
Forbes, I. and Smith, S., (eds), *Politics and Human Nature*, (Frances Pinter, 1983).
Fromm, E., *Fear of Freedom*, (RKP, 1960).
Gallie, W.B., 'Essentially contested concepts', *Proceedings of the Aristotelian Society*, vol. LVI, (1955–6).
Gaus, G.F., *The Modern Liberal Theory of Man*, (Croom Helm, 1983).
Geach, P.T., 'Good and evil', in Phillippa Foot (ed.), *Theories of Ethics*, (OUP, 1967).
Geach, P.T., *The Virtues*, (CUP, 1977).
Gilmour, I., *Inside Right*, (Quartet Books, 1978).
Graham, G., *Politics in its Place*, (OUP, 1986).
Gray, J., *Liberalism*, (OUP, 1986).
Green, M., (ed.), *The Truth of God Incarnate*, (Hodder & Stoughton, 1977).
Green, T.H., *Lectures on the Principles of Political Obligation*, (Longman, 1963).
Halevy, E., *The Growth of Philosophical Radicalism*, (Faber, 1972).
Halle, L.J., *The Ideological Imagination*, (Chatto & Windus, 1971).
Hamilton, M.B., 'The elements of the concept of ideology', *Political Studies*, vol. XXXV, (March 1987).
Hare, R.M., *The Language of Morals*, (OUP, 1952).
Hare, R.M., *Freedom and Reason*, (OUP, 1963).
Hare, R.M., 'Rawl's theory of justice', in Norman Daniels (ed.), *Reading Rawls*, (Blackwell, 1975).
Hare, R.M., *Moral Thinking*, (OUP, 1981).
Hassner, P., 'Immanuel Kant', in J. Cropsey and L. Strauss (eds), *History of Political Philosophy*, (2nd edn), (Chicago University Press, 1981).
Hattersley, R., *Choose Freedom: The Future of Democratic Socialism*, (Michael Joseph, 1987).
Hayek, F.A., *The Road to Serfdom*, (RKP, 1944).
Hayek, F.A., *The Constitution of Liberty*, (RKP, 1960).
Heidegger, M., *An Introduction to Metaphysics*, (Anchor Books, 1961).
Hicks, J., (ed.), *The Myth of God Incarnate*, (SCM, 1977).
Hobbes, T., *Leviathan*, (Penguin edn, 1968).
Hobhouse, L.T., *Liberalism*, (OUP, 1941).
Hollis, M., *Models of Man*, (CUP, 1977).
Hudson, W.D., *Modern Moral Philosophy*, (2nd edn), (Macmillan, 1983).
Jackel, E., *Hitler's World View*, (Harvard University Press, 1981).
Kant, I., 'Groundwork of the metaphysics of morals', in H.G. Paton (ed.), *The Moral Law*, (Hutchinson, 1948).
Kant, I., *Critique of Pure Reason*, trans. Norman Kemp-Smith, (Macmillan, 1933).
Kant, I., *The Metaphysical Elements of Justice*, trans. J. Ladd, (Bobbs Merrill, 1965).
Kant, I., *On History*, Lewis White Beck (ed.), (Bobbs Merrill, 1963).
Kuhn, T., 'The function of dogma in scientific research', in A. C. Crombie (ed.), *Scientific Change*, (Heinemann, 1963).
Kuhn, T., *The Structure of Scientific Revolutions*, (2nd edn), (University of Chicago Press, 1970).
Laslett, P. (ed.), *Philosophy, Politics and Society*, first series, (Blackwell, 1956), Introduction.
Lichtheim, G., *The Concept of Ideology and Other Essays*, (Vintage Books, 1968).
Lipset, S.M., *Political Man*, (Heinemann, 1960).

Locke, J., *A Letter Concerning Toleration*, (Bobbs Merrill, 1955).
Locke, J., *Two Treatises on Government*, (Mentor, 1965).
Lucas, J.R., *The Principles of Politics*, (OUP, 1966).
Machiavelli, N., *The Prince*, (Penguin, 1961).
MacIntyre, A., *A Short History of Ethics*, (RKP, 1966).
MacIntyre, A., *After Virtue*, (Duckworth, 1981), (2nd edn, 1985).
Mackenzie, W.J.M., *Political Identity*, (Penguin, 1978).
McLellan, D., *Ideology*, (Open UP, 1986).
Macquarrie, J., *Existentialism*, (Penguin, 1973).
MacRae, D., *Ideology and Society*, (Heinemann, 1961).
Mannheim, K., *Ideology and Utopia*, (RKP, 1936).
Manning, D.J., *Liberalism*, (Dent, 1976).
Manning, D.J. and Robinson, T.J., *The Place of Ideology in Political Life*, (Croom Helm, 1985).
Marx, K., *Economic and Philosophic Manuscripts*, (Lawrence and Wishart, 1973).
Marx, K. and Engels, F., *The German Ideology*, C.J. Arthur, (ed.), (Lawrence and Wishart, 1970).
Marx, K., *The Poverty of Philosophy*, (Progress Publishers, Moscow, 1955).
Marx, K. and Engels, F., *The Communist Manifesto*, (Penguin, 1967).
Marx, K., Preface to 'A contribution to a critique of political economy', in L.S. Feuer (ed.), *Marx and Engels: Basic Writings on Politics and Philosophy*, (Fontana, 1969).
Marx, K., 'The eighteenth Brumaire of Louis Bonaparte', in David McLellan (ed.), *Karl Marx: Selected Writings*, (OUP, 1977).
Marx, K., *Capital*, vol. I, (Lawrence & Wishart, 1970).
Miller, D. and Siedentop, L., (eds), *The Nature of Political Theory*, (OUP, 1983).
Minogue, K., *Alien Powers: The Pure Theory of Ideology*, (Weidenfeld & Nicholson, 1985).
Mounce, H.O., 'Theory and practice', in *Proceedings of the Philosophy of Education Society of Great Britain*, (July 1976).
Murphy, J.G., *Kant: The Philosophy of Right*, (Macmillan, 1970).
Nisbet, R., *Conservatism*, (Open UP, 1986).
Nozick, R., *Anarchy, State and Utopia*, (Blackwell, 1974).
Oakeshott, M., 'Rationalism in politics', in *Rationalism in Politics and Other Essays*, (Methuen, 1962).
Oakeshott, M., 'The activity of being an historian', in *Rationalism in Politics and Other Essays*, (Methuen, 1962).
Oppenheim, F., *Political Concepts*, (Basil Blackwell, 1981).
Parekh, B., 'The problems of ideology', in Robert Benewick *et al.* (eds), *Knowledge and Belief in Politics*, (Allen & Unwin, 1973).
Parekh, B., (ed.), *The Concept of Socialism*, (Croom Helm, 1975), Introduction.
Parekh, B., *Marx's Theory of Ideology*, (Croom Helm, 1982).
Paton, H.J., (ed.), *The Moral Law*, (Hutchinson, 1948).
Pelling, H., *Origins of the Labour Party*, (2nd edn), (OUP, 1965).
Phillips, D.Z. and Mounce, H.O., *Moral Practices*, (RKP, 1970).
Plamenatz, J., (ed.), *Readings from Liberal Writers*, (Allen & Unwin, 1965).
Plamenatz, J., 'The uses of political theory', in Anthony Quinton (ed.), *Political Philosophy*, (OUP, 1967).
Plamenatz, J., *Ideology*, (Macmillan, 1970).
Plant, R., 'The resurgence of ideology', in Henry Drucker *et al.* (eds), *Developments in British Politics*, (Macmillan, 1983).
Plant, R., 'Scientific claims', *The Times Higher Educational Supplement*, 28.6.85.
Plato, *The Republic*, trans. F.M. Cornford, (OUP, 1941).
Popper, K., *The Poverty of Historicism*, (2nd edn), (RKP, 1960).
Popper, K., *The Open Society and its Enemies*, (5th edn), vol. II, (RKP. 1966).
Popper, K., *Conjectures and Refutations*, (RKP, 1963).
Popper, K., *The Logic of Scientific Discovery*, (6th edn), (Hutchinson, 1972).

Putman, R.D., 'Studying elite political culture: the case of ideology', *The American Political Science Review*, vol. LXV, 3, (1971).

Quinton, A., (ed.), *Political Philosophy*, (OUP, 1967), Introduction.

Raphael, D.D., *The Problems of Political Philosophy*, (2nd edn), (Macmillan, 1976).

Rawls, J., *A Theory of Justice*, (OUP, 1972).

Reiss, H., (ed.), *Kant's Political Writings*, (CUP, 1970).

Rousseau, J.-J., 'The social contract', in *The Social Contract and Discourses*, (Dent, 1973).

Ryan, A., '"Normal" Science or Political Ideology', P. Laslett *et al.* (eds), *Philosophy, Politics and Society*, fourth series, (Basil Blackwell, 1972).

Ryan, A., 'Two concepts of politics and democracy', in Martin Fleisher (ed.), *Machiavelli and the Nature of Political Thought*, (Croom Helm, 1973).

Ryan, A., 'The nature of human nature in Hobbes and Rousseau', in J. Benthall (ed.), *The Limits of Human Nature*, (Allen Lane, 1973).

Ryle, G., *The Concept of Mind*, (Penguin, 1963).

Sartori, G., 'Politics, ideology and belief systems', *The American Political Science Review*, vol. LXIII, 2 (1969).

Sartre, J.-P., *Being and Nothingness*, trans. Hazel Barnes, (Methuen, 1958).

Sartre, J.-P., 'No Exit' in *Two Plays*, trans. Stuart Gilbert, (Hamish Hamilton, 1946).

Sartre, J.-P., *Existentialism and Humanism*, trans. Philip Mairet, (Eyre Methuen, 1948).

Sarte, J.-P., *Critique of Dialectical Reason*, trans. Alan Sheridan-Smith, (New Left Books, 1976).

Sarte, J.-P., *Search for a Method*, trans. Hazel Barnes, (Alfred Knopf, 1963).

Schapiro, J.S., (ed.), *Liberalism: Its Meaning and History*, (Van Nostrand, 1958).

Seliger, M., *Ideology and Politics*, (Allen & Unwin, 1976).

Shils, E., 'Ideology and civility: on the politics of the intellectual', *The Sewanee Review*, vol. LXVI, 3, (1958).

Shils, E., 'The concept and function of ideology', in *The International Encyclopedia of the Social Sciences*, vol. VII, (1968).

Skinner, B.F., *Beyond Freedom and Dignity*, (Penguin, 1973).

Skinner, B.F., *Walden Two*, (2nd edn), (Macmillan, New York, 1976).

Spencer, H., *Man Versus the State*, (Penguin, 1969).

Spencer, H., *The Data of Ethics*, (1907), (no publisher given); cited in Frederick Copleston, *A History of Philosophy*, vol. 8, pt 1, (Doubleday, New York, 1967).

Stafford, W., 'Utopianism and human nature', in Ian Forbes and S. Smith (eds), *Politics and Human Nature*, (Frances Pinter, 1983).

Steintrager, J., *Bentham*, (Allen & Unwin, 1977).

Stevenson, C.L., *Ethics and Language*, (Yale, 1944).

Stevenson, L., *Seven Theories of Human Nature*, (OUP, 1974).

Strawson, P.F., 'Social morality and personal ideal', in *Freedom and Resentment and Other Essays*, (Methuen, 1974).

Toulmin, S.E., 'Does the distinction between normal and revolutionary science hold water?', in I. Lakatos and A. Musgrave (eds), *Criticism and the Growth of Knowledge*, (CUP, 1970).

Tudor, H., *Political Myth*, (Pall Mall Press, 1972).

Weber, M., 'Science as a vocation', in H.H. Gerth and C. Wright Mills (eds), *From Max Weber*, (RKP, 1948).

Williams, B., *Moral Luck*, (CUP, 1981).

Williams, H., *Kant's Political Philosophy*, (Basil Blackwell, 1983).

Winch, P., *Ethics and Action*, (RKP, 1972).

Wolin, S., 'Paradigms and political theories', in Preston King and Bhikhu Parekh (eds), *Politics and Experience*, (CUP, 1968).

Wolin, S., 'Political theory as a vocation', in Martin Fleisher (ed), *Machiavelli and the Nature of Political thought*, (Croom Helm, 1973).

Wood, A., *Karl Marx*, (RKP, 1981).

INDEX